AF573957

The Bird of Self-Knowledge

The Bird of Self-Knowledge

Folk Art and Current Artists' Positions

Edited by Peter Weiermair

With essays by
Wolfgang Brückner
Jean-Hubert Martin
Saul Ostrow
Marie-Louise von Plessen
Peter Weiermair
Beat Wyss

EDITION STEMMLE

Zurich – New York

Preface

The Bird of Self-Knowledge, the work which inspired the puzzling, thought-provoking title of our exhibition, offers us words of wisdom that might be expressed somewhat differently in the language of our time: "Tend to your own business. Don't get involved in things that don't concern you."

Is it appropriate, then, to invite artists from all over the world, to whom the folk art of the Tyrol and the museum itself were virtually unknown before preparations for the exhibition began, to get involved and to intervene in the existing museum collections – to get involved by changing, rearranging, undermining and perhaps even provoking? I think the answer is yes. We should indeed tend to our own business. That will help us avoid succumbing to self-righteousness and superficiality.

The idea of presenting the collection of the Tiroler Volkskunstmuseum founded in 1888, in an international exhibition began to take shape within the "Freundeskreis des Tiroler Volkskunstmuseums" some time ago. The objective was to bring the collection to the attention of a broader public in a new approach that would be in tune with contemporary concerns. It soon became clear that 1998 would be an ideal time for such an event. Our museum celebrates its 100th anniversary this year, and Austria will advance to the foreground of European interest as it assumes the Presidency of the EU during the latter half of the year.

What could be more fitting, therefore, than to present an exhibition of European, indeed international scope. In giving substance and shape to this idea, the Tyrolean artist Anton Christian, a member of the "Freundeskreis des Tiroler Volkskunstmuseums" intimately familiar with the museum and its rich collections for many years, has realized a highly unique project, and I wish to express my gratitude to him for doing so.

I would also like to thank all of the artists and the exhibition team, whose members eagerly committed themselves to this exciting undertaking.

Never before has an existing museum collection been complemented – indeed, undermined and perhaps even fundamentally altered – through the presentation of contemporary art. This invasion of the past by the present takes place in an attitude of respect for tradition and with the goal of "intervening" in order to make visible what is often taken for granted, to teach us to see what we ordinarily perceive without a great deal of reflection.

The symposium planned in Innsbruck on October 9th and 10th, to which numerous experts have been invited to discuss the theme of "Folk Art – Contemporary Art," is an integral part of our "Self-Knowledge" project.

It is my hope that the months of fruitful preparation will culminate in interesting and exciting discussions on all aspects of folk art and its significance within the context of a common European landscape. I wish the Tiroler Volkskunstmuseum a great many visitors and am confident that the interventions of the present will enable those visitors to see the treasures of the past, preserved there with loving care and professional expertise, in an entirely new light.

Franz Fischler
EU Commissioner and Chairman of
the "Freundeskreis des Tiroler Volkskunstmuseums"

Contents

Introduction

Peter Weiermair

Aside from documenting the installations of 25 international artists, this catalogue, with its extensive textual material, is the primary publication of a professional symposium dedicated, like the exhibition itself, to an investigation into the relationship between contemporary art and authentic, anonymous folk culture.

The exhibition title – "The Bird of Self-Knowledge" – alludes to one of the most interesting and allegorically puzzling objects on exhibit at this museum, the site of an "invasion" by a group of artists invited to spend the summer and autumn of 1998 at the institution. The artists' objective is to set in motion, with the aid of their interventions, a process of self-discovery and self-recognition in museum visitors, who are thereby encouraged to reconsider fundamental values of life and reflect upon the relationship between tradition and the present on the basis of these staged dialogues. The artists invited to participate in this endeavor do not see themselves as administrators of the museum, home to one of the most beautiful collections of ethnic art in Europe. Unlikely to be embraced with loving arms by the real museum administrators, they are regarded rather as intruders. Yet they take the objects they have selected very seriously, viewing them with eager, alert eyes and opening new avenues of approach to them by creating new contexts. They penetrate the sanctuary of the museum from the outside (Jetelová), give new life to the exhibition rooms (Christian, Iseli, Katase, Ontani), build assemblages (Friedmann, Proença, Souza), appropriate museum pieces (Siebel, Schmidt) or create, with their own works, new contextual links within the collection as a whole (e. g. Mol, Trenkwalder).

"Setting scenes" is perhaps the best way to describe what these 25 artists from Europe, North and Central America and Japan have in mind for the museum. The museum itself, robbed of its peace in the interest of an attempt to gain new experiences and insights – artists are, after all, the most discerning visitors – becomes the showplace for a dialogue of unprecedented scope. The collection is more than merely a set or backdrop for the events that unfold here; indeed, the objects comprised within it become playmates, in a sense, for the new works distributed throughout the museum and created, in most cases, especially for the Innsbruck presentation. Marie-Louise von Plessen cites "unheard-of juxtapositions" upon which the artists focus in exploring the estrangement of archaic Christian values and objects expressive of old ways of life. The artists are not concerned with evoking feelings of nostalgia based upon enmity towards progress and civilization or with promoting mere aesthetic pleasure; instead, they aim to "demystify and permeate the particularity of the object without bowing to its own autonomous meaning." As an individualist, the artist gives these anonymous things new life and a special appeal by dissolving, staging, linking, creating assemblages, illuminating and augmenting. In the past, new assessments of existing collections have frequently been undertaken by persons who do not share the conventional view of professional curators or scholars. Ever since Andy Warhol's "Raid the Icebox" show, philosophers, film-makers and artists have been invited to rub against the grain of conventional museum practice. For the exhibition at the Tiroler Volkskunstmuseum, 25 contemporary artists representing several different generations have chosen certain situations, departments or objects from the museum to which they wished to respond. This particular selection of artists is an experiment. Naturally, we looked at the backgrounds of the respective artists and took their inclinations and their cultural origins into account as well, yet our aim in doing so was simply to determine how likely they might be to catch the spark of enthusiasm. The project has involved considerable risk from the outset, and it has truly been an experimental undertaking. I believe we are justified in claiming today that the experiment has been a success.

At the same time, the exhibition offers a panoramic view of the broad spectrum of media strategies available to the contemporary artist today. These range from evidence preservation – the presentation of the objects themselves as illustrations of particular states or conditions (Spoerri, Lang) – assemblages comprising links between artificial objects and real things (Dimitrijevic, Friedmann, Souza), masks and paintings (Ontani, Tàpies), drawings in unusual form (Proença) and staged object presentations (Parmiggiani, Quiñones) to video projections (Cibulka) and retouched (Rainer) or staged photographs (Cravo Neto). The wonderful richness of the exhibition is a function of the diversity of approaches used.

Anton Christian, who initiated this project, distributes his "rag dolls" throughout the museum and thus creates a domestic context, yet he makes the dolls available in such a way that children will accept them and take them along proudly when they leave the museum.

A number of artists have discovered the historical rooms as exhibition sites. Iseli, who sees rust, the toad-stool and the beehive as elements of object imagery and metaphors of time (as fundamental references to the vanity theme), creates a tableau out of cross, clock and birdhouse in the historical rooms to evoke a mood that heightens the intentions inherent in the images. Tàpies has frequently responded to anonymous signs, scribbled forms and traces of decay and decline in his oeuvre, often integrating rudimentary furniture, beds or doors in his object images as well, and his exhibits here affirm that interest. Elmar Trenkwalder, an artist who takes a highly unusual approach to the medium of ceramics, presents a "ceramic chair" and figural formations that place him in close proximity to the traditional art of Tyrolean potters, with whom he shares a mannerist vocabulary of forms and figures.

The Dutch artist Pieter Laurens Mol places his poetic objects near other exhibition pieces, practicing a kind of mimicry that triggers a productive irritation in the viewer's mind. These non-functional aesthetic objects, full of Surrealist object-magic, positioned within the contexts of functional tools or objects of folk culture invigorate their counterparts and permit us to look at them in entirely new ways.

When an artist exhibits his or her work, as Hermann Nitsch does his "tools of his actions," in showcases identical to those used to display items in the permanent exhibit, the context of the museum department plays an important role, for the viewer's gaze moves back and forth between these objects and the pieces in the permanent exhibit. Other artists, such as Pavel Schmidt, establish temporary marriages of objects, questioning the historical dimension in comparisons with items from contemporary popular culture or modern technology (tools). While the evidence collector Nikolaus Lang deposits the inventory of a museum storage hold in a demonstrative quantitative presentation on the museum floor, the Portuguese artist Pedro Proença encircles a showcase full of grotesque figures that have inspired his baroque hybrid and fabulous beings with a drawing that runs around the entire wall. Pablo Siebel establishes a link between cradles from the alpine region and upright Mediterranean sails, while Claudio Parmiggiani employs the simple placement of a mirror to assist the viewer in creating associations between his view of the allegorical image of the "Bird of Self-Knowledge" and his own presence. Reflection and perception, observation and emerging thought come together. The Mexican artist Néstor Quiñones also uses mirrors to heighten the memento-mori quality of an object – specifically a towel-holder incorporating the head of a human figure, half of its face in the full bloom of beauty, the other half a skull. Quiñones' fascination with this figure in particular is not surprising, since he, like a number of other artists, comes from a country where an earlier pagan culture was subsumed under the mantle of Catholicism. Thus the photographs of the Brazilian artist Mario Cravo Neto communicate the exotic character of Afro-Brazilian culture to the extent that they reflect the magic of tribal shamanism and the baroque sensibilities of Portuguese-Brazilian culture with which black magic and religion imported from Africa intermingled. Cravo Neto is presented within the context of this exhibition because his work is suggestive of the fundamental animism, altered by Catholicism yet appropriating it at the same time, that underlies local popular beliefs and many old customs. Whereas Cravo Neto stages his photographs, Rainer retouches photos of masks from the museum collection. Rainer is fascinated by the vocabulary of facial expressions he finds in these masks. In retouching the photographic images, he accentuates and comments upon these expressions. In his pictures and masks, Luigi Ontani intermixes a wide variety of cultural languages. Recently, particularly in response to his sojourns in Trento, he has focused his attention on the iconography of the alpine region. A number of artists, including Braco Dimitrijevic and Henk Visch, confront items from the museum collection with documents from a different ethnic region. Braco Dimitrijevic presents time-worn souvenirs of African culture; Henk Visch exhibits portraits from the culture of the Maoris in New Zealand. While Henk Visch's succinct visual quotations call upon the viewer to make comparisons, Braco Dimitrijevic combines his aesthetic documents with natural materials, such as fruits, to create a situation of ontological imbalance. Nature, as a symbol of a different geography, is played off against culture – the objects in the museum.

In Gloria Friedmann's installation, which dominates the entire second floor, the ubiquitous presence of our media world is represented by the CNN program shown on the television screen and transformed in combination with the past, seen in the stuffed stag and bleached bones suspended in a kind of mobile, into an ironic, polemical ensemble. Whereas the video program reflects international political reality, Heinz Cibulka has, in his "audio-visual installation" converted the principle of the static visual poem into a series of rapidly changing impressions with the aid of stills shown on two different monitors. Full of interwoven associations, his photographic material is the product of his on-site research at the museum. Many artists have chosen the authentic exhibits of rooms in peasants' homes as the site for their installations. The experience of space and of specific objects is the primary concern of the Japanese artist Katase. He incorporates the oversized model of a house into a subtly altered room, thus enclosing the real interior space in the monumental (for a model) outer skin of a house. Light, scent and color play an important role in his installations.

Again and again, artists call attention to the function, form and material qualities of objects in the museum collection. Thus Martin Gostner confronts the once functional storage bins of the museum with a modern-style model kitchen, "ennobled" by the magical light that radiates from its interior. One might see this as an appeal to the viewer to see and to reassess museum objects from the standpoint of their former function; at the same time, it may serve as a reference to the possibility that this kitchen will someday also be worthy of exhibition in a museum. Not only does Michael Kienzer present a showcase containing a rolled-up red rope, emphasizing its material quality and its functional beauty, he also employs the same rope as a barrier between traditional museum pieces.

It can be said of all of the participating artists that their interventions make us aware of something, that they evoke an experience that goes beyond aesthetic reception. The significance of the individual materials and interventions is of essential importance and must be kept in mind at all times. This applies to Al Souza's wads of newspaper stored behind iron grids and to the view into the building made possible by Magdalena Jetelová. Jetelová has had a wide, open wooden stairway built at the rear side of the museum, offering the visitor a (forbidden) view of the peasants' living rooms originally incorporated into the former monastery building. Like visitors to a theater permitted to go behind the stage, we are given a view of the space between the architecture of the peasants' rooms and the monastery. A video presentation offers insight into the position in cosmic space. In this way, Jetelová creates links between times and spaces, calling upon the viewer to look behind the things themselves – an aim shared by all of the 25 participating artists, albeit in widely differing approaches.

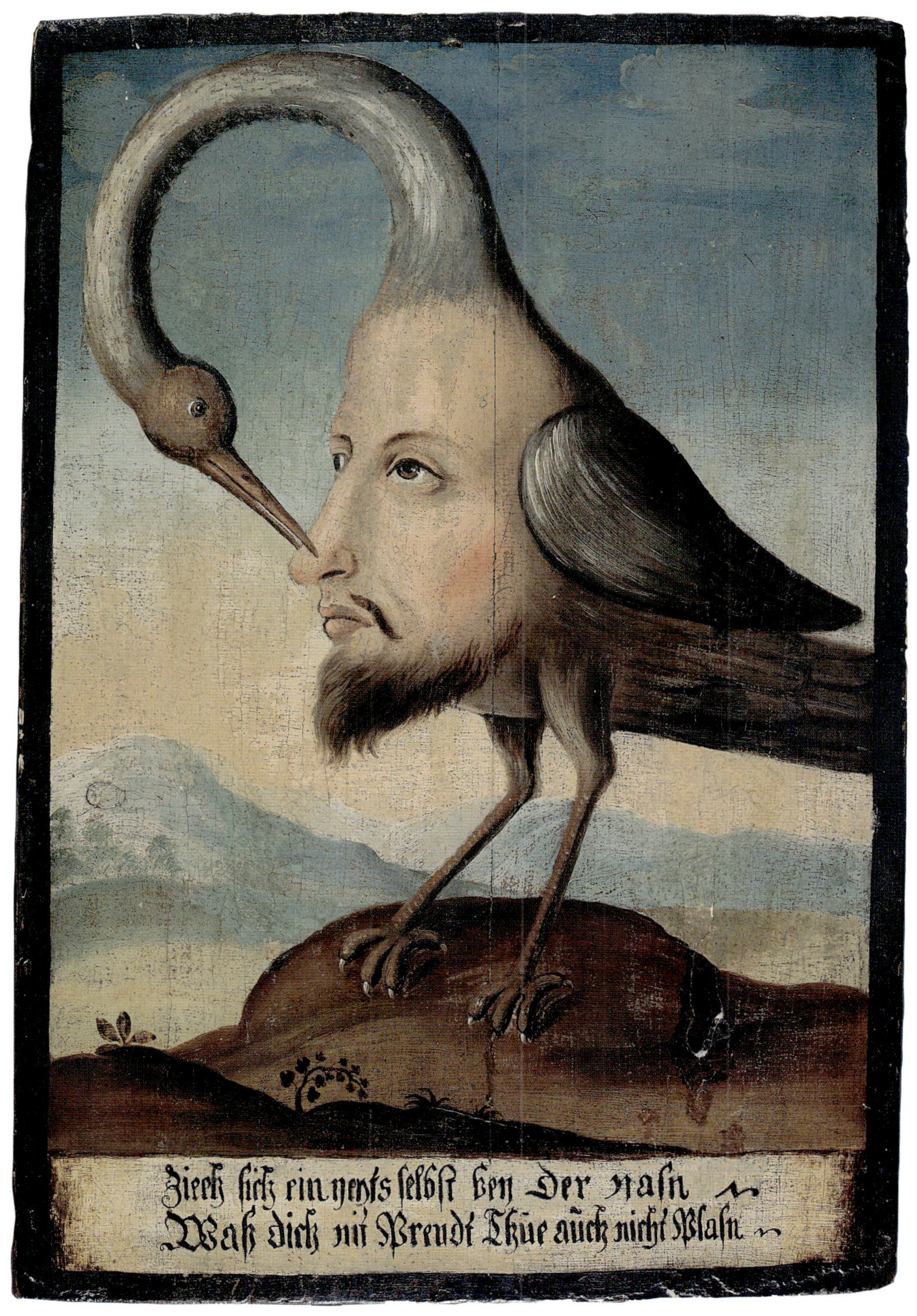
Ziech sich ein yeder selbst bey der Nasn
Was dich nit freudt thue auch nicht Blasn

Anton Christian
Heinz Cibulka
Mario Cravo Neto
Braco Dimitrijevic
Gloria Friedmann
Martin Gostner
Rolf Iseli
Magdalena Jetelová
Kazuo Katase
Michael Kienzer
Nikolaus Lang
Pieter Laurens Mol
Hermann Nitsch
Luigi Ontani
Claudio Parmiggiani
Pedro Proença
Néstor Quiñones
Arnulf Rainer
Pavel Schmidt
Pablo Siebel
Al Souza
Daniel Spoerri
Antoni Tàpies
Elmar Trenkwalder
Henk Visch

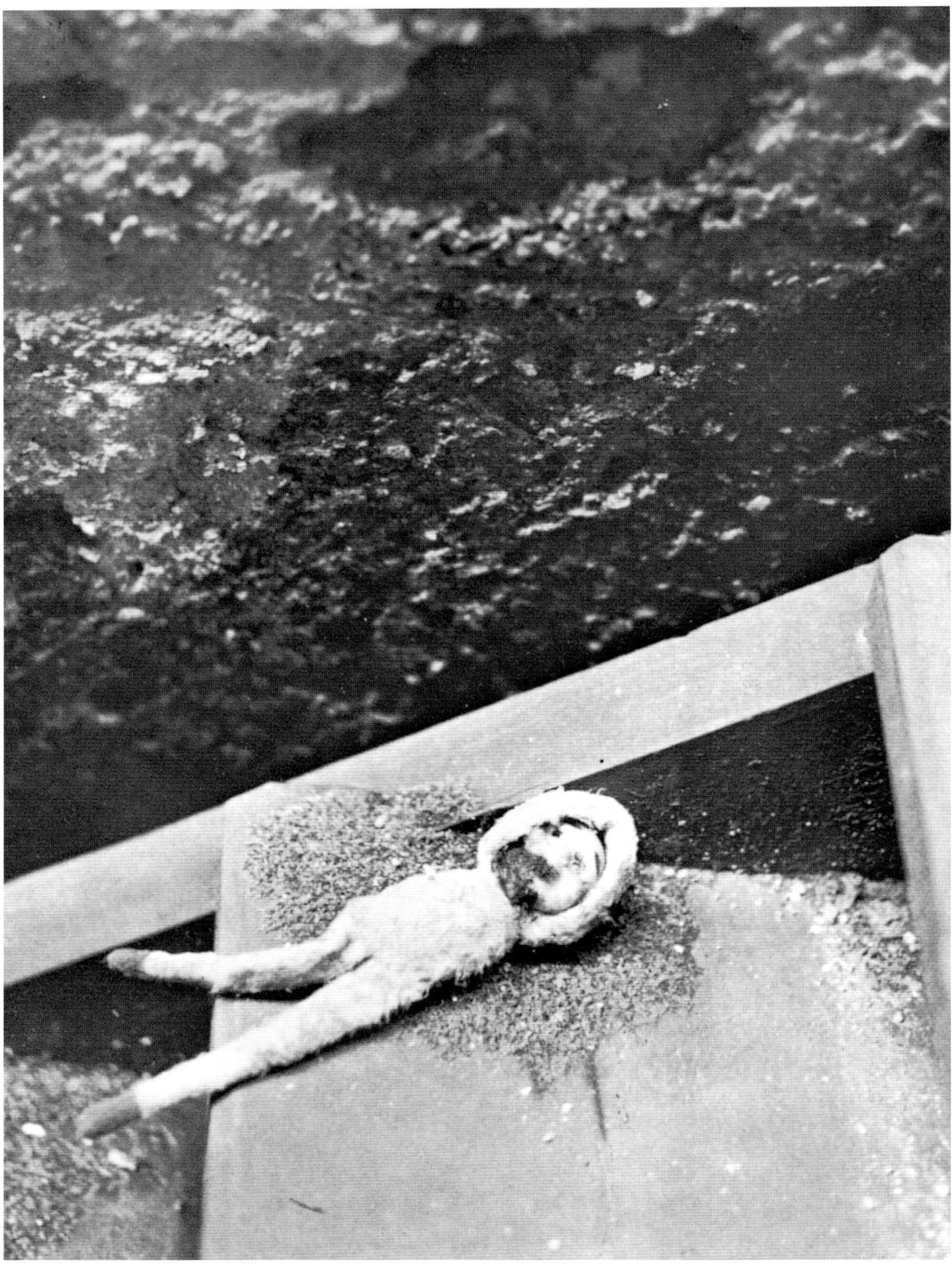

Puppen, 1998

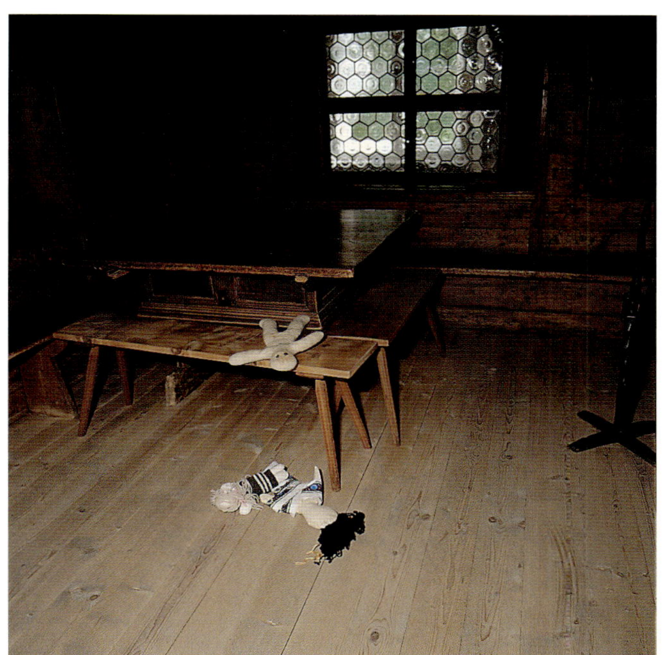

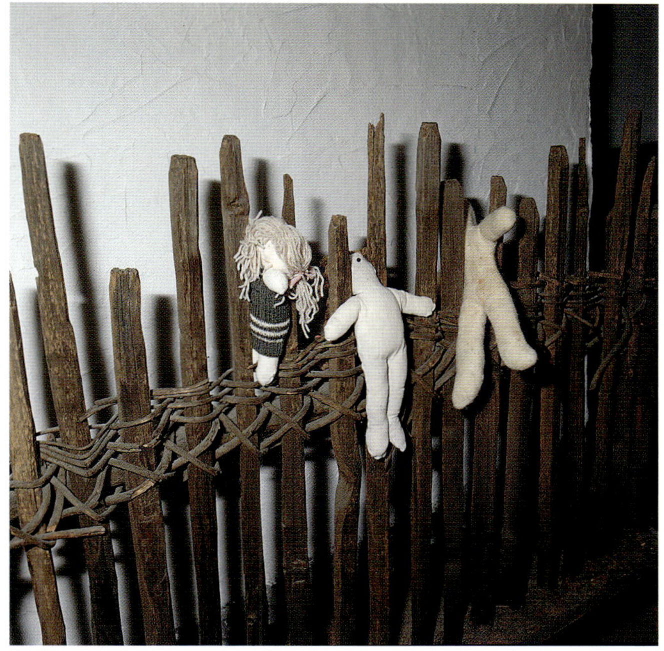

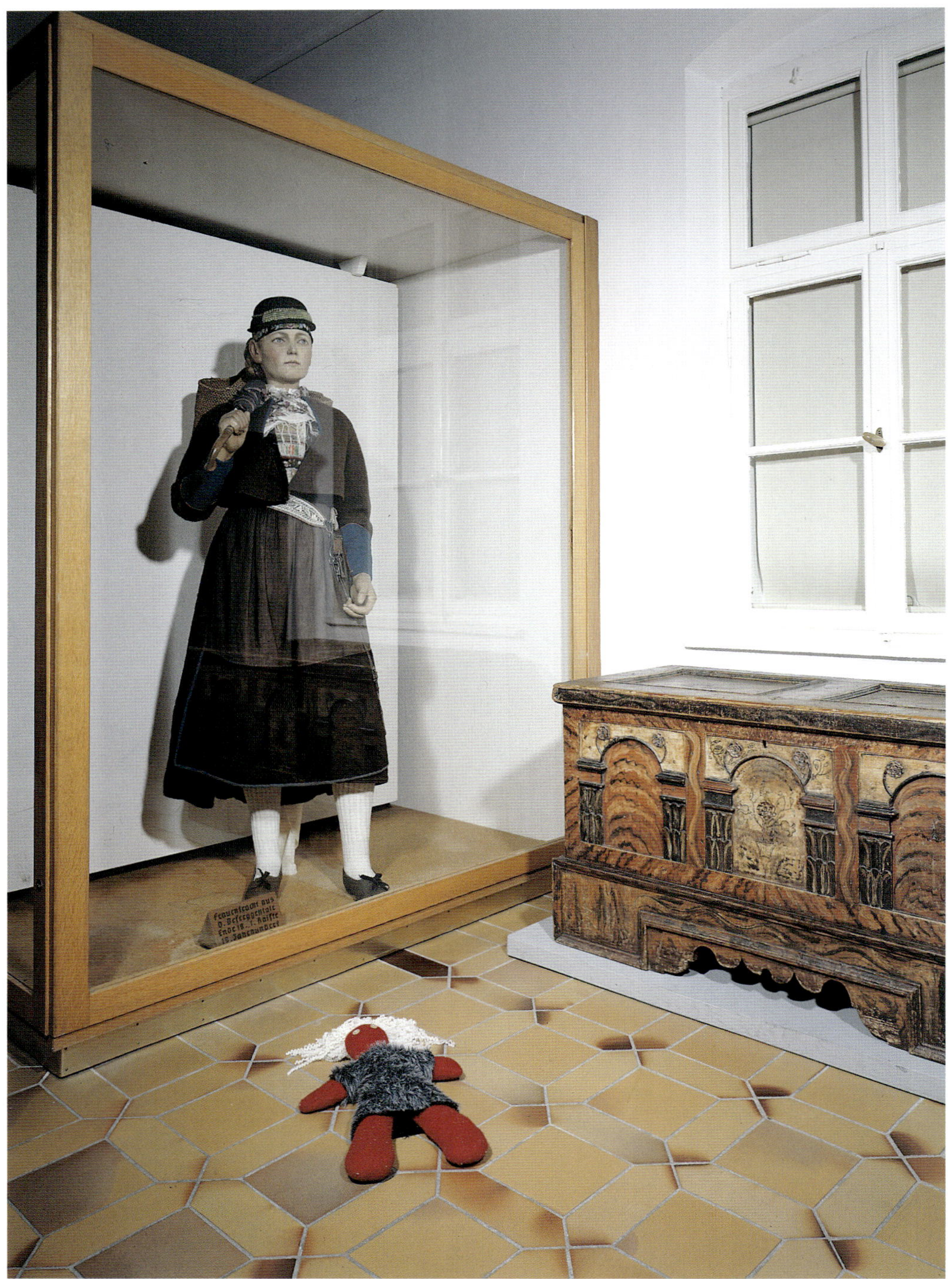

Puppen, 1998

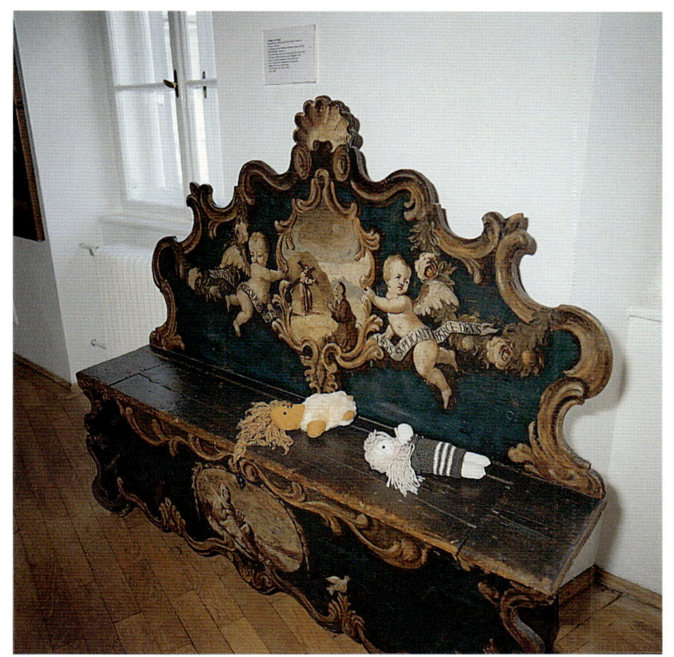

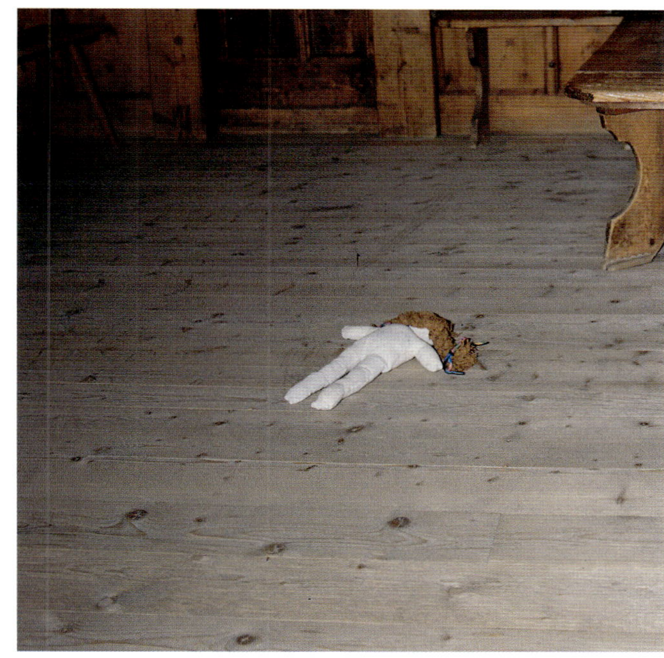

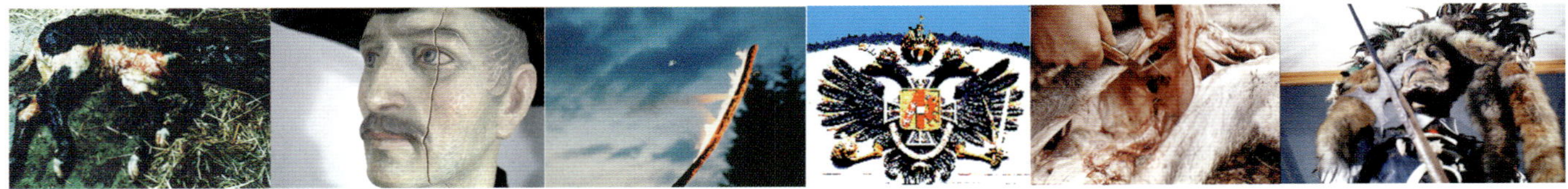

DOPPEL BRENNER

4 bildsprachlich gesetzte Bildfolgen auf 8 Monitoren
zu Zeitstrukturen von 4 als Musik komponierten Tonmontagen

Konzept:
Heinz Cibulka

Bild:
Heinz Cibulka
Ton:
Raimund Suchanek

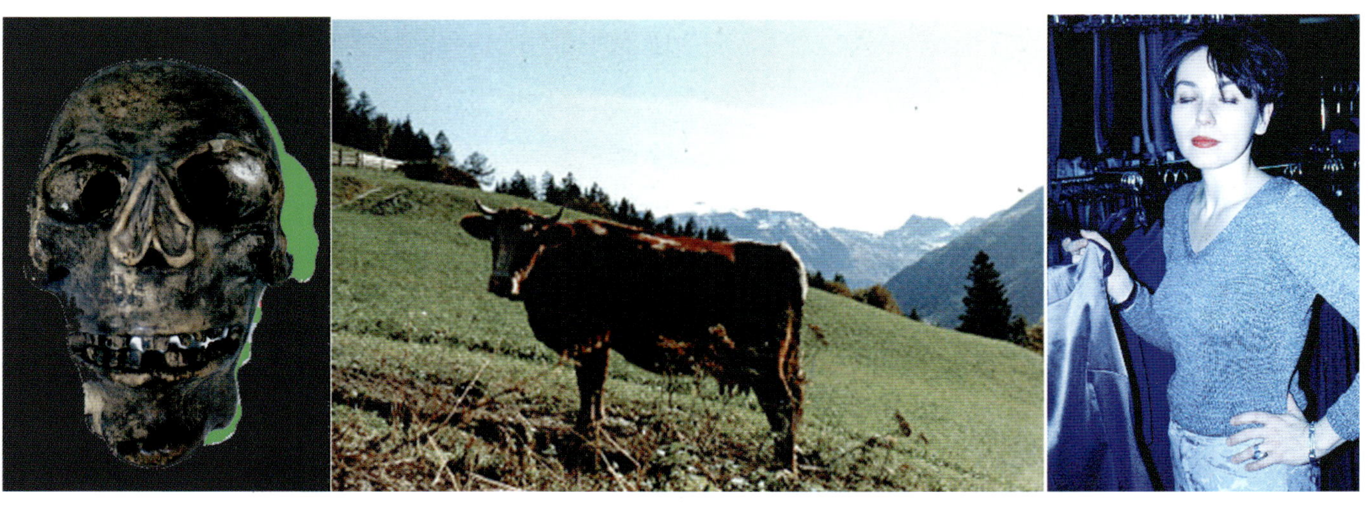

Doppel-Brenner, 1998

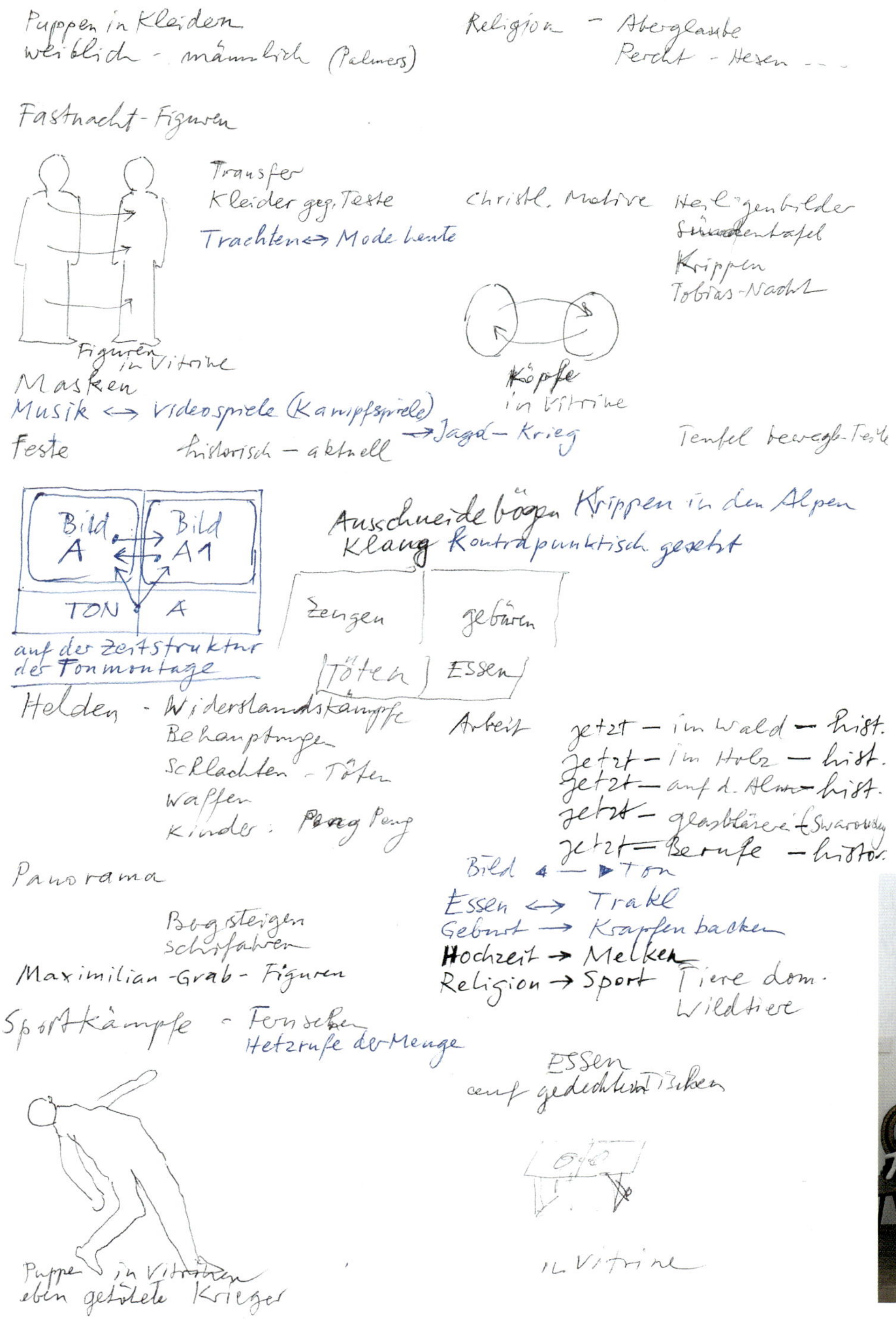

Puppen in Kleidern
weiblich – männlich (Palmers)

Religion – Aberglaube
Percht – Hexen ...

Fastnacht-Figuren

Transfer
Kleider geg. Teste
Trachten ↔ Mode heute

christl. Motive
Heiligenbilder
Sündentafel
Krippen
Tobias-Nacht

Figuren in Vitrine

Köpfe in Vitrine

Masken
Musik ↔ Videospiele (Kampfspiele) → Jagd – Krieg
Feste historisch – aktuell

Teufel beweglich-Teste

Bild A ⇄ Bild A1
TON A
auf der Zeitstruktur der Tonmontage

Ausschneidebögen Krippen in den Alpen
Klang kontrapunktisch gesetzt

Zeugen | gebären
Töten | Essen

Helden – Widerstandskämpfe
Behauptungen
Schlachten – Töten
Waffen
Kinder: Ping Pong

Arbeit
jetzt – im Wald – hist.
jetzt – im Holz – hist.
jetzt – auf d. Alm – hist.
jetzt – Glasbläserei Swarovsky
jetzt – Berufe – histor.

Panorama

Bild ←→ Ton
Essen ↔ Trakl
Geburt → Krapfen backen
Hochzeit → Melken
Religion → Sport

Tiere dom.
Wildtiere

Bergsteigen
Schifahren

Maximilian-Grab-Figuren

Sportkämpfe – Fernsehen
Hetzrufe der Menge

Essen auf gedeckten Tischen

Puppe in Vitrinen
eben getötete Krieger

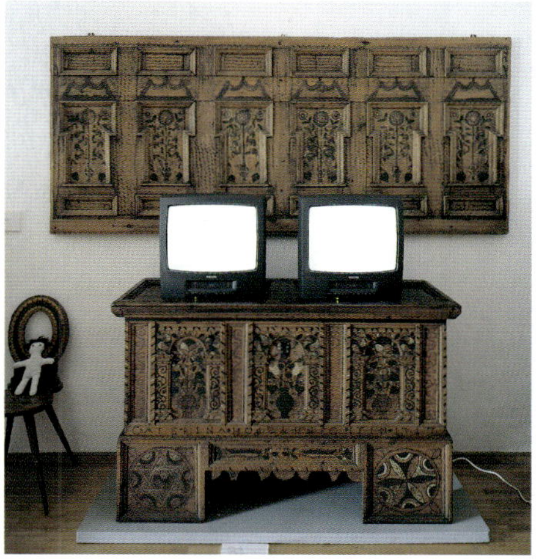

in Vitrine

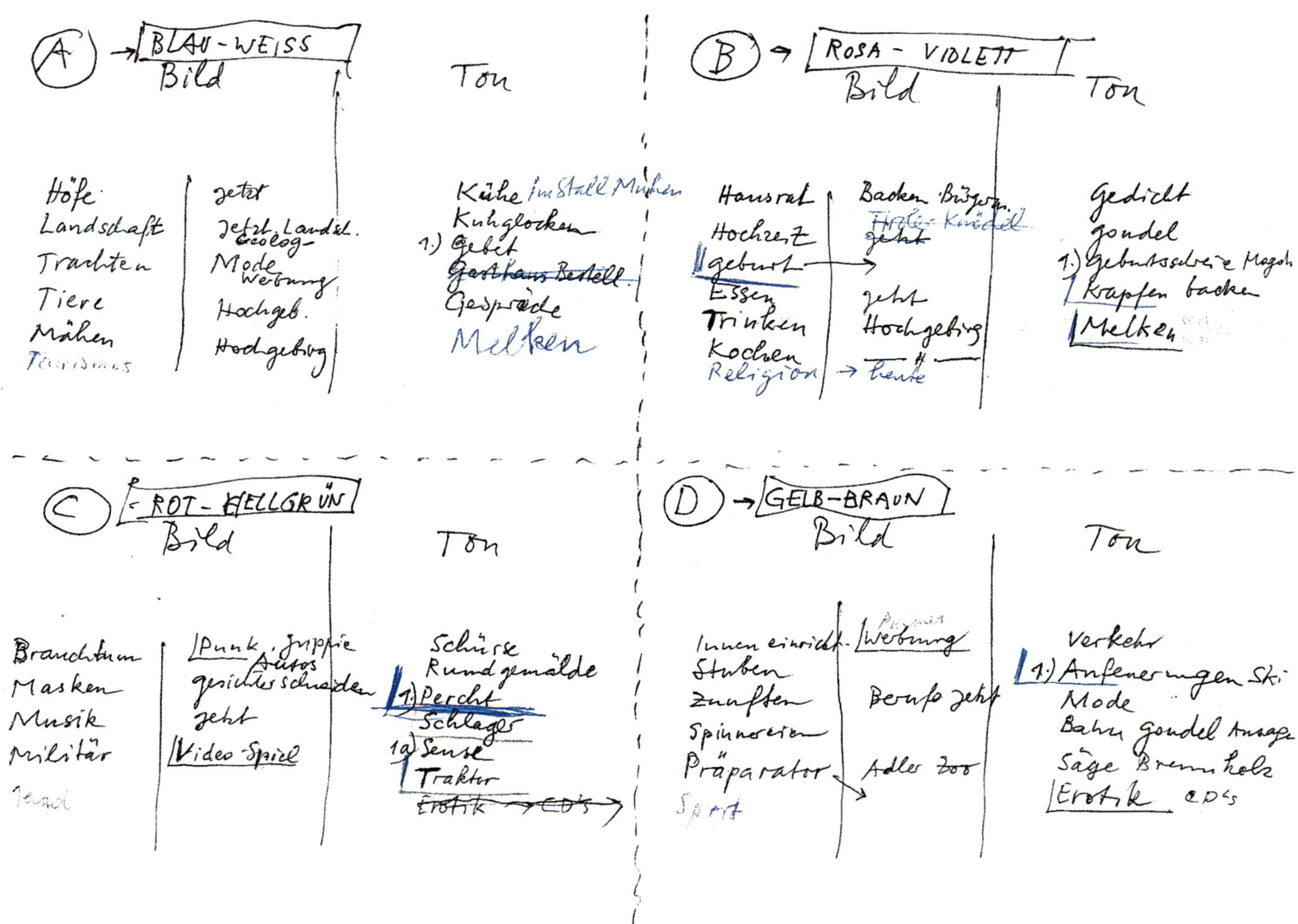

Doppel-Brenner, 1998

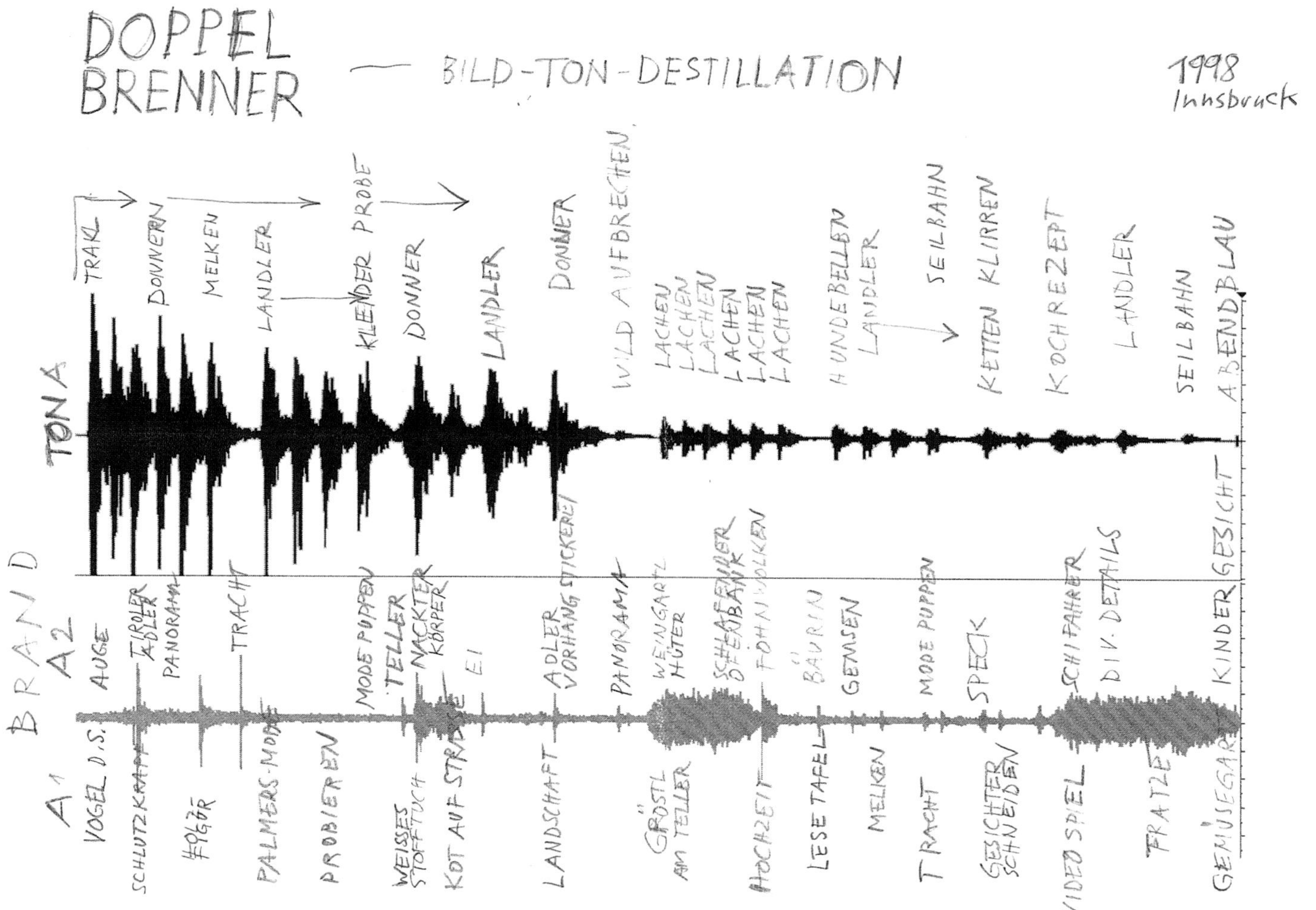

Konzept: H. Cibulka
Bild: Cibulka
Ton: Suchanek

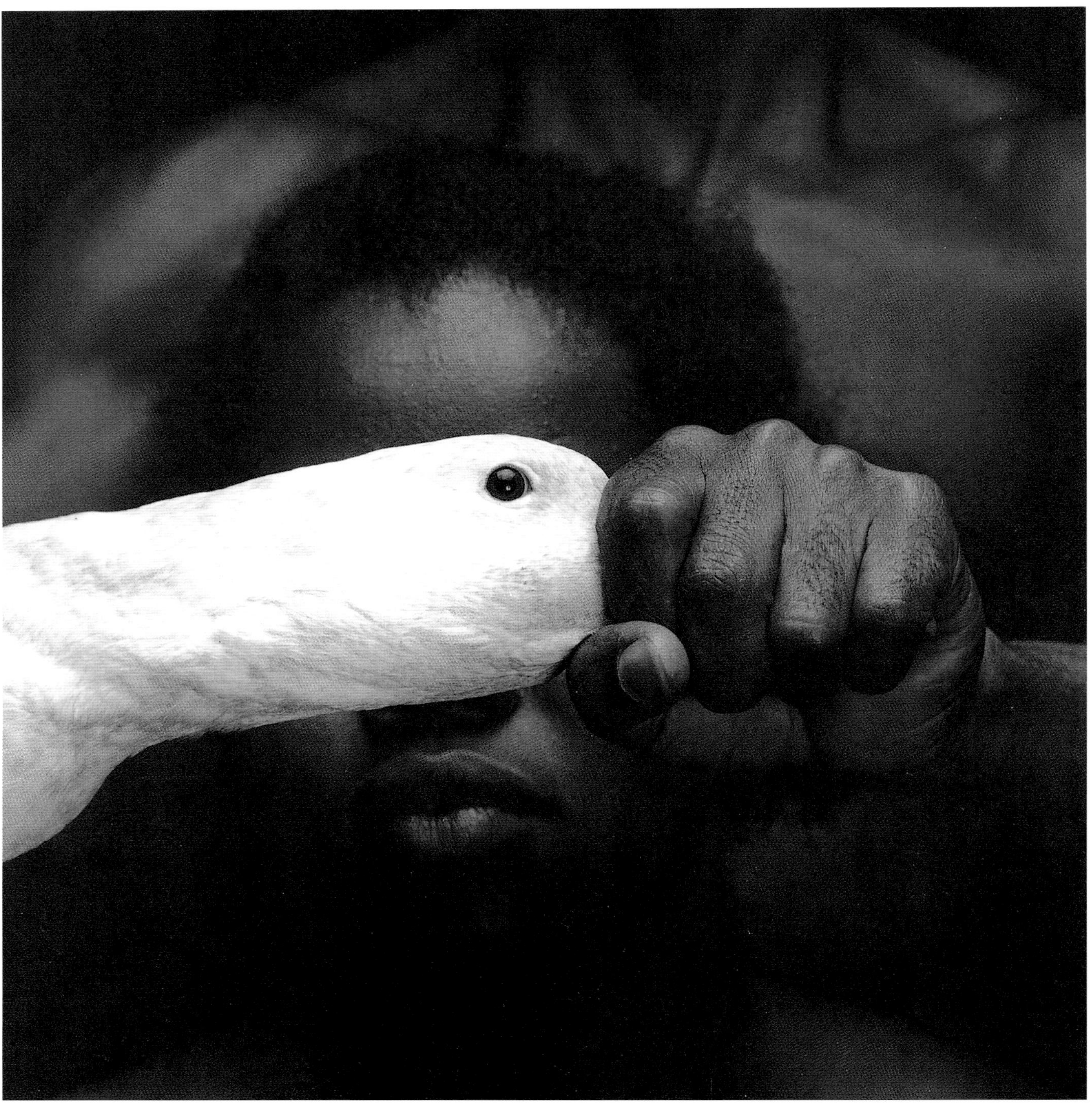

Odé, 1989

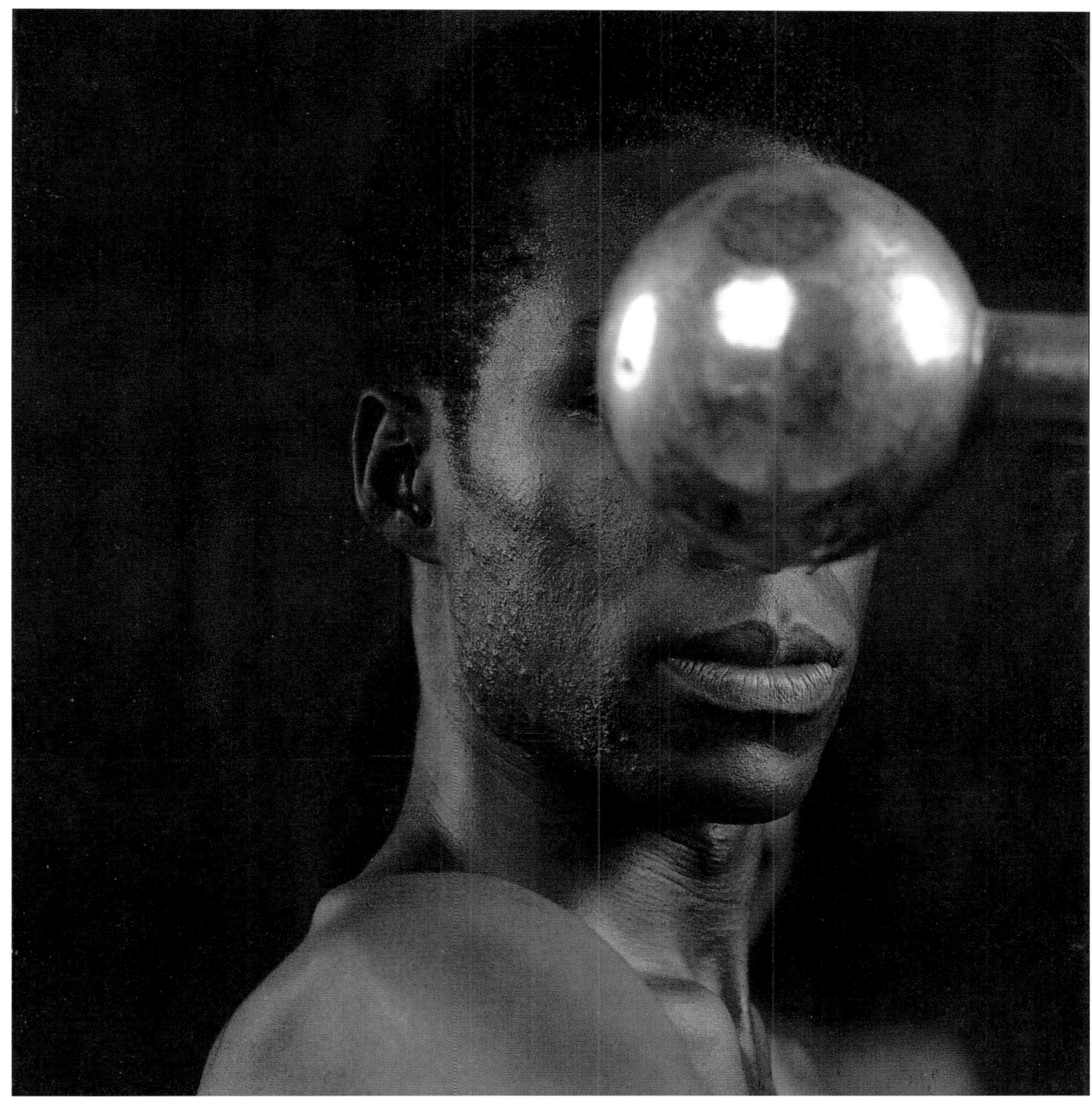

Pandang, 1991

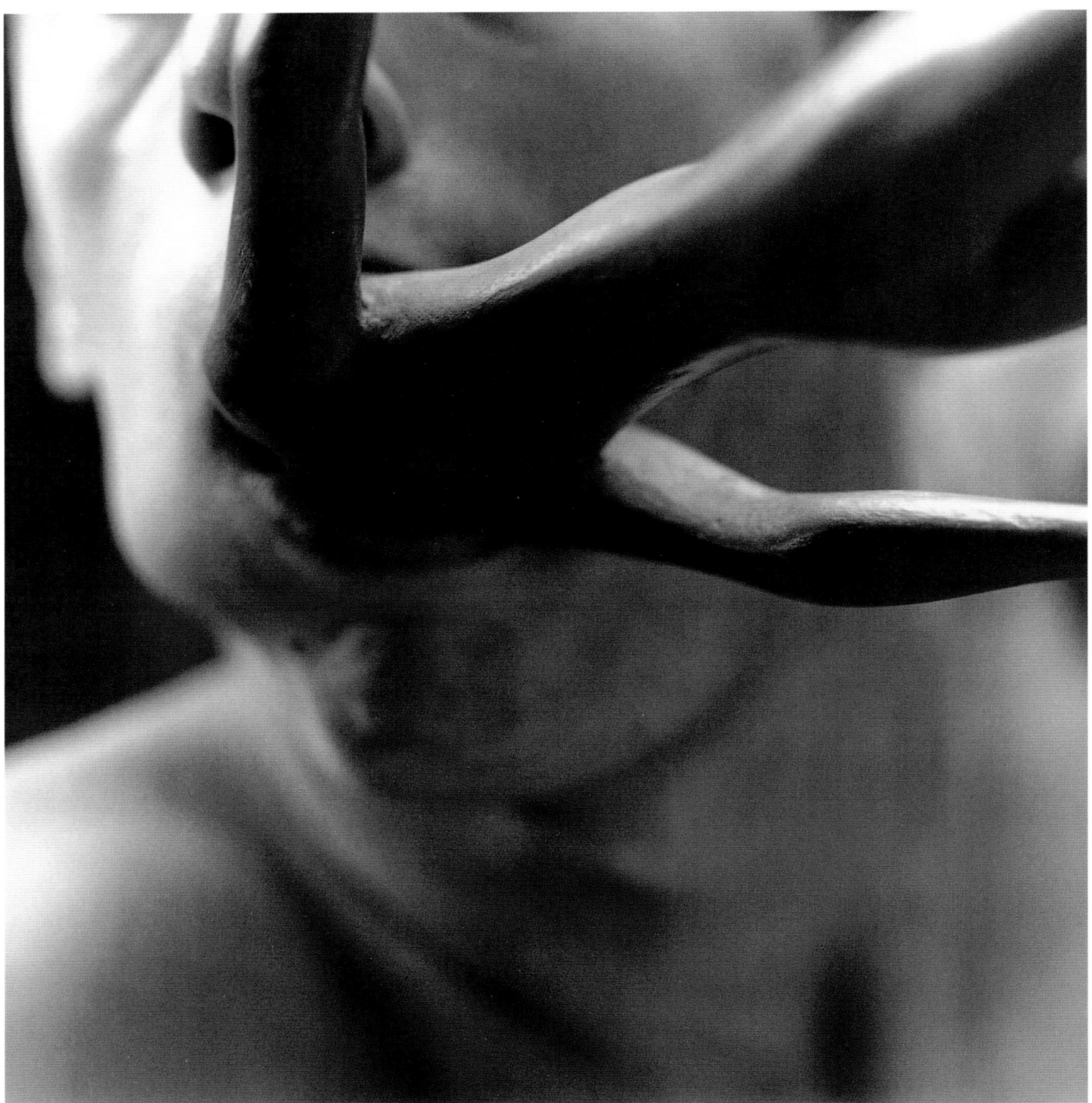

Saturno, 1992

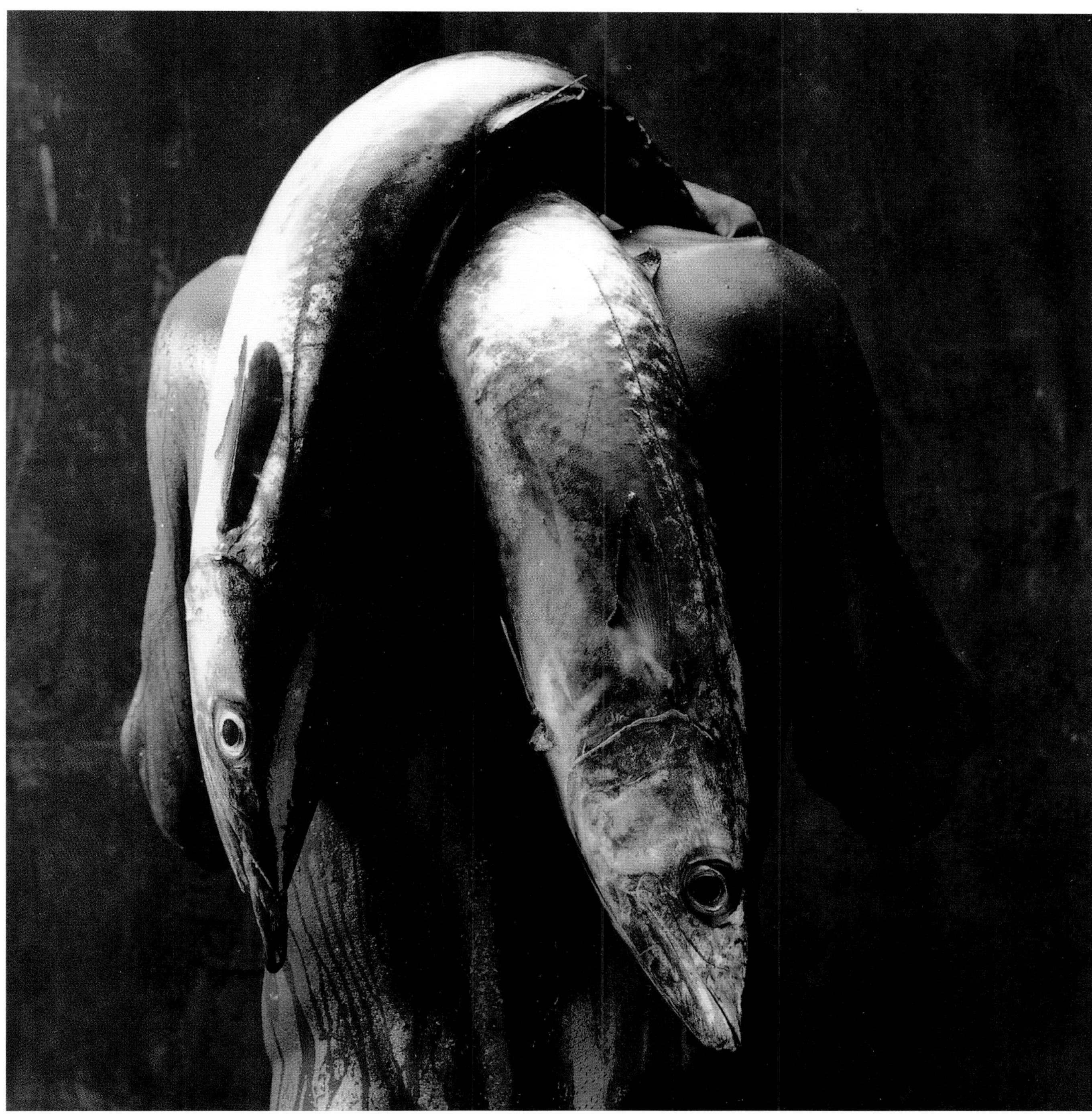

Man with Two Fish, 1992

Andy Warhol as a Tiroler Volkskunstler,
while Dead Picasso is still Scoring on Coconuts,
1998

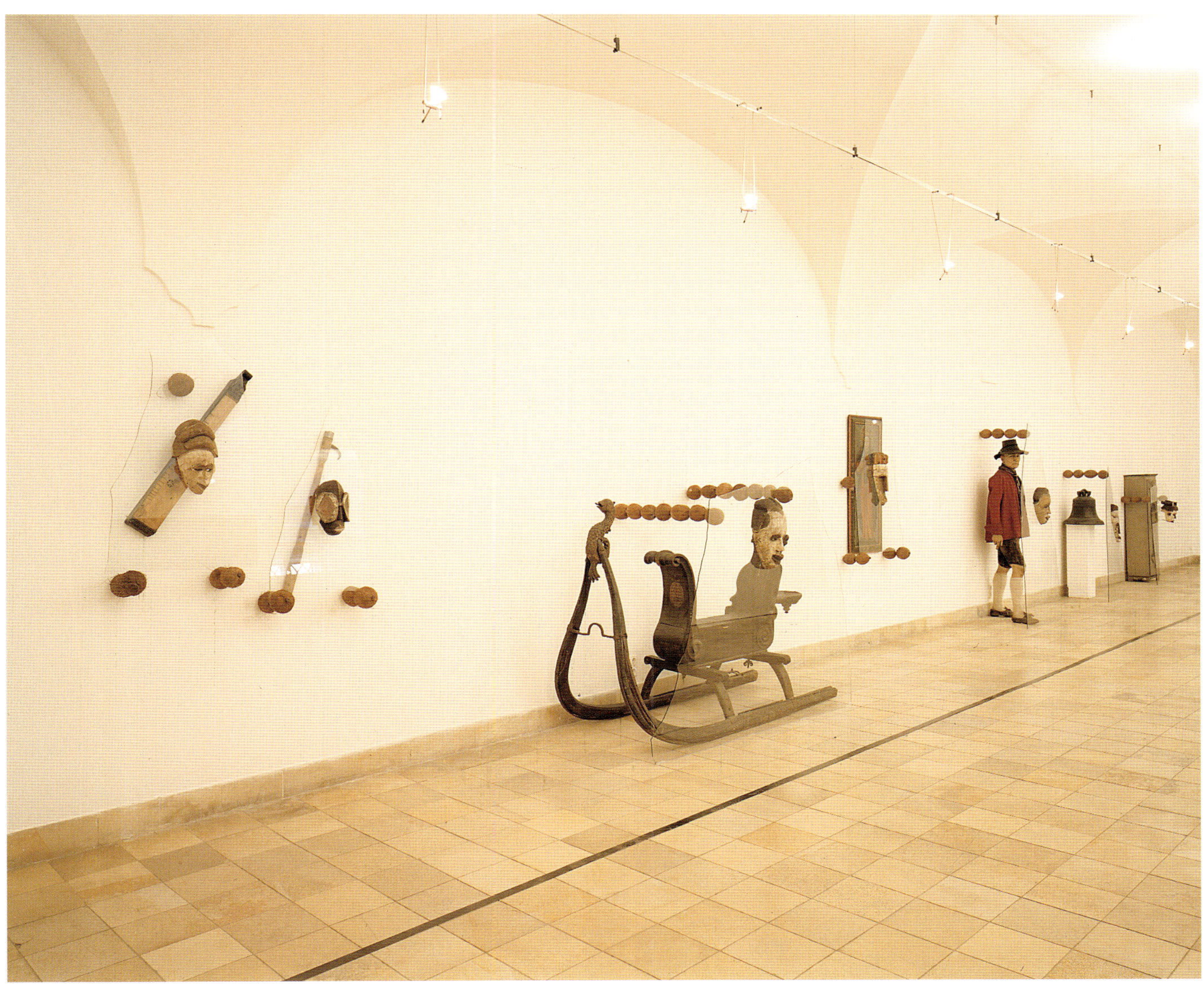

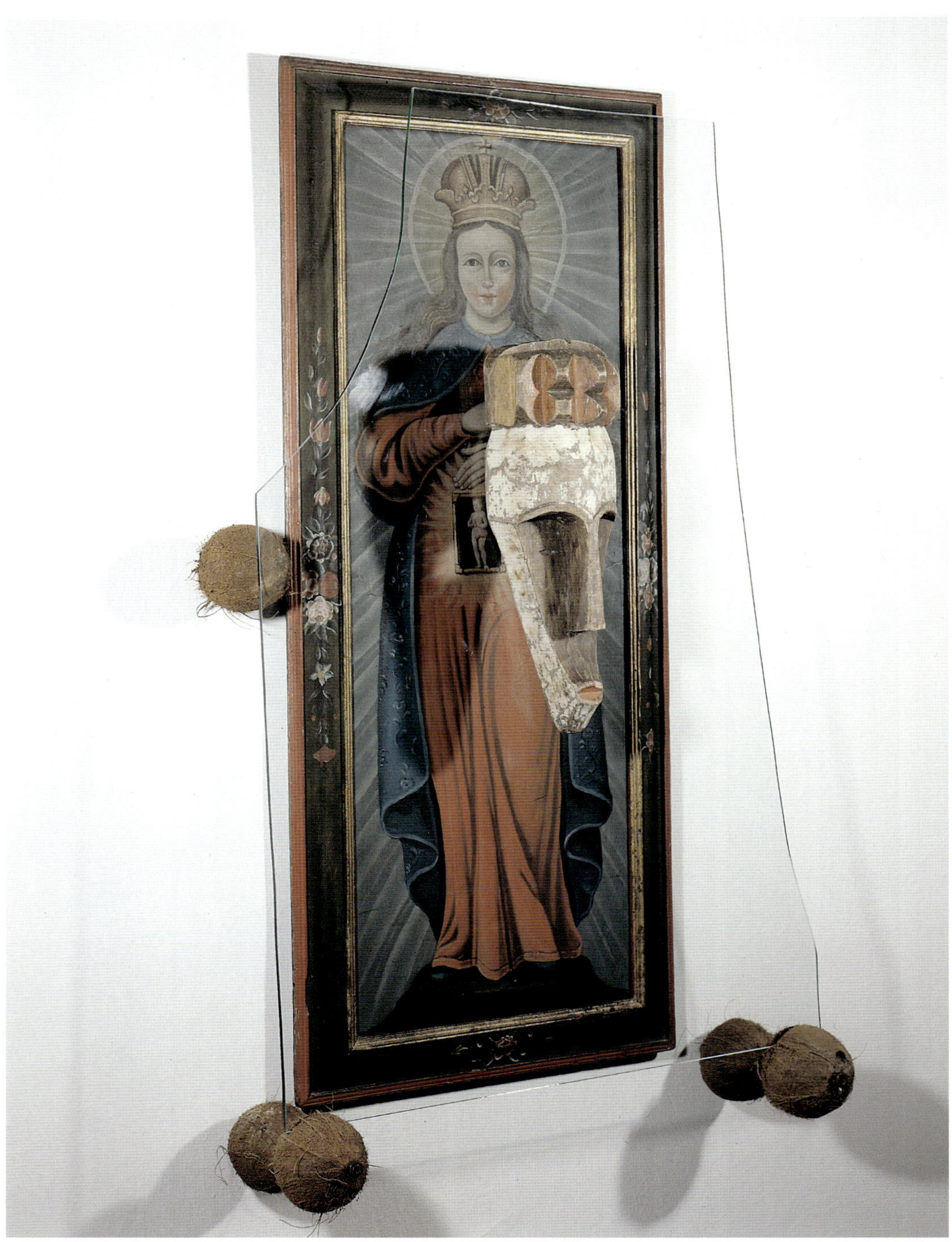

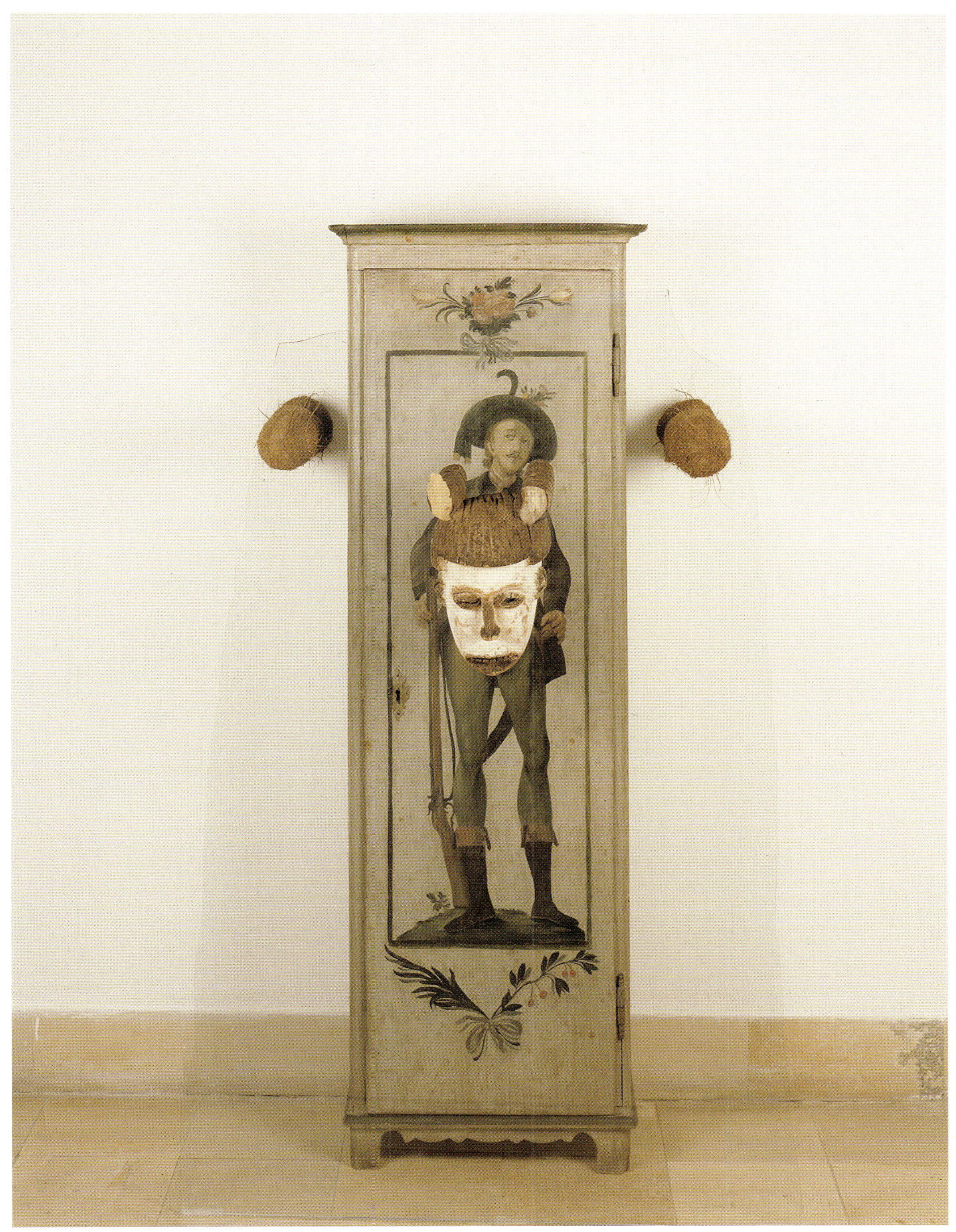

Handwerker, Trachtenhersteller, Bauern, Häuserbauer sind wie ich Rohstoff-Umwandler, also Kollegen. Die Nachbarschaft der hier gezeigten Symbolträger empfinde ich als ein Plus. Hier geht es um das, was den Menschen universal zur Verfügung steht. Neben Gebrauchsgegenständen die ungleichen Partner Knochen und Blut, die Gleichsetzung von Mensch und Tier, die Wanderung des Menschen vom Diesseits zum Jenseits. Diesen «Gen-Pool» verstehe ich, hier gibt es Gegenentwürfe zur Anonymität der Massengesellschaft.

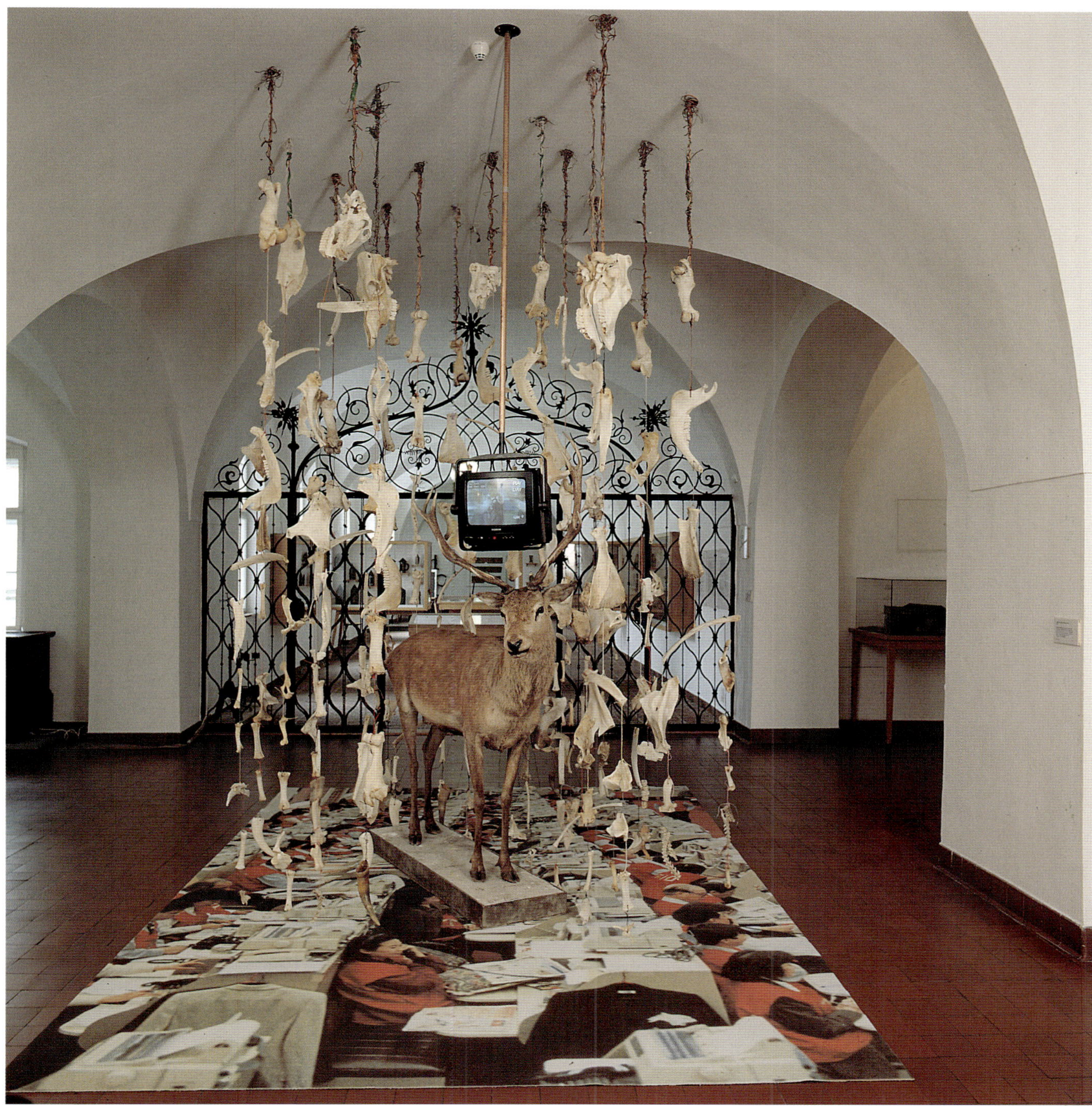

Global Village, 1998

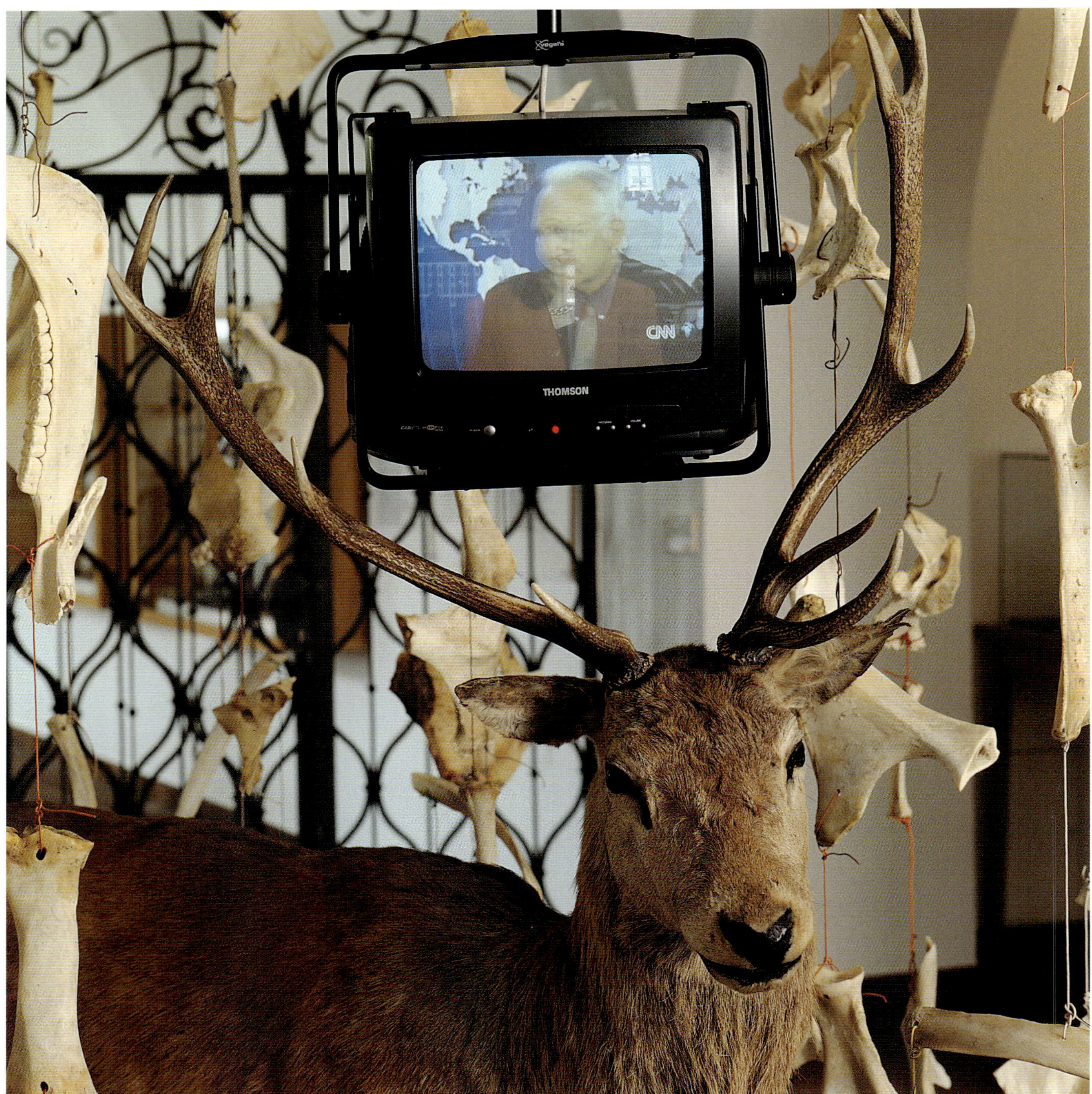

Global Village, 1998 (Detail)

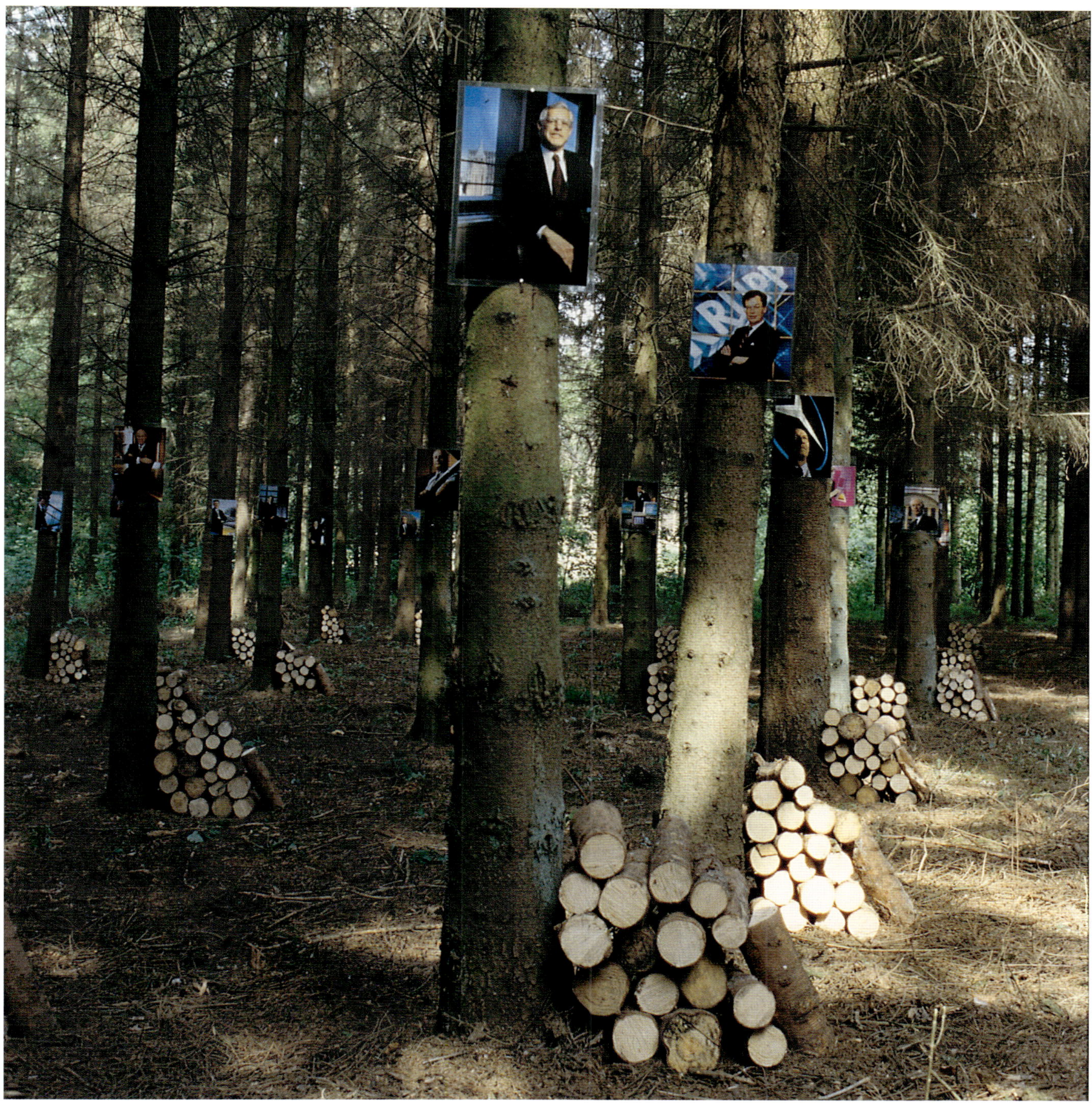

Global / Lokal, 1998

Old Democritus under a tree,
Sits on a stone with book on knee;
About him hang there many features,
Of cats, dogs, and such-like creatures,
Of which he makes anatomy,
The seat of black choler to see.
Over his head appears the sky,
And Saturn, Lord of melancholy.

Robert Burton, *The Anatomy of Melancholy*

Wann endlich der Gram keinen bestimmten Gegenstand mehr hat,
sondern über das Ganze des Lebens sich verbreitet;
dann ist er gewissermaßen ein In-sich-Gehen, ein Zurückziehen,
ein allmähliches Verschwinden des Willens, dessen Sichtbarkeit, den Leib,
er sogar leise, aber im Innersten untergräbt, wobei der Mensch eine gewisse Ablösung
seiner Banden spürt, ein sanftes Vorgefühl des sich als Auflösung
des Leibes und des Willens zugleich ankündigenden Todes;
daher diesen Gram eine heimliche Freude begleitet, welche es, wie ich glaube, ist,
die das melancholischste aller Völker the joy of grief genannt hat.

Arthur Schopenhauer, *Die Welt als Wille und Vorstellung*

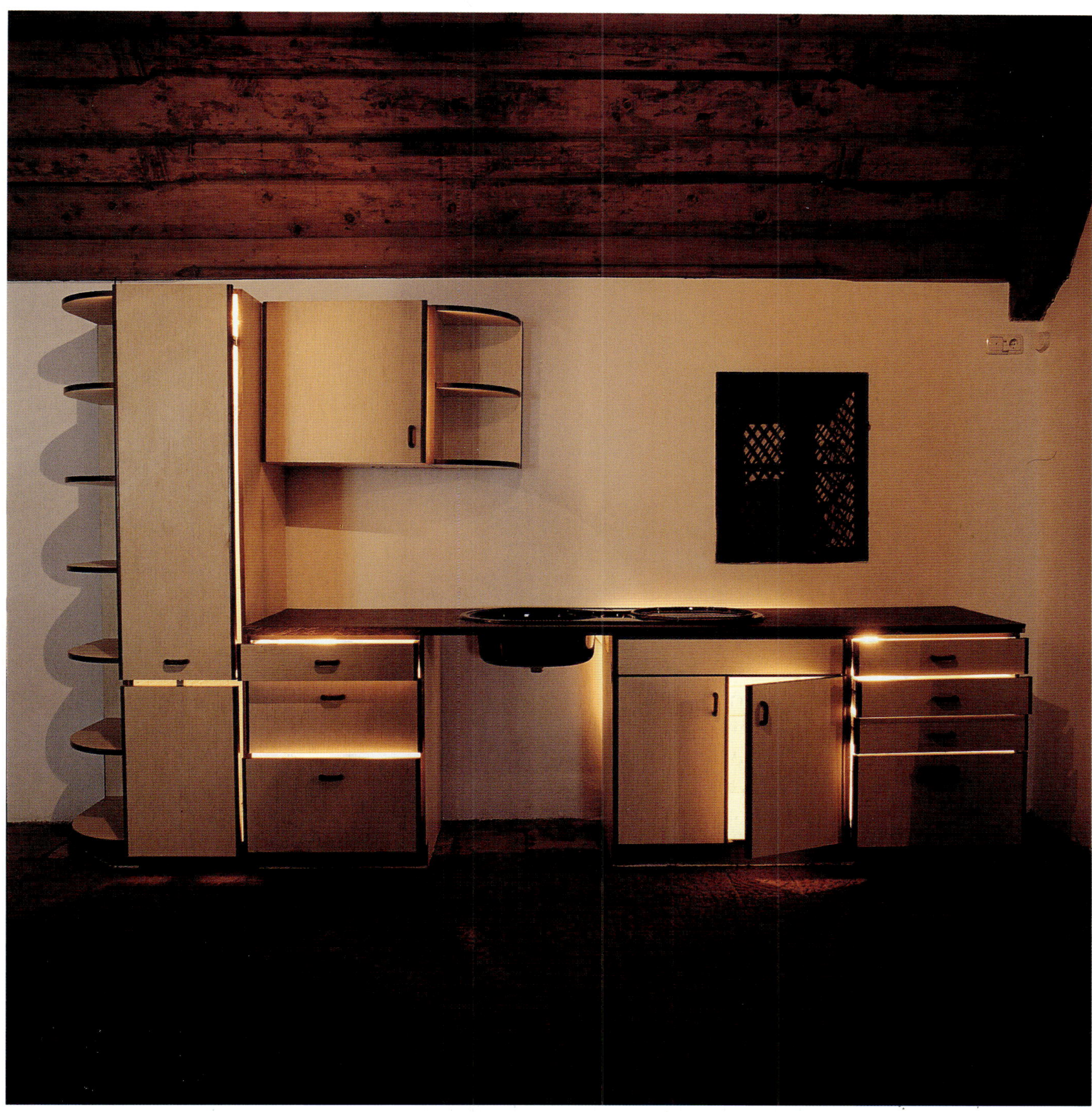

Öde Gallenküche II, 1998

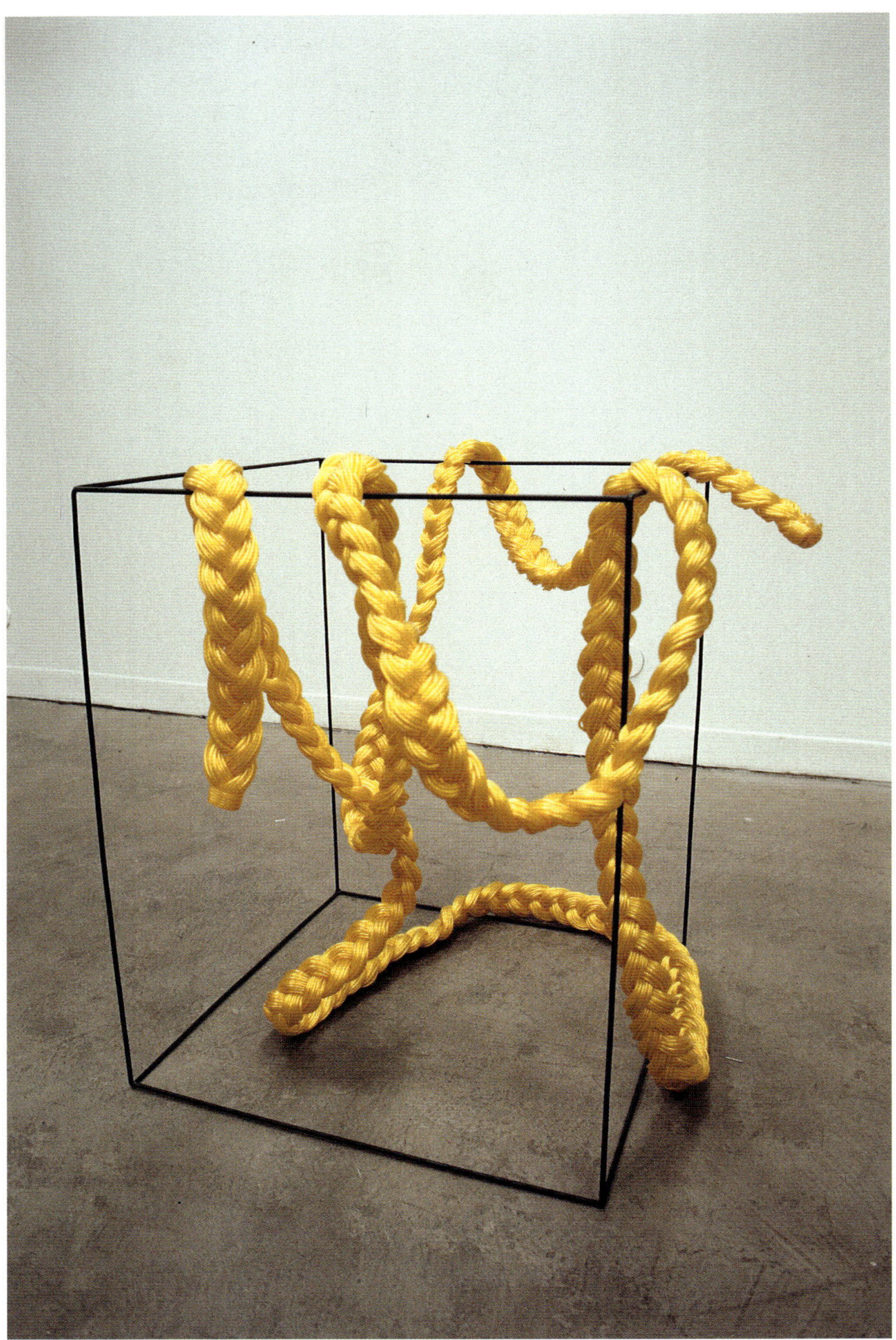

Dem Rat der Philosophen zu folgen, 1997

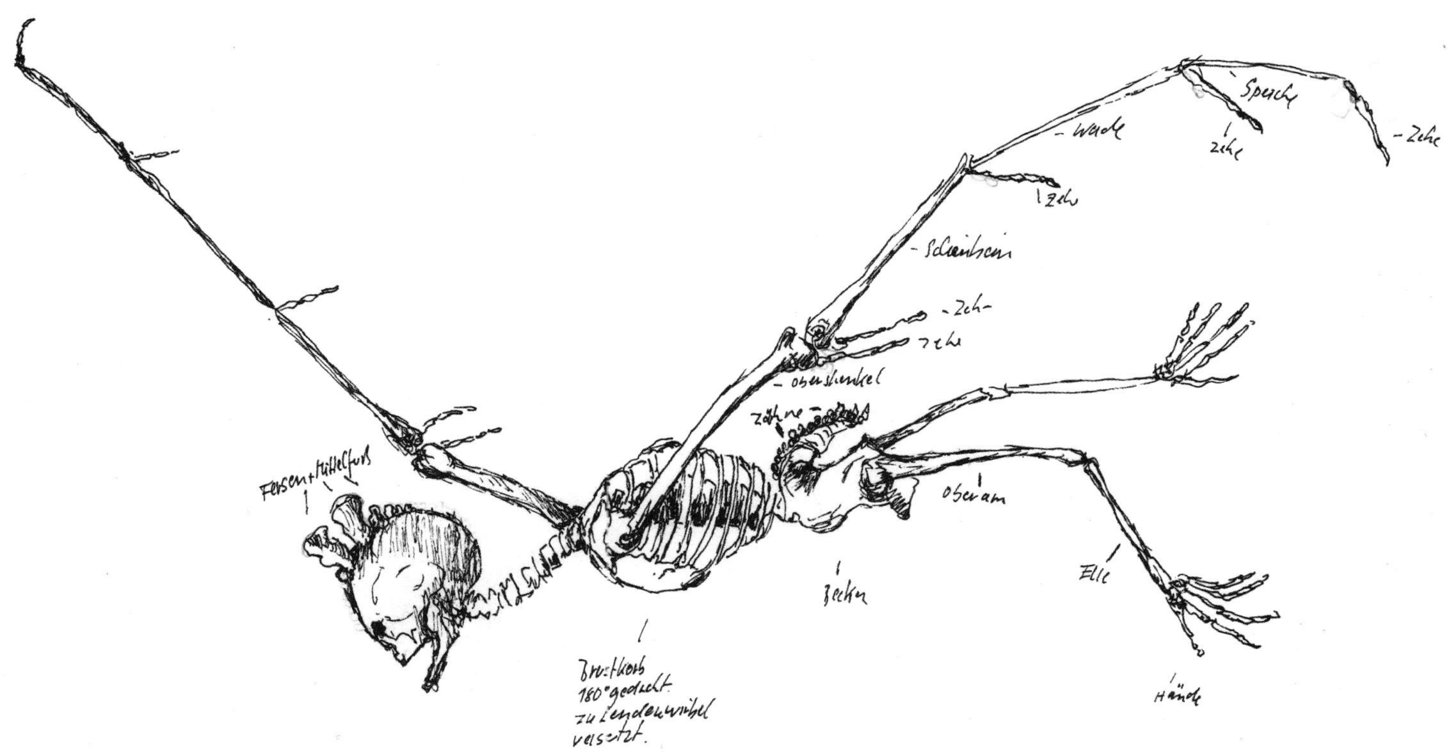

Vorstellung (Ihre Anatomie), 1998

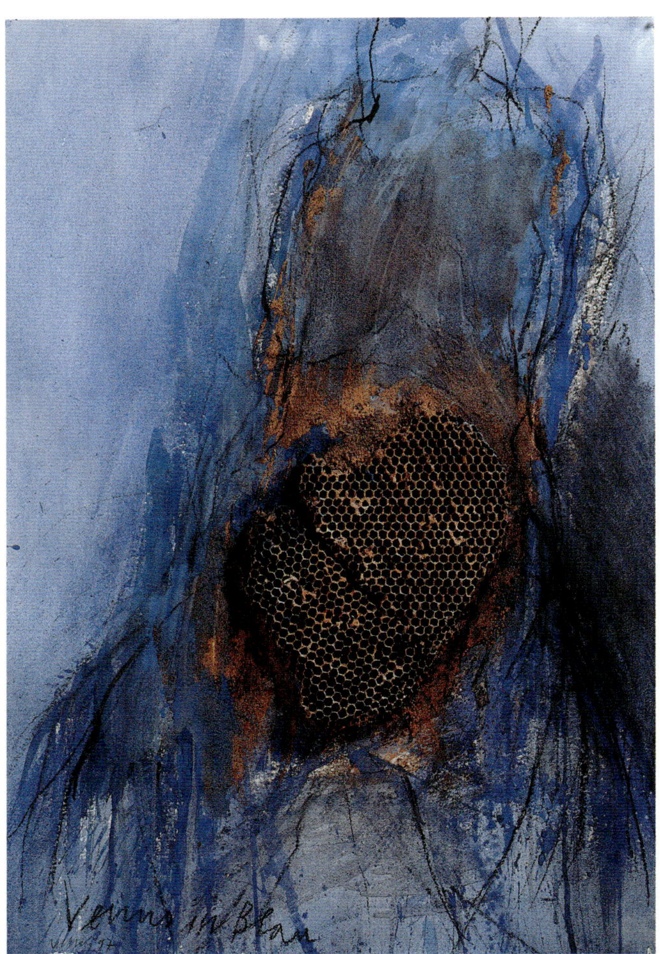

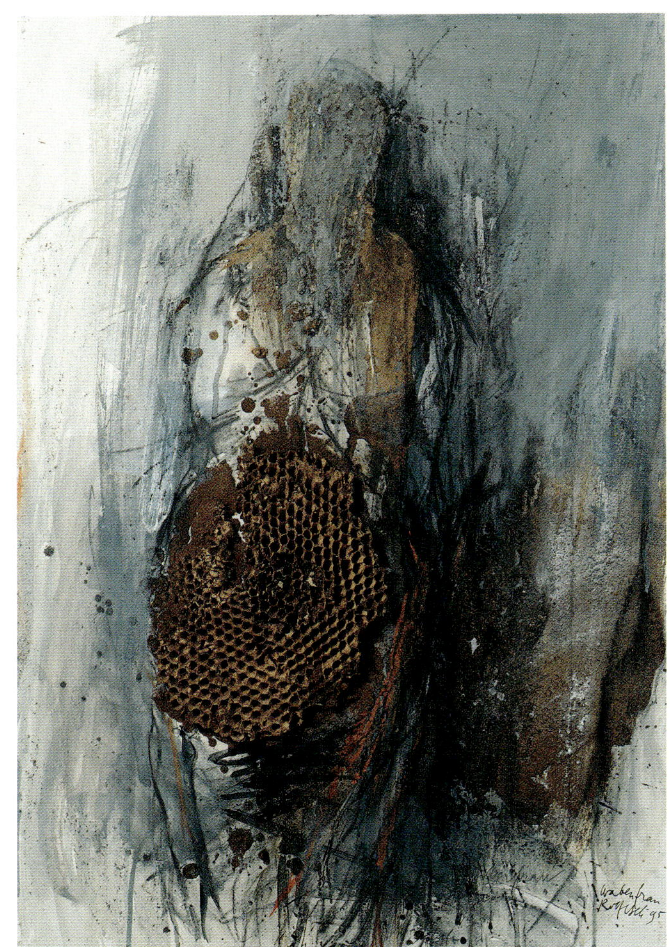

Venus in Blau, 1997

Wabenfrau, 1995

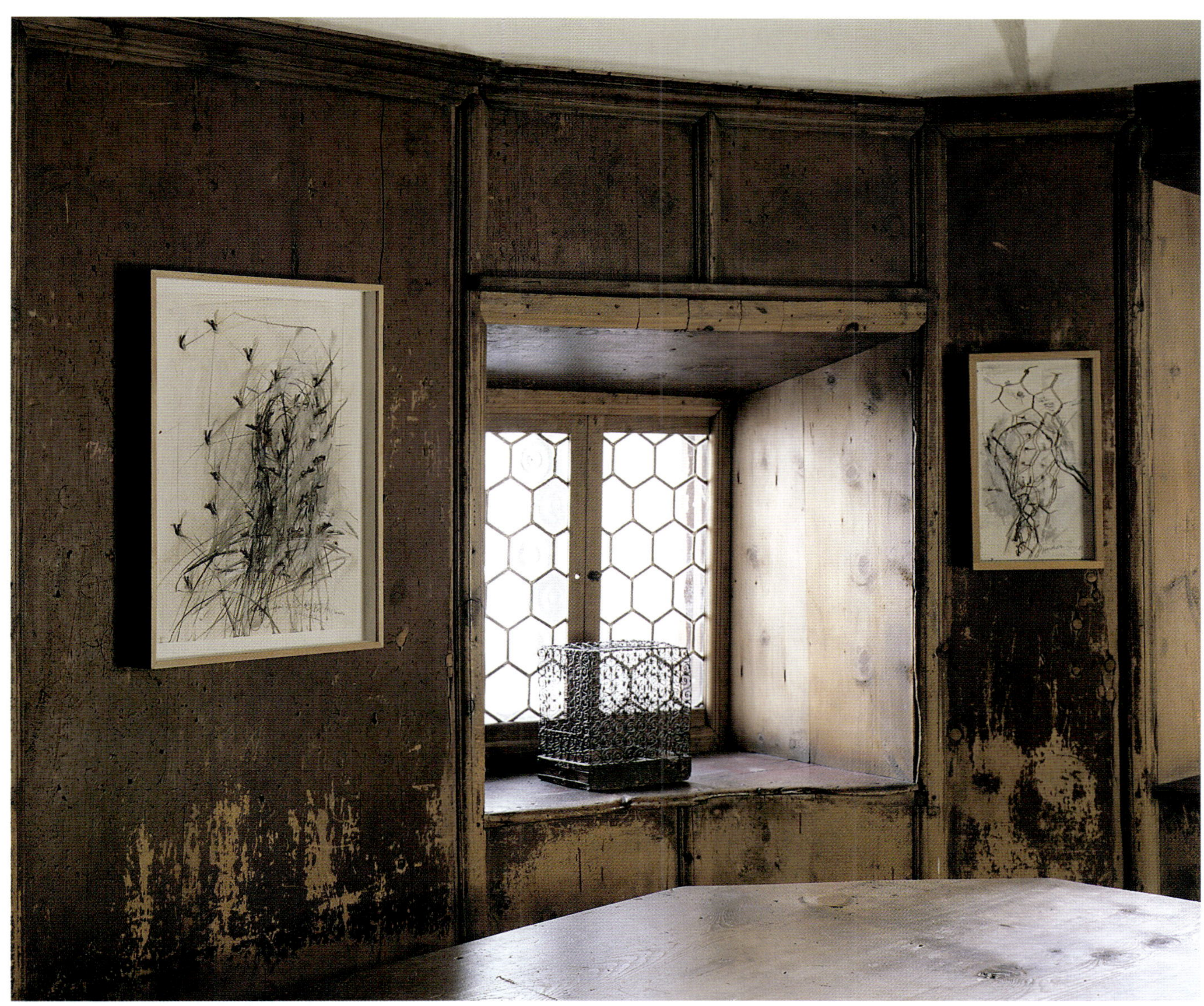

Installation mit

Ablesbar, 1994

Horcher, 1982-83

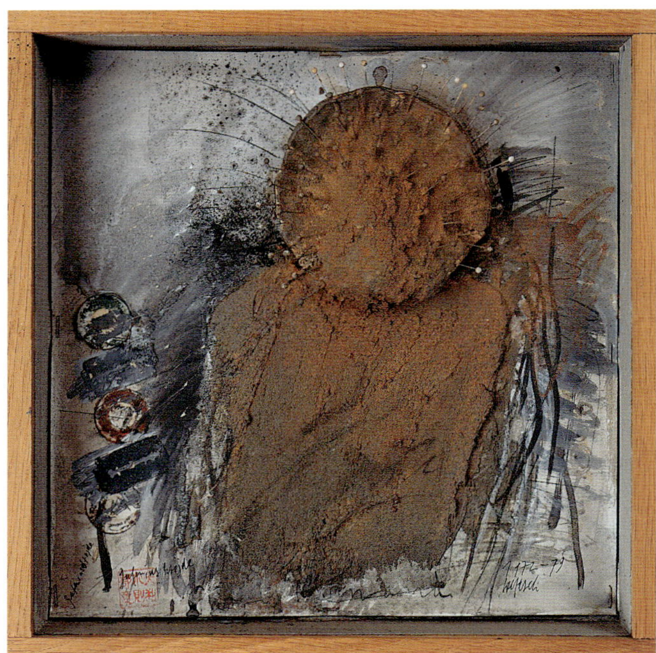

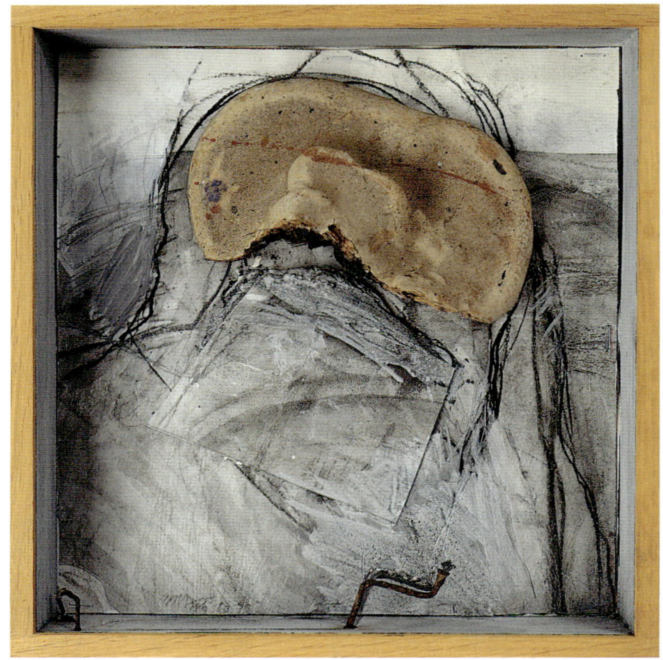

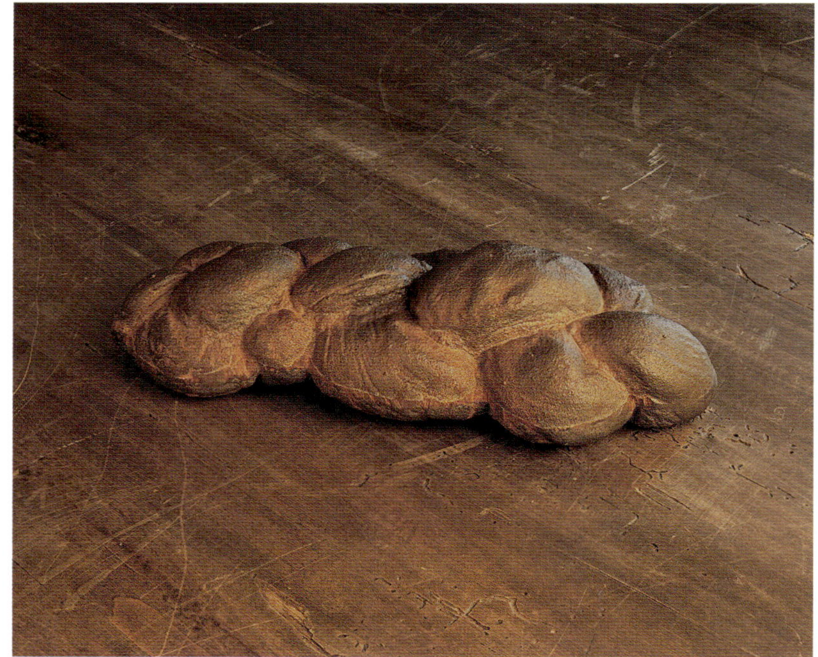

Gufen-Insektoide, 1972–79

Schwummkopf, 1983

Eisenzüpfe, 1970

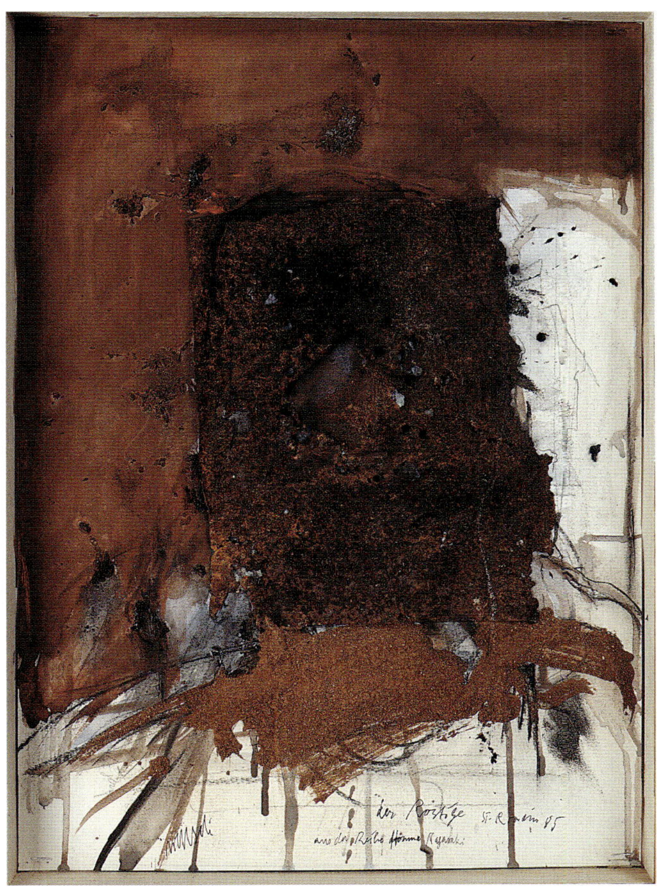

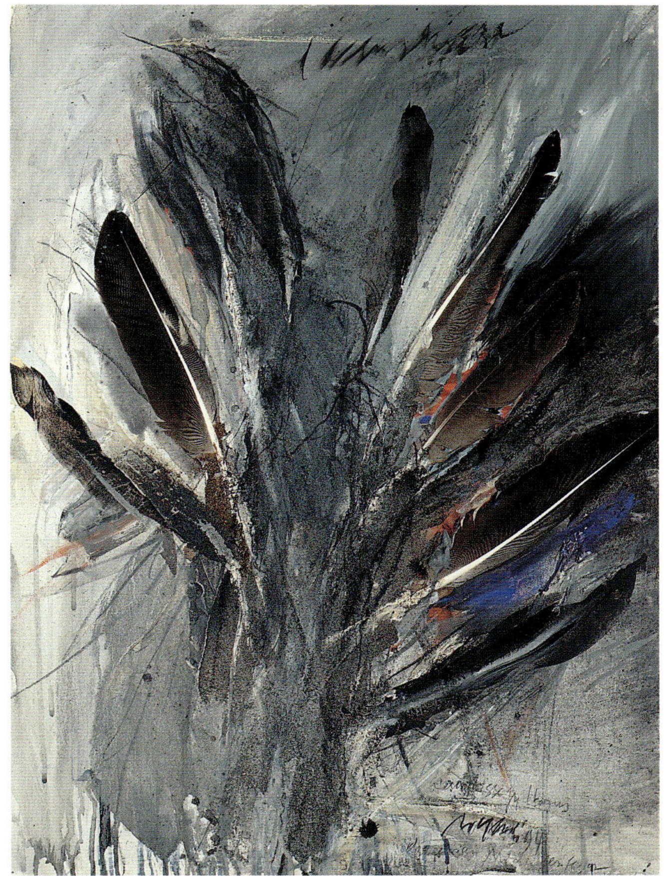

Der Rostige, 1985

Die ewigen Möchtegernflieger, 1994

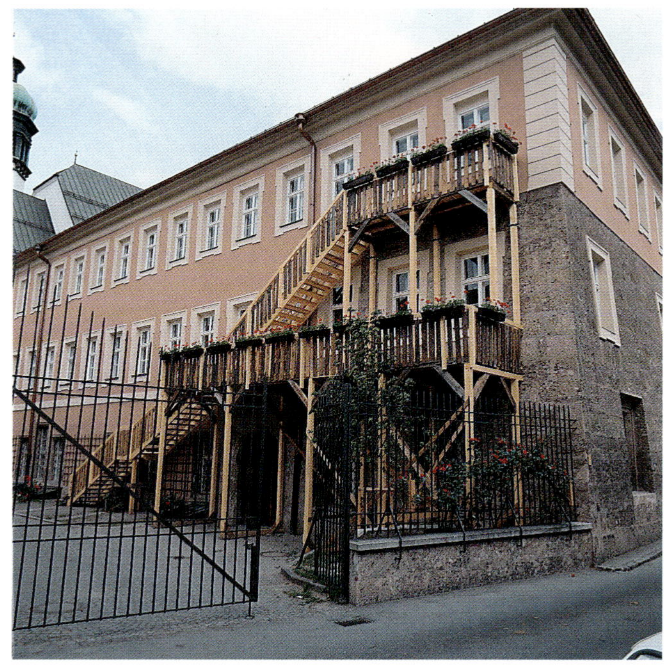

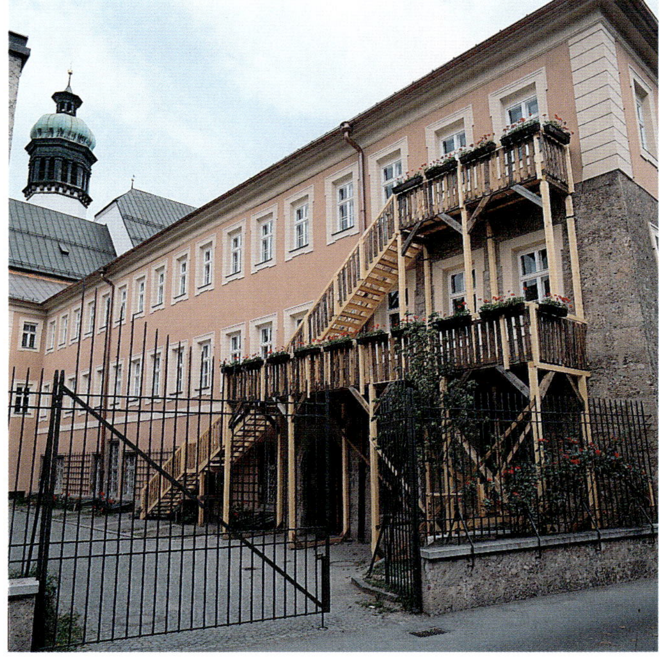

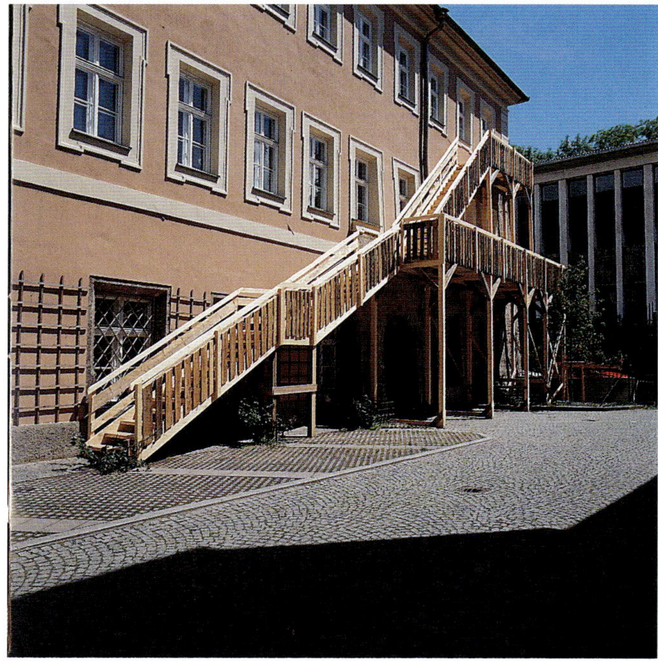

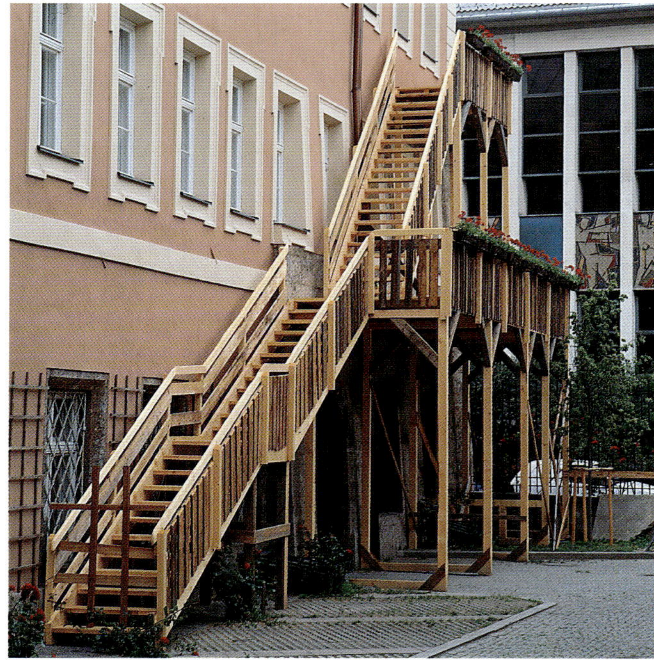

Zwischenraum, 1998

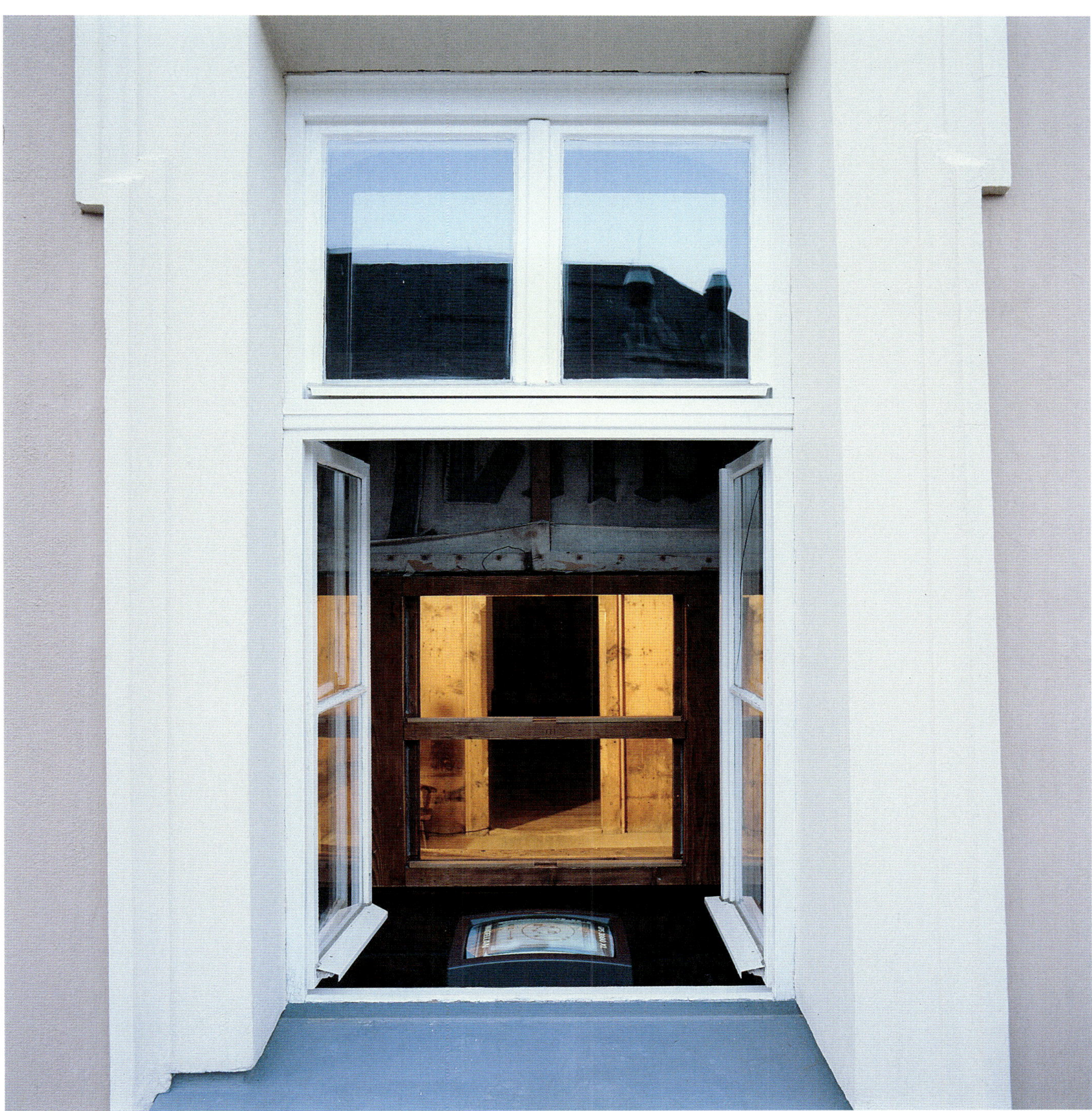

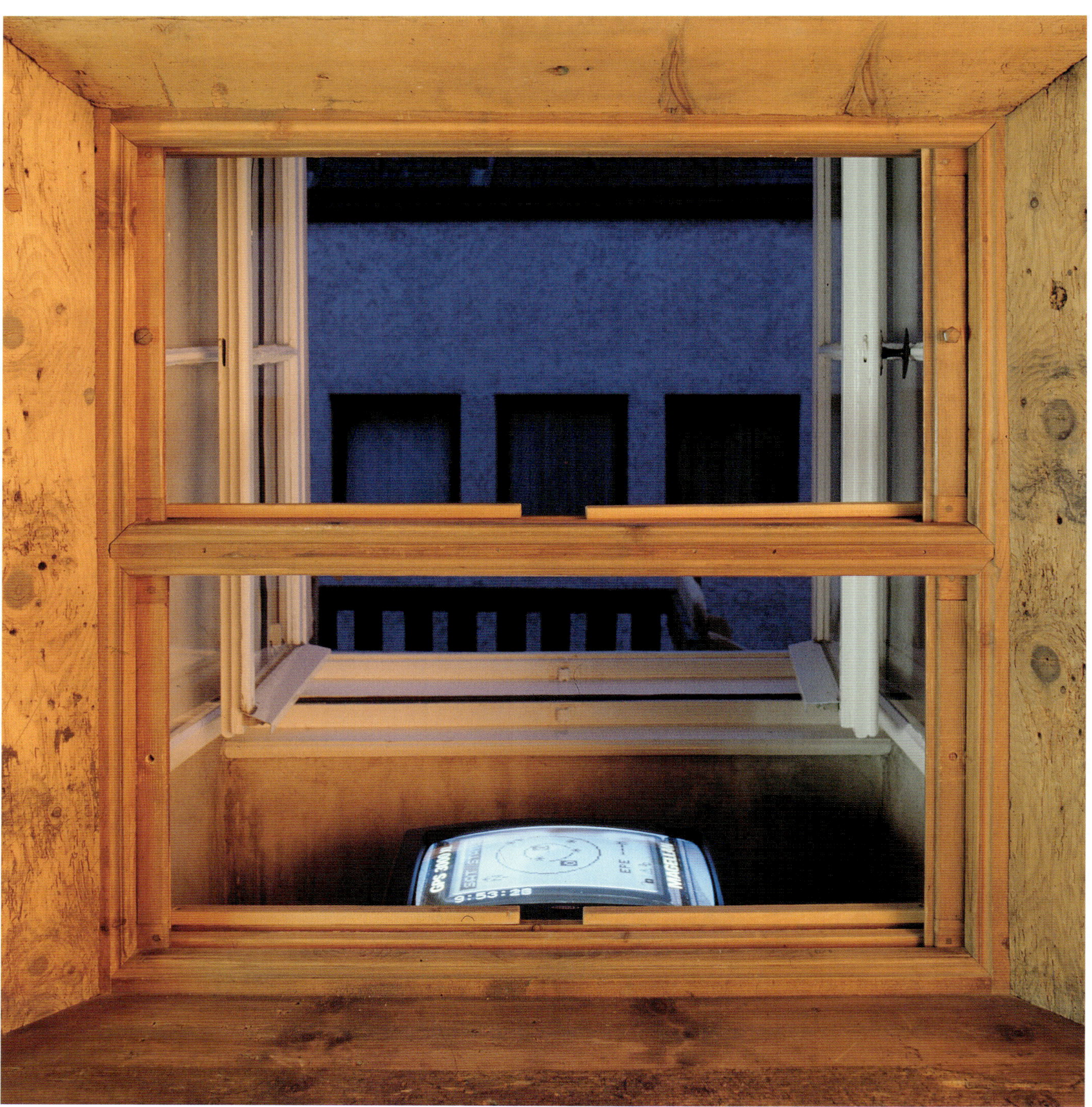

Zwischenraum, 1998

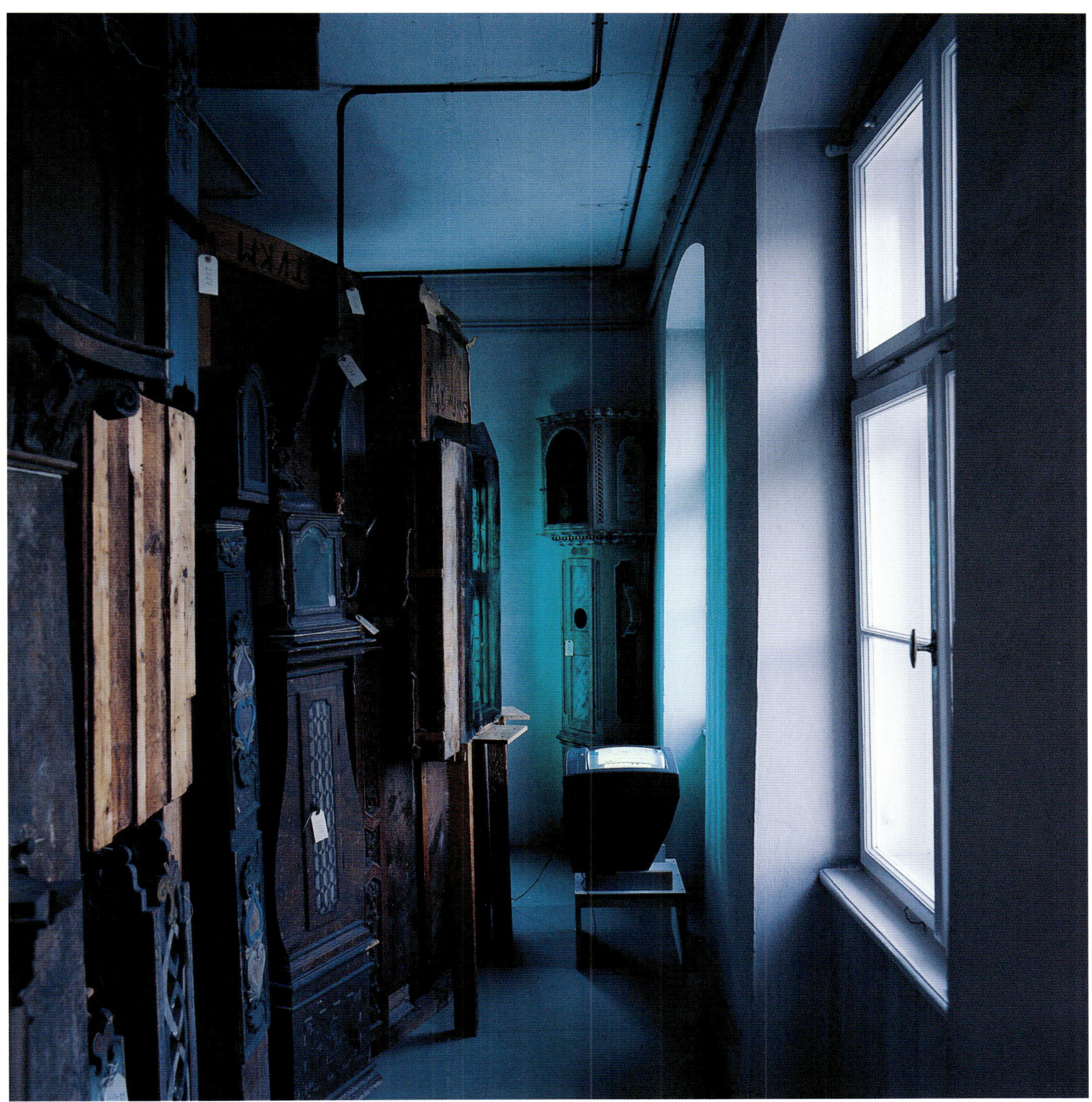

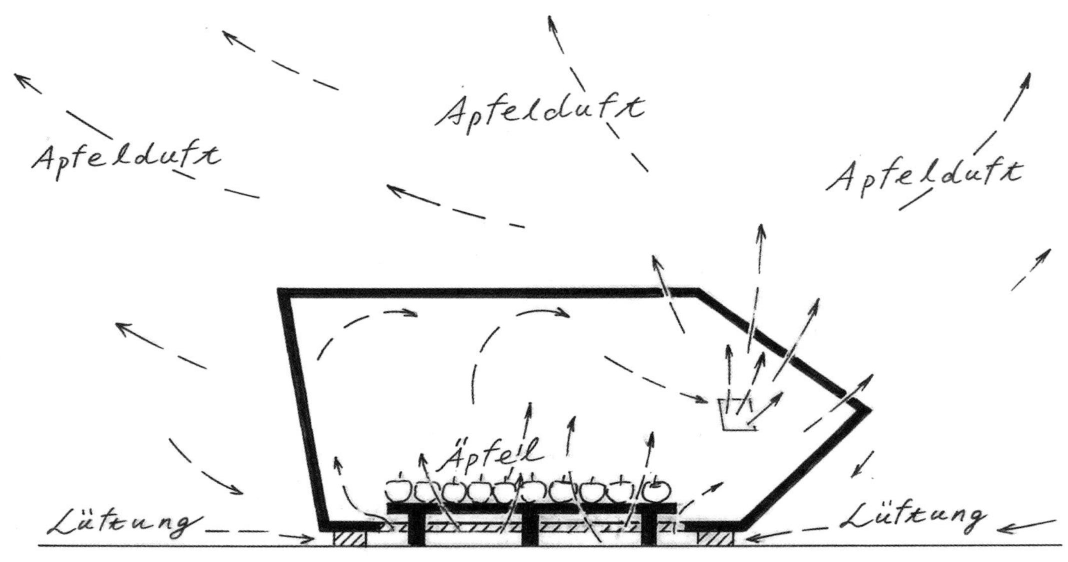

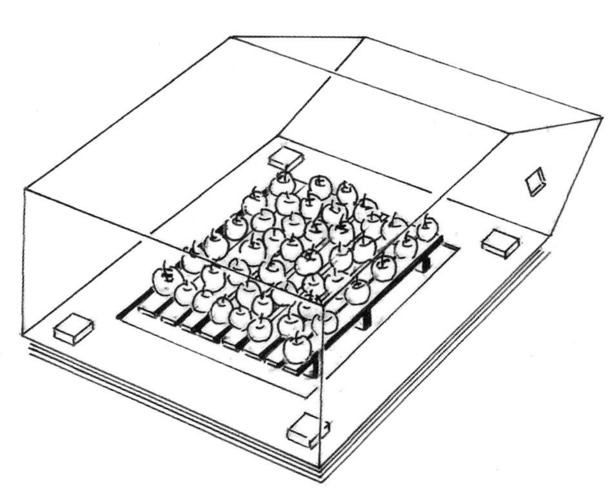

Ort-Raum "Apfelgarten (Die Suche nach der verlorenen Zeit)" 1998

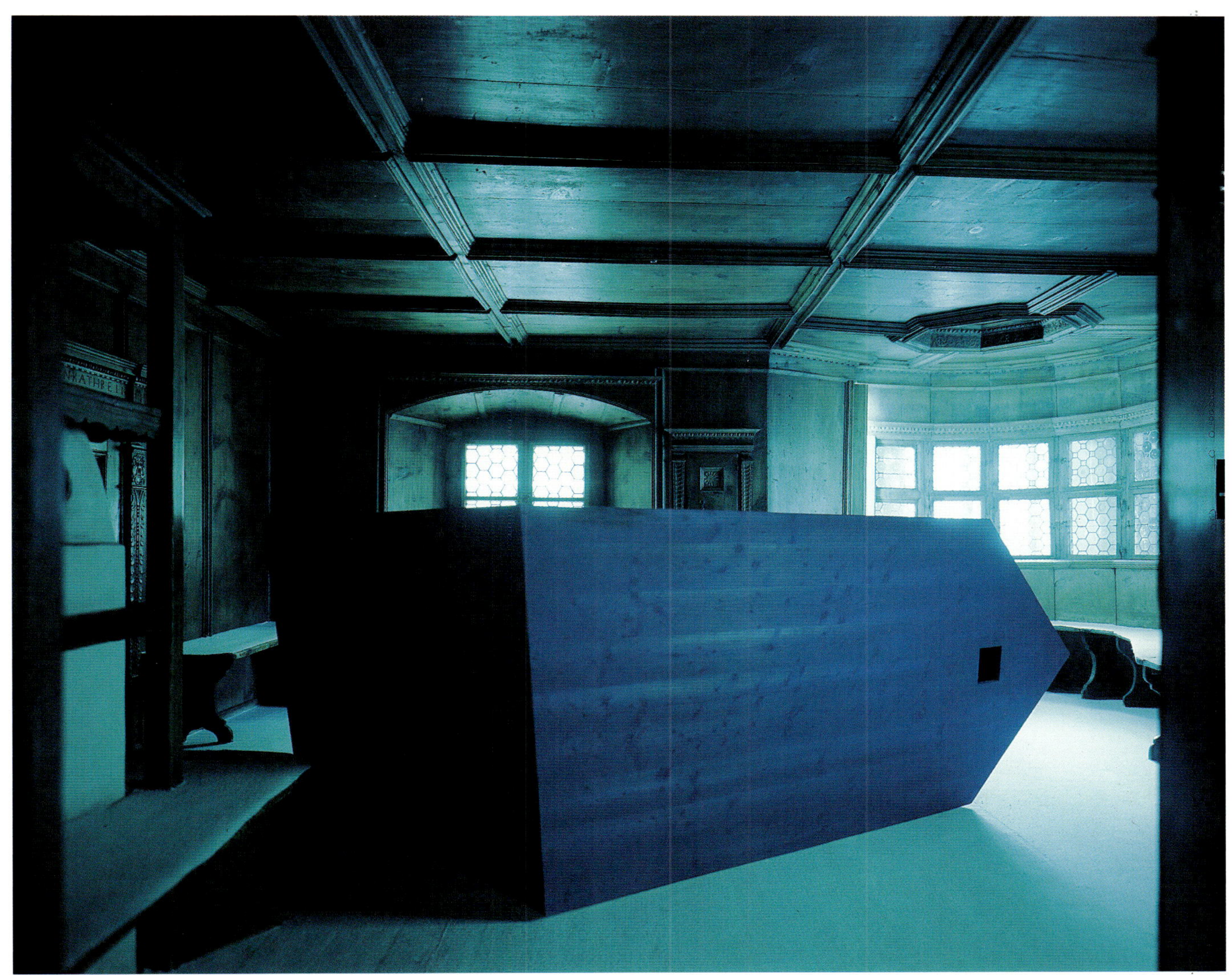

Ort-Raum: Apfelgarten (Die Suche nach der verlorenen Zeit), 1998

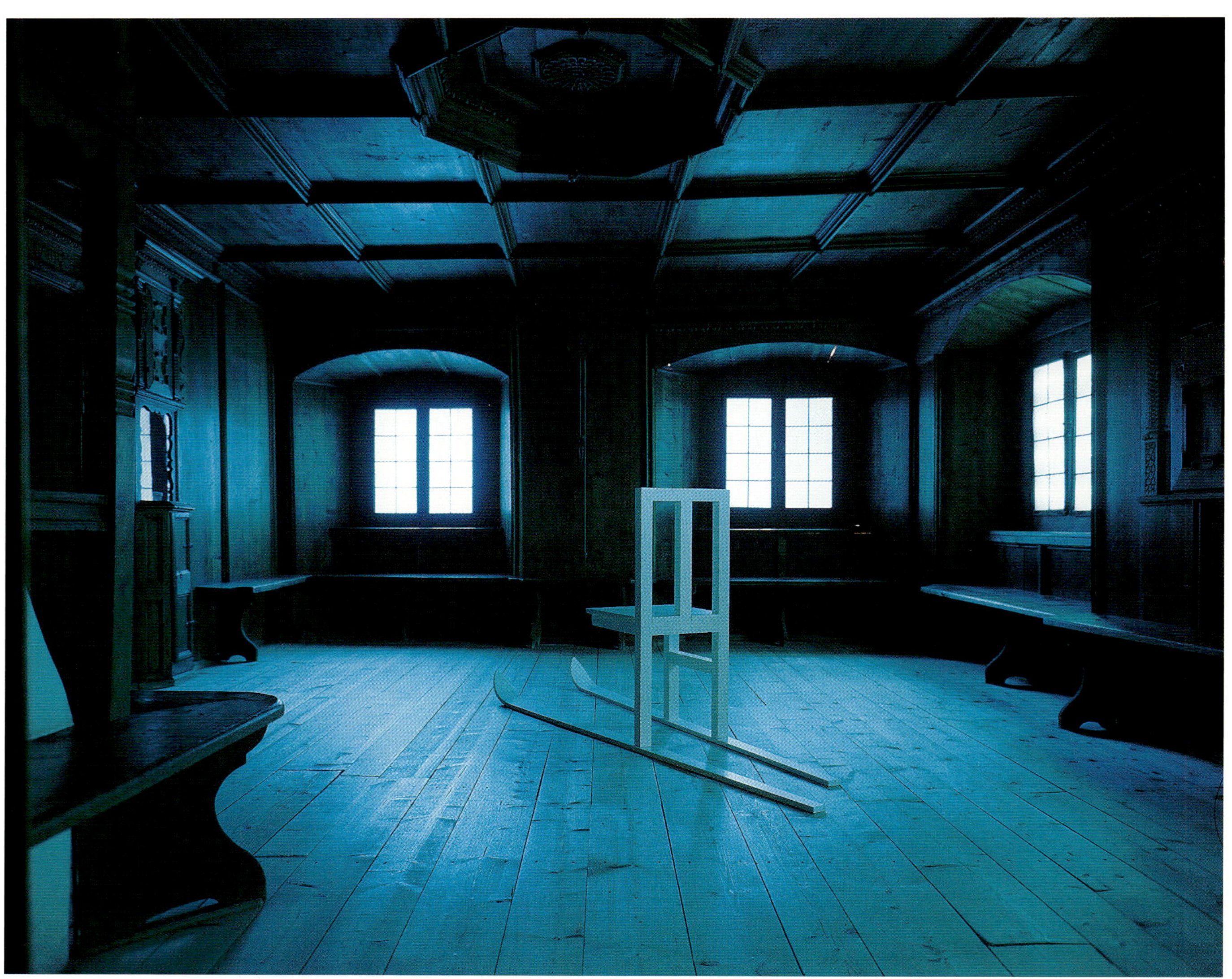

Ort-Raum: Apfelgarten (Die Suche nach der verlorenen Zeit), 1998

Stawrogin: «… In der Apokalypse verkündet der Engel, daß es keine Zeit mehr geben werde.»

Kirillow: «Ich weiß. Das steht dort sehr nachdrücklich, unmißverständlich und klar. Wenn jeder Mensch glücklich ist, dann wird es auch keine Zeit mehr geben, weil sie dann gar nicht mehr gebraucht werden wird. Ein sehr richtiger Gedanke.»

Stawrogin: «Aber wo wird man sie dann verstecken?»

Kirillow: «Man wird sie nirgends verstecken. Die Zeit ist schließlich kein Ding, sondern eine Idee. Sie wird im Verstand verlöschen.»

F. M. Dostojewskij, *Die Dämonen*

Ohne Titel (Museumskordel), 1998

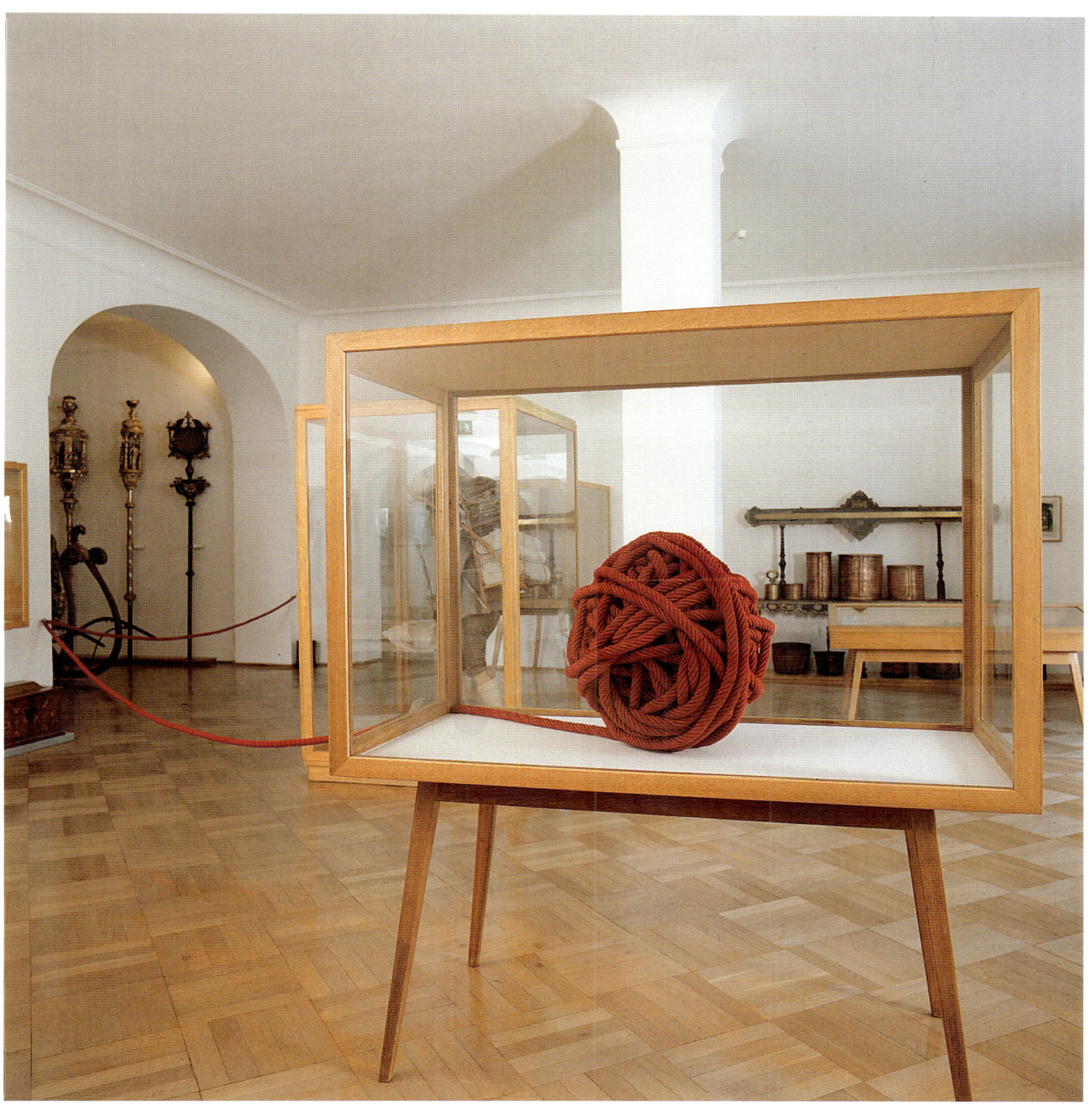

Roter Teppich, 1996
Installation im Museum des 20. Jahrhunderts, Wien, zur Ausstellung «Coming Up»

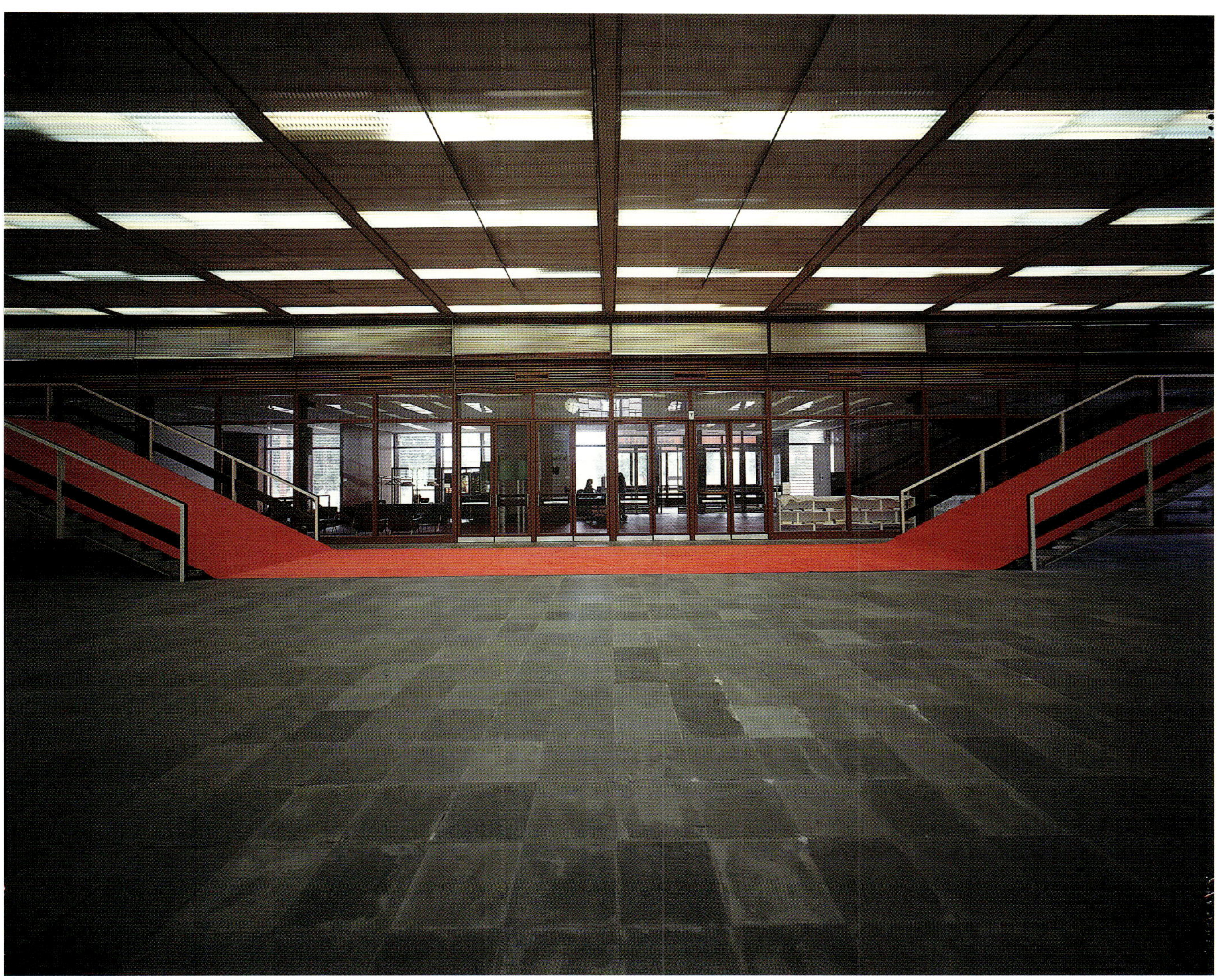

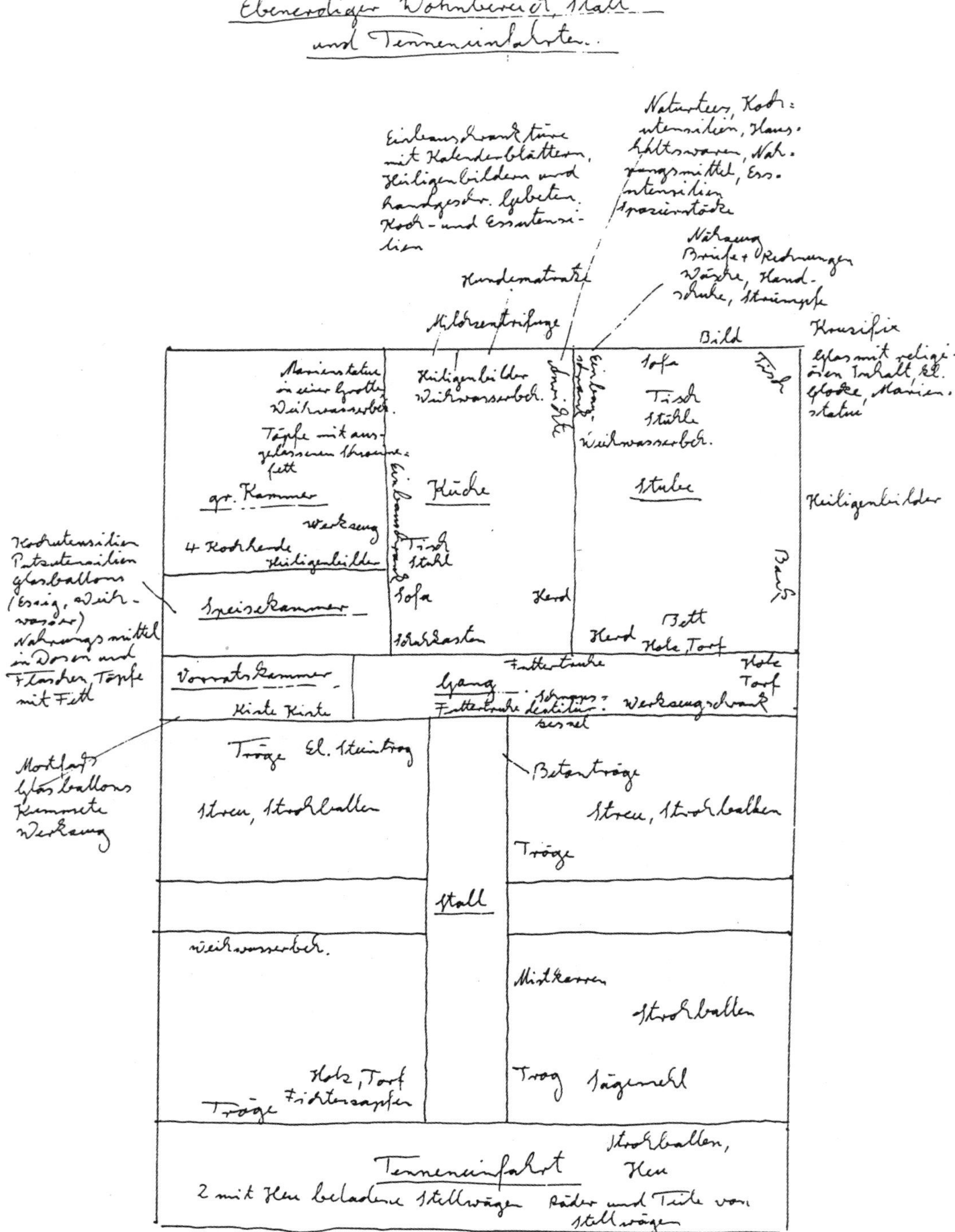

Für Frau G. «Nachlaß – Lebensmittel- und religiöser Hort», 1981/82
Courtesy: Staatliche Museen zu Berlin,
Nationalgalerie, Eigentum des Vereins der Freunde der Nationalgalerie

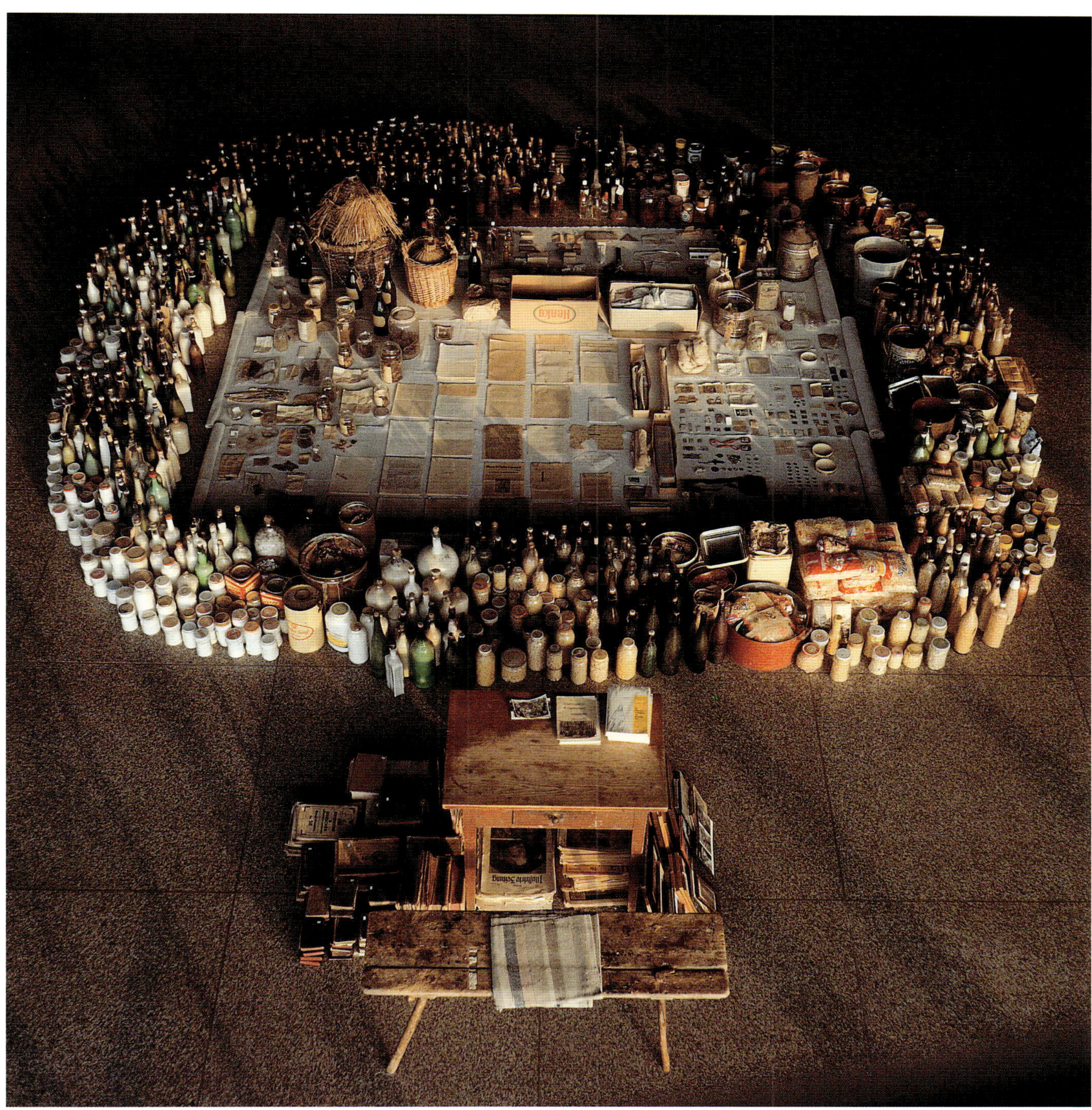

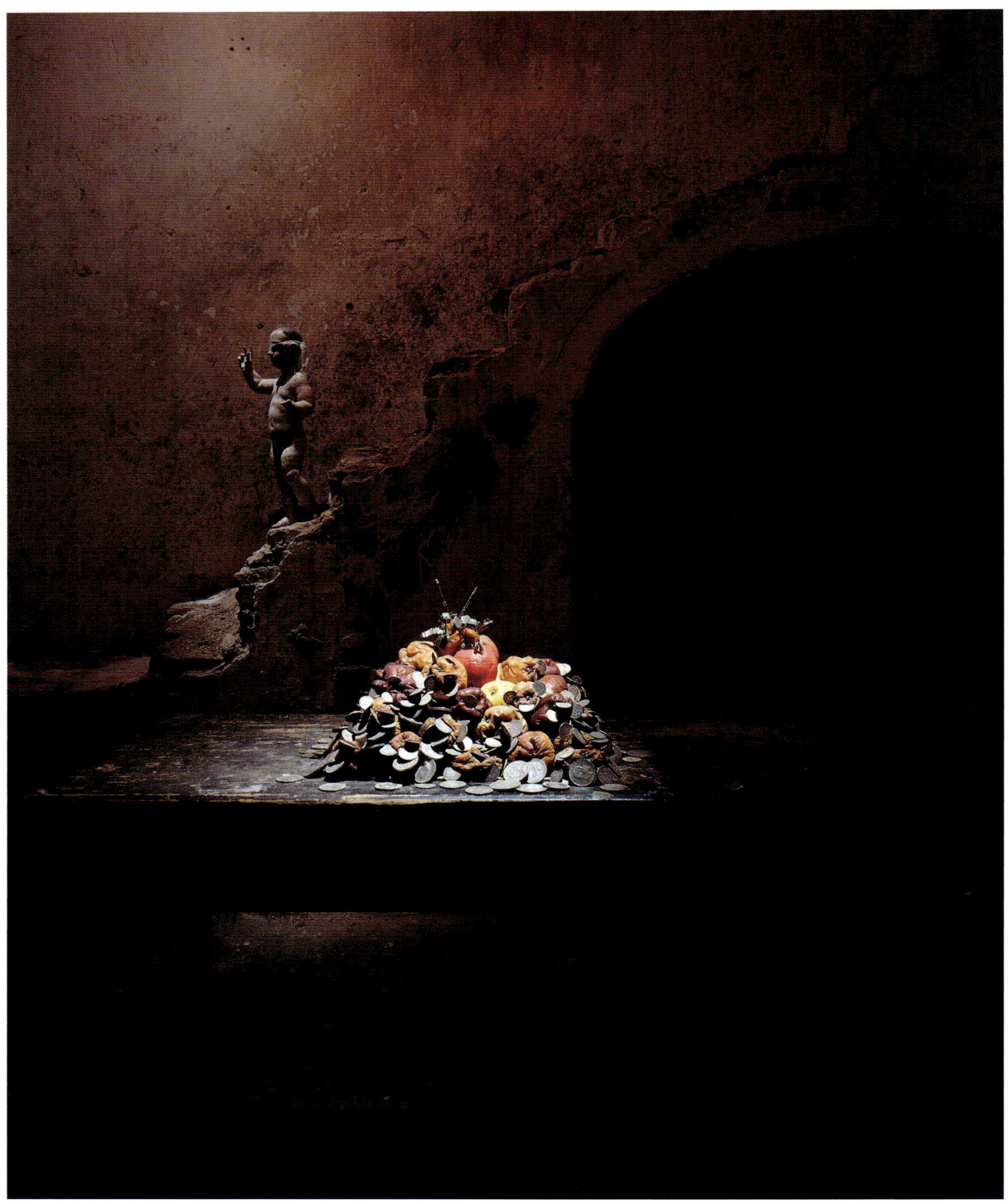

Für Frau G. «Hausschatz», gefunden Juni 1997, Grundbauernhof

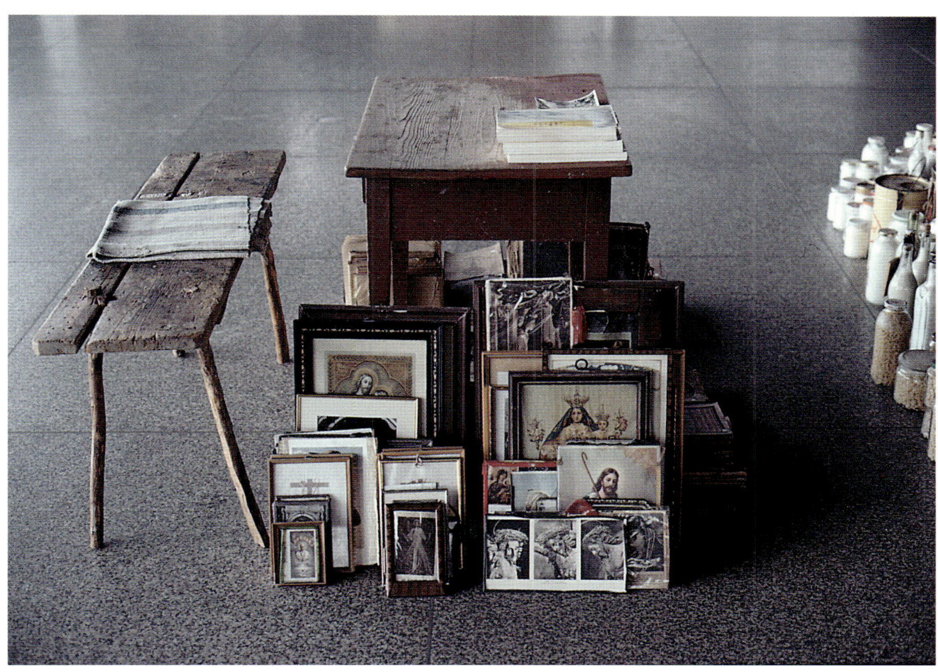

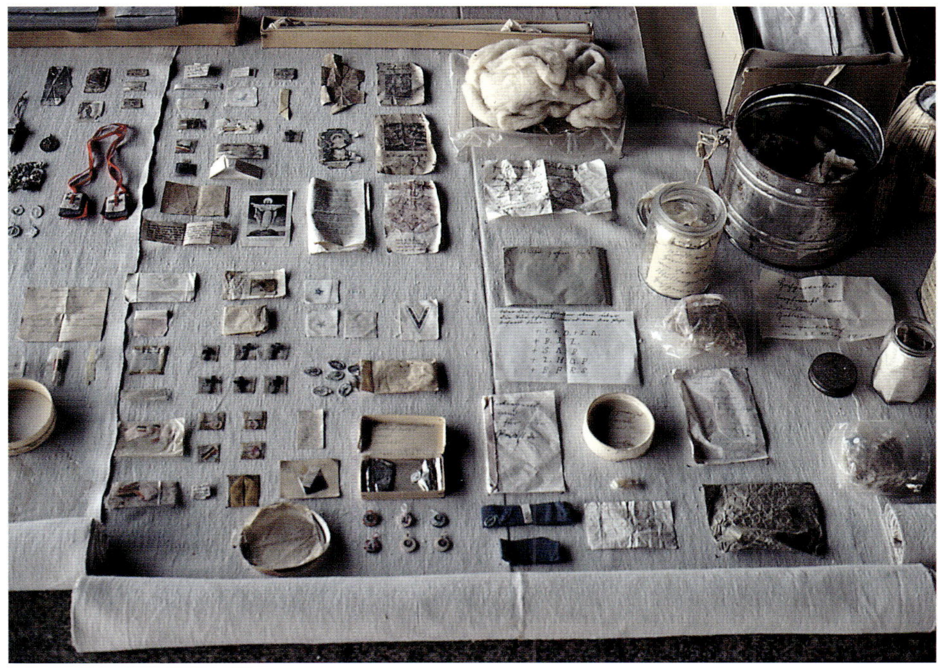

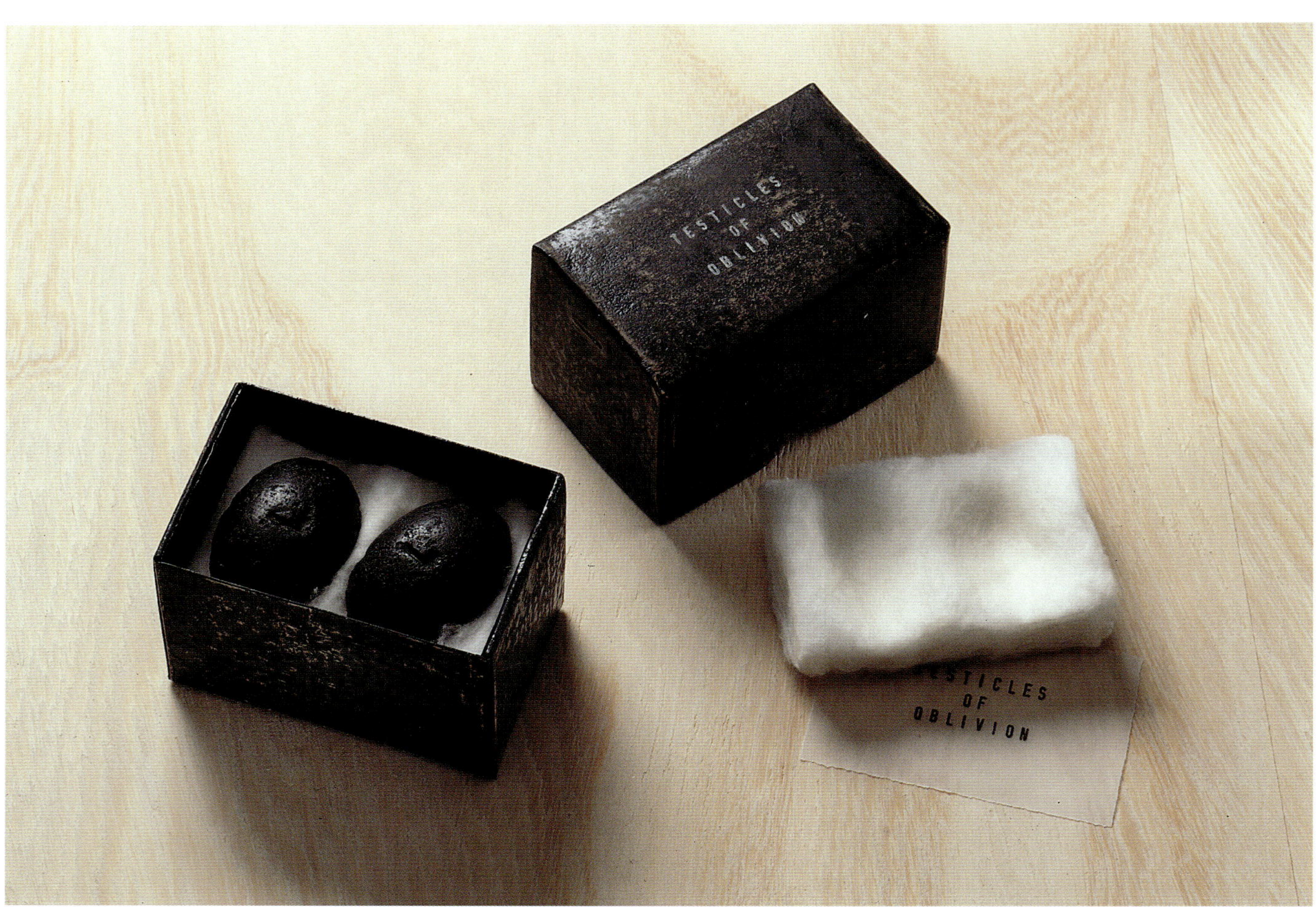

Testicles of Oblivion, 1987

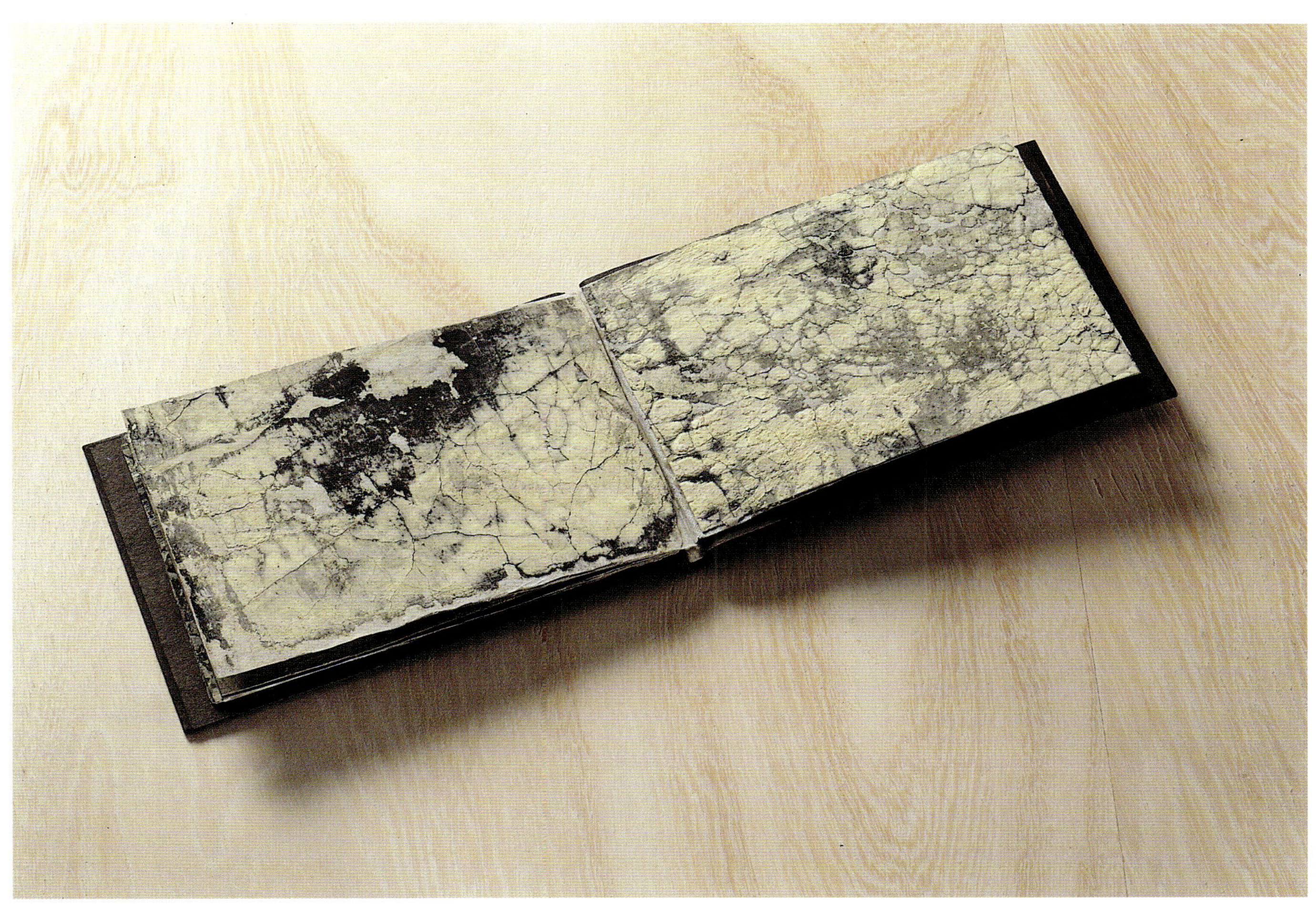

Hellegids, 1986

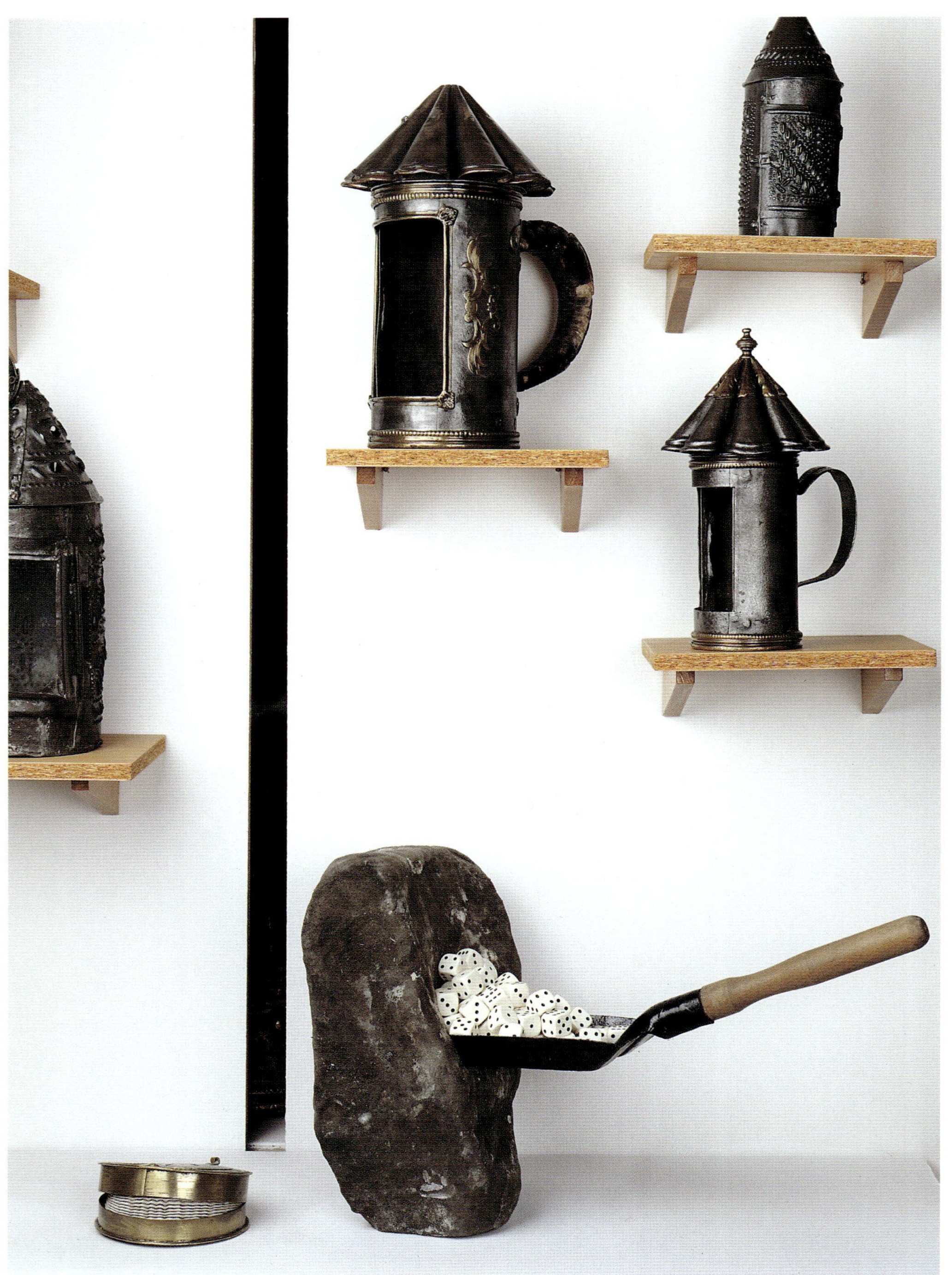

Installation mit

Duivelsdag Delver, 1992

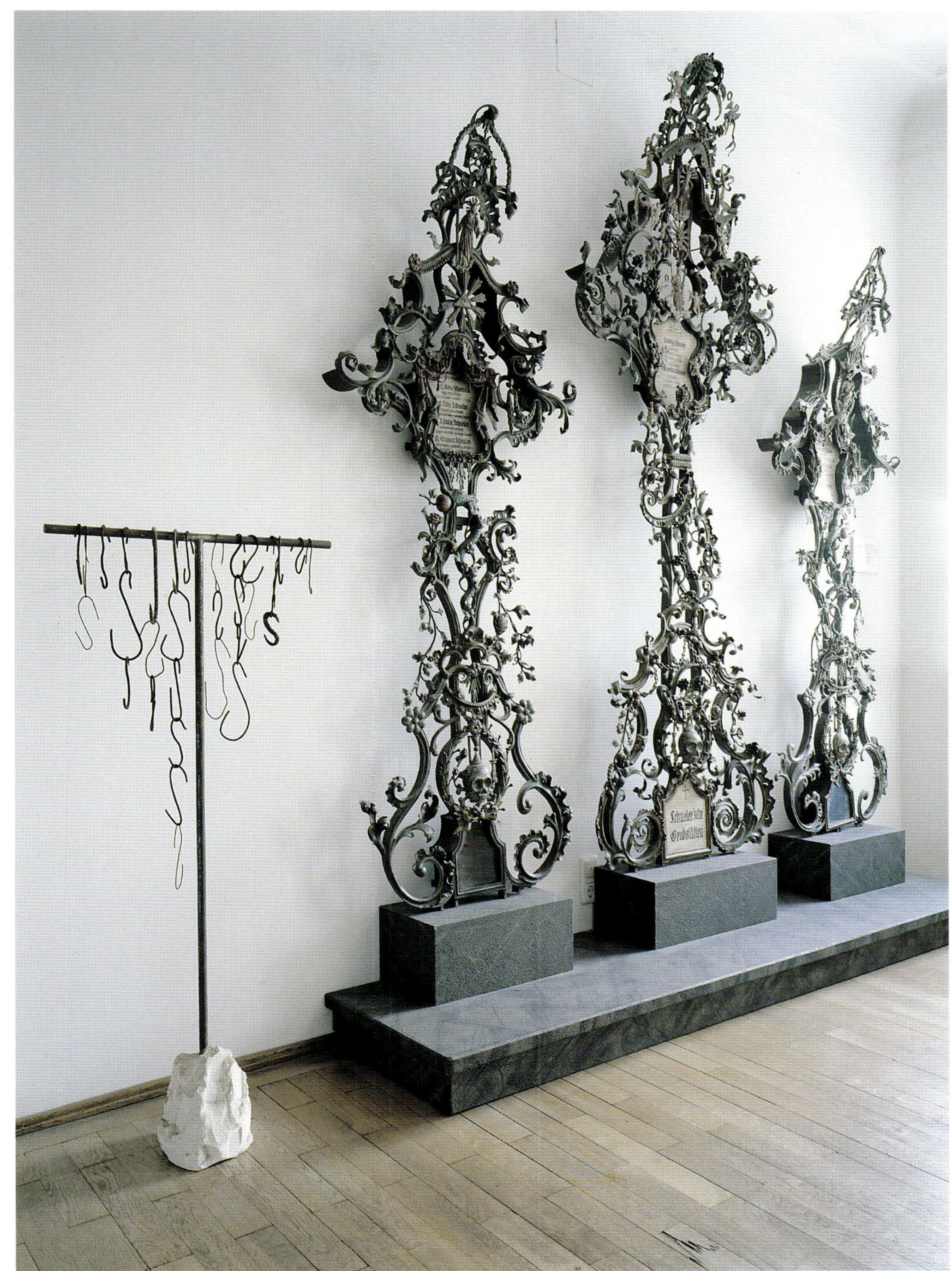

Installation mit

Sssssst (Stilte-beeld), 1974

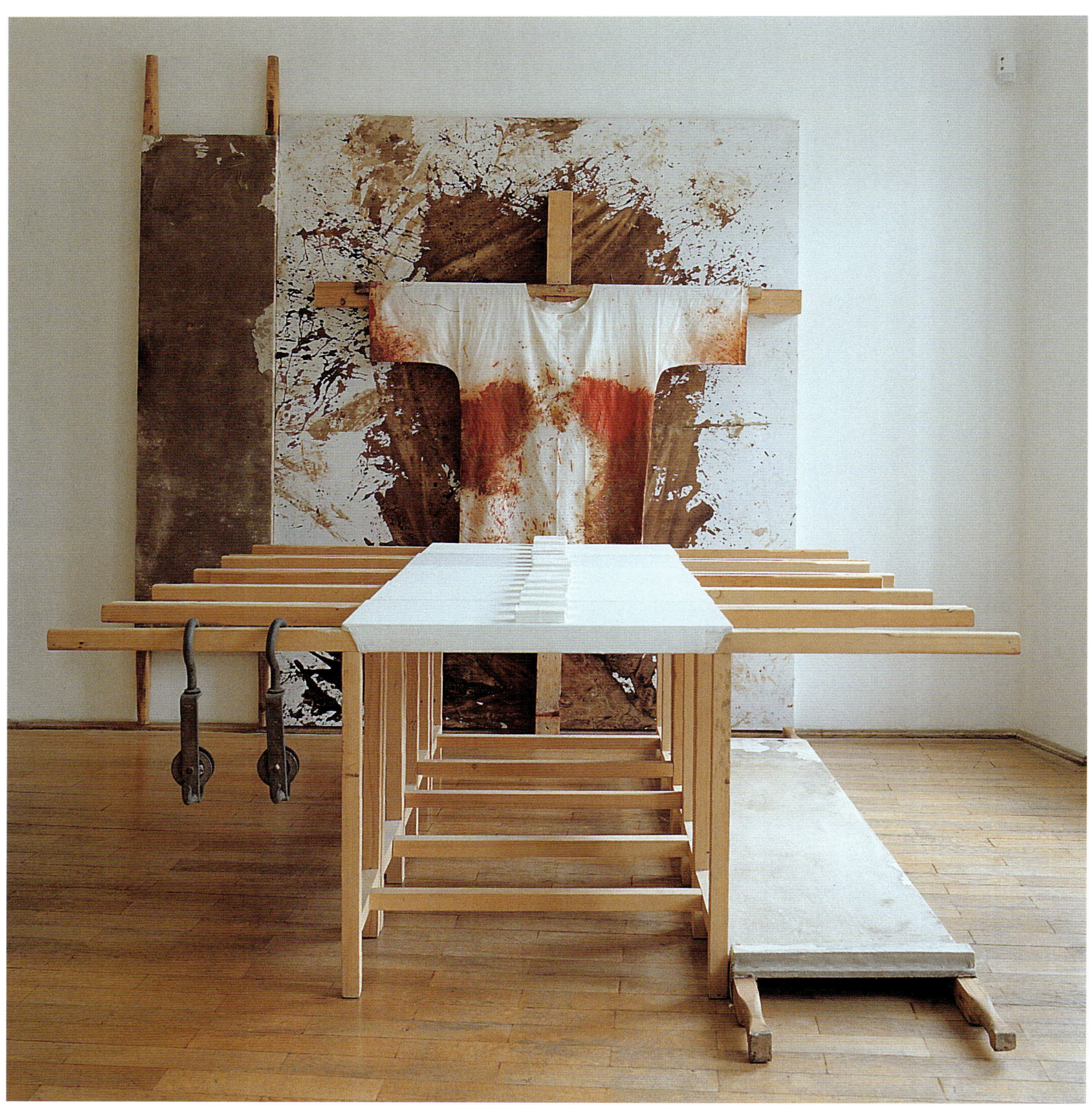

Orgien Mysterien Theater, Reliktinstallation, 1996–98

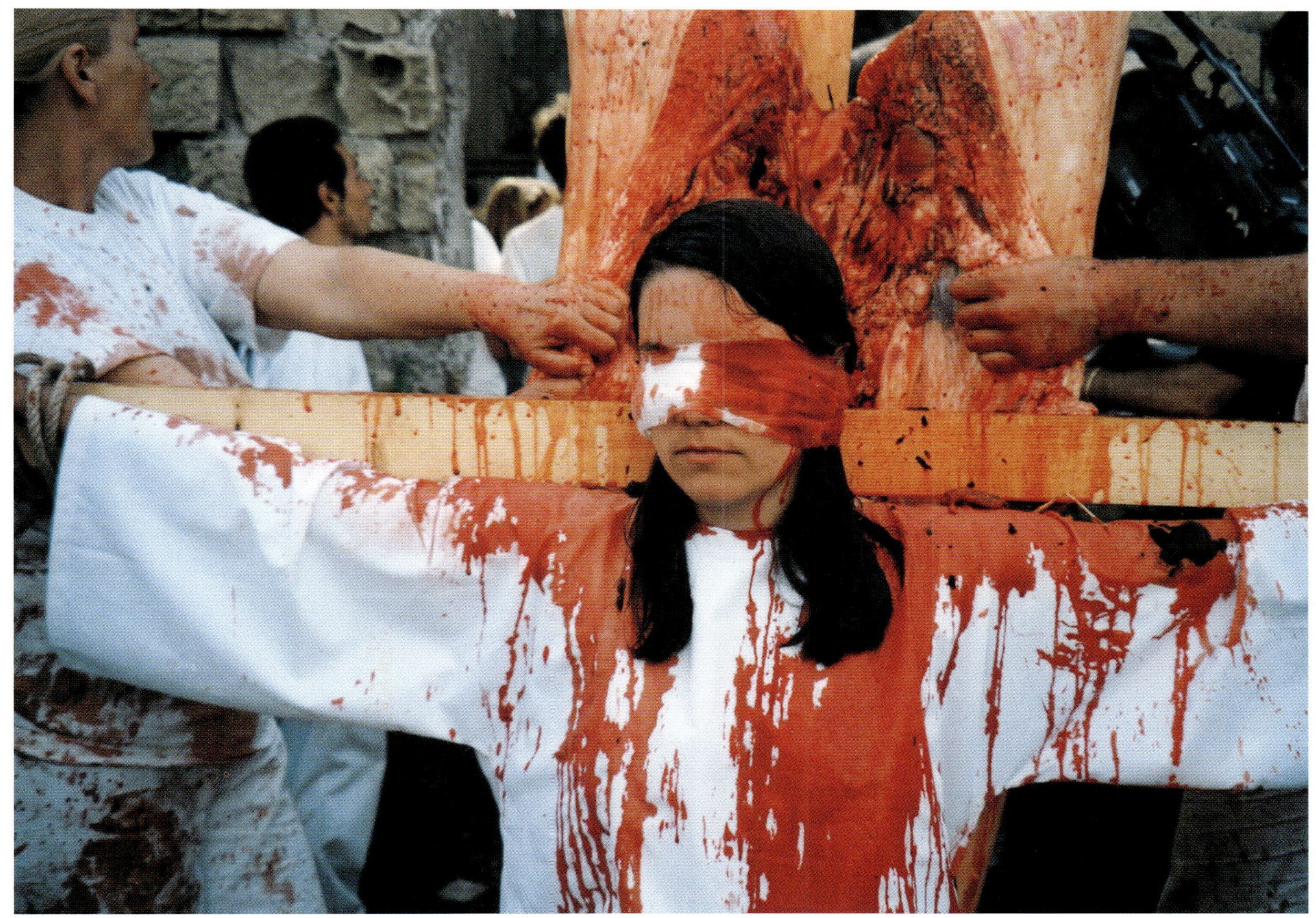

96. Aktion des Orgien Mysterien Theaters, Neapel, 1996

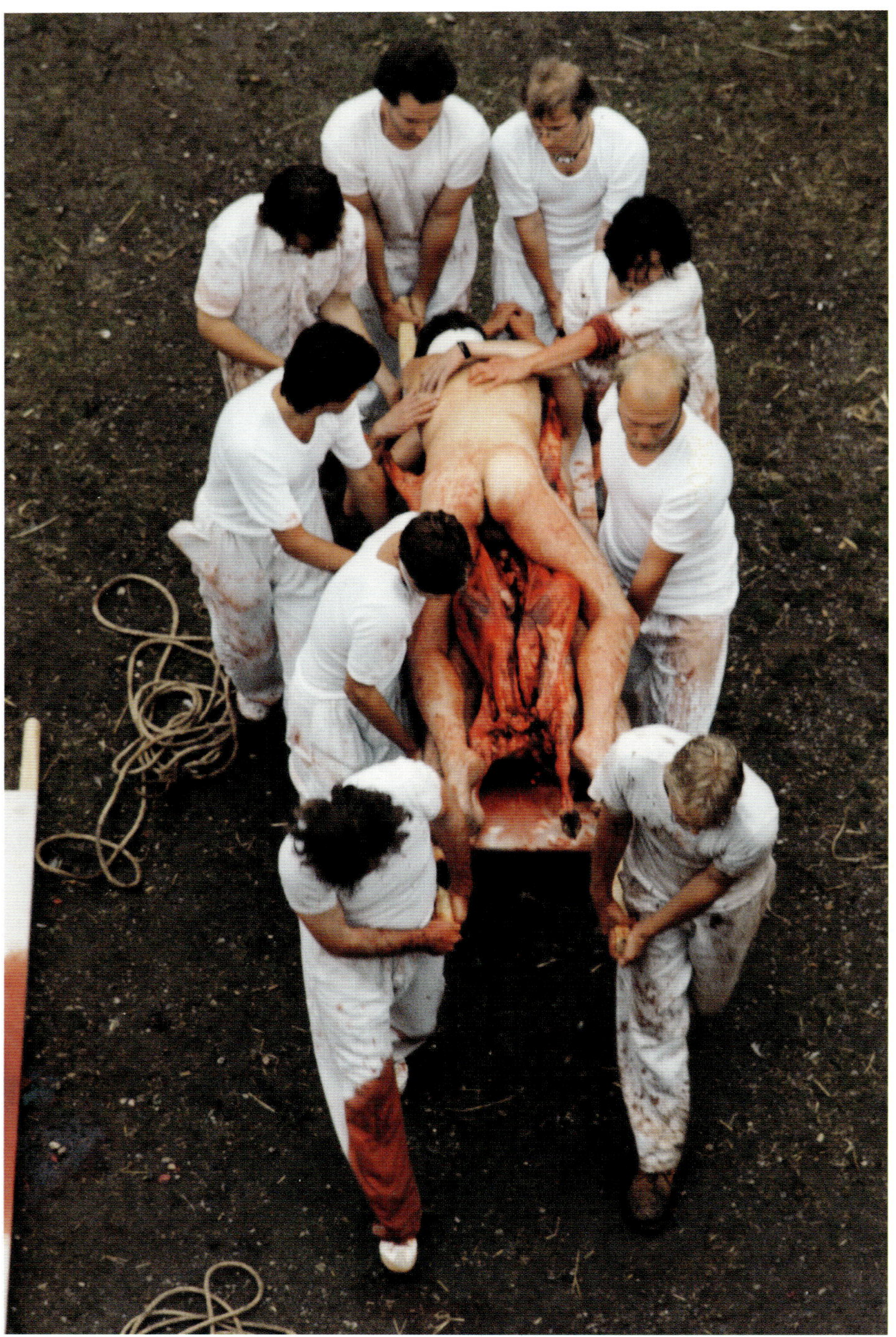

80. Aktion des Orgien Mysterien Theaters, Prinzendorf, 1984

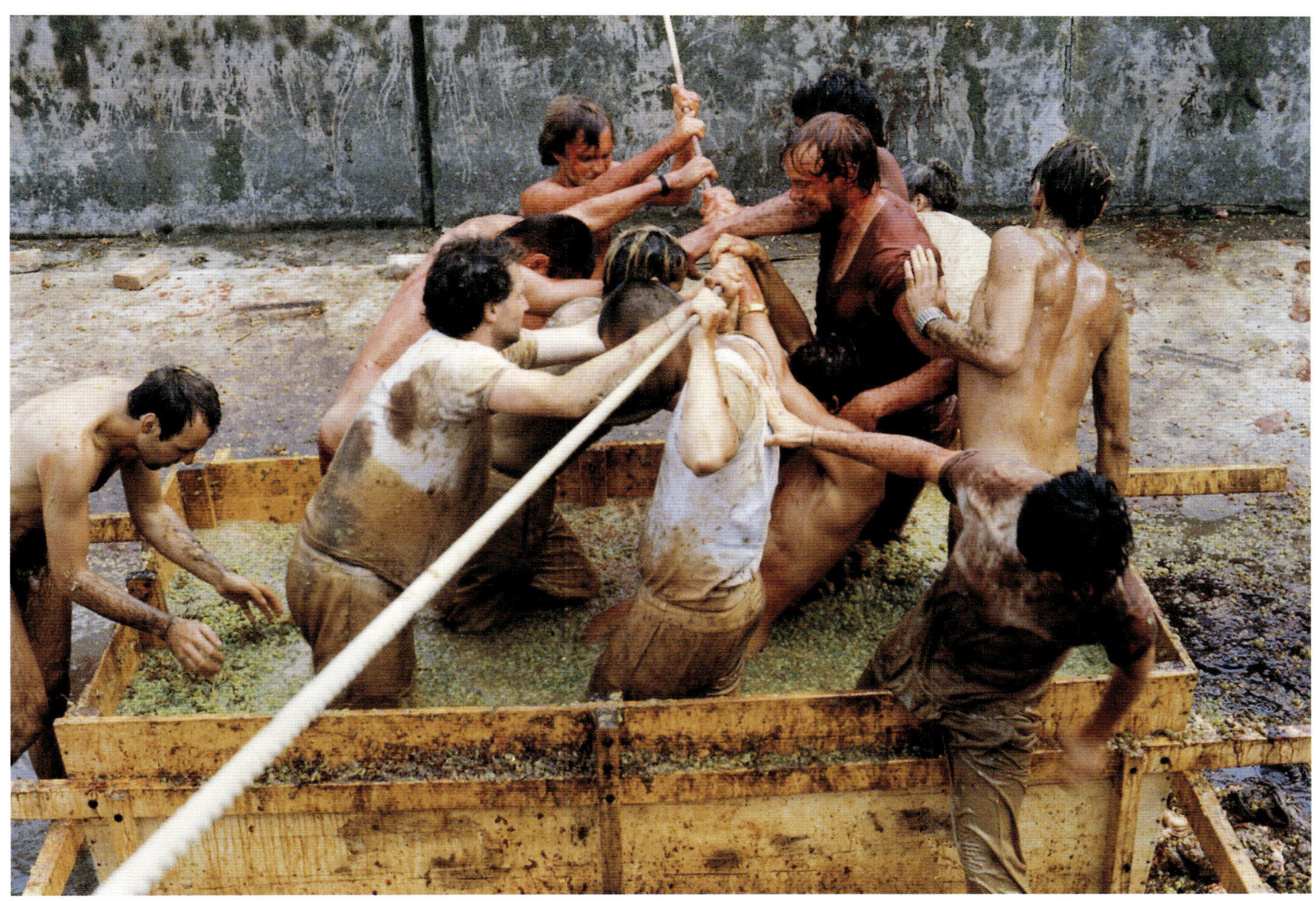

80. Aktion des Orgien Mysterien Theaters, Prinzendorf, 1984

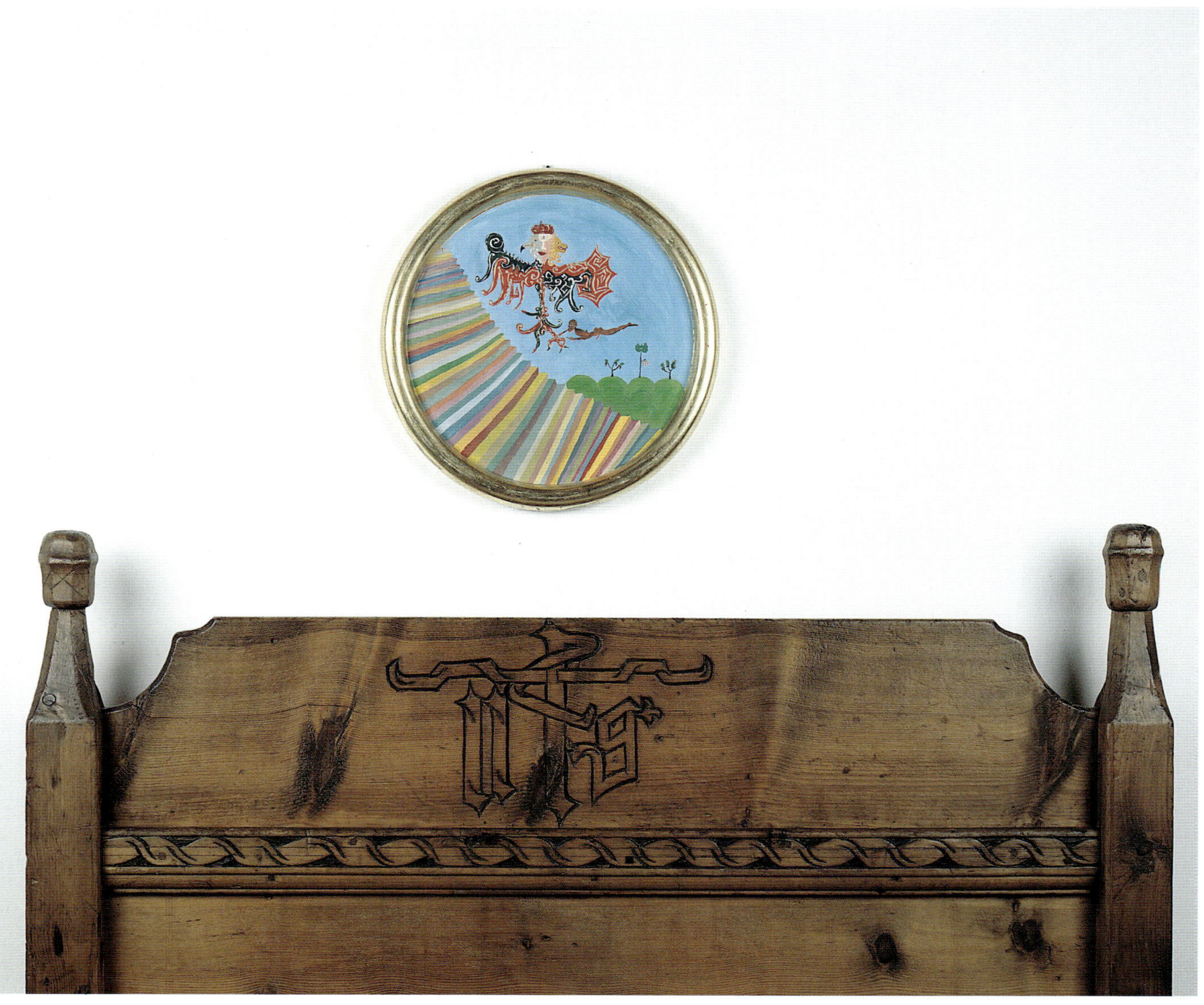

Installation mit

Castò e buon consiglio di dado Davide a Golia goliardia, 1994

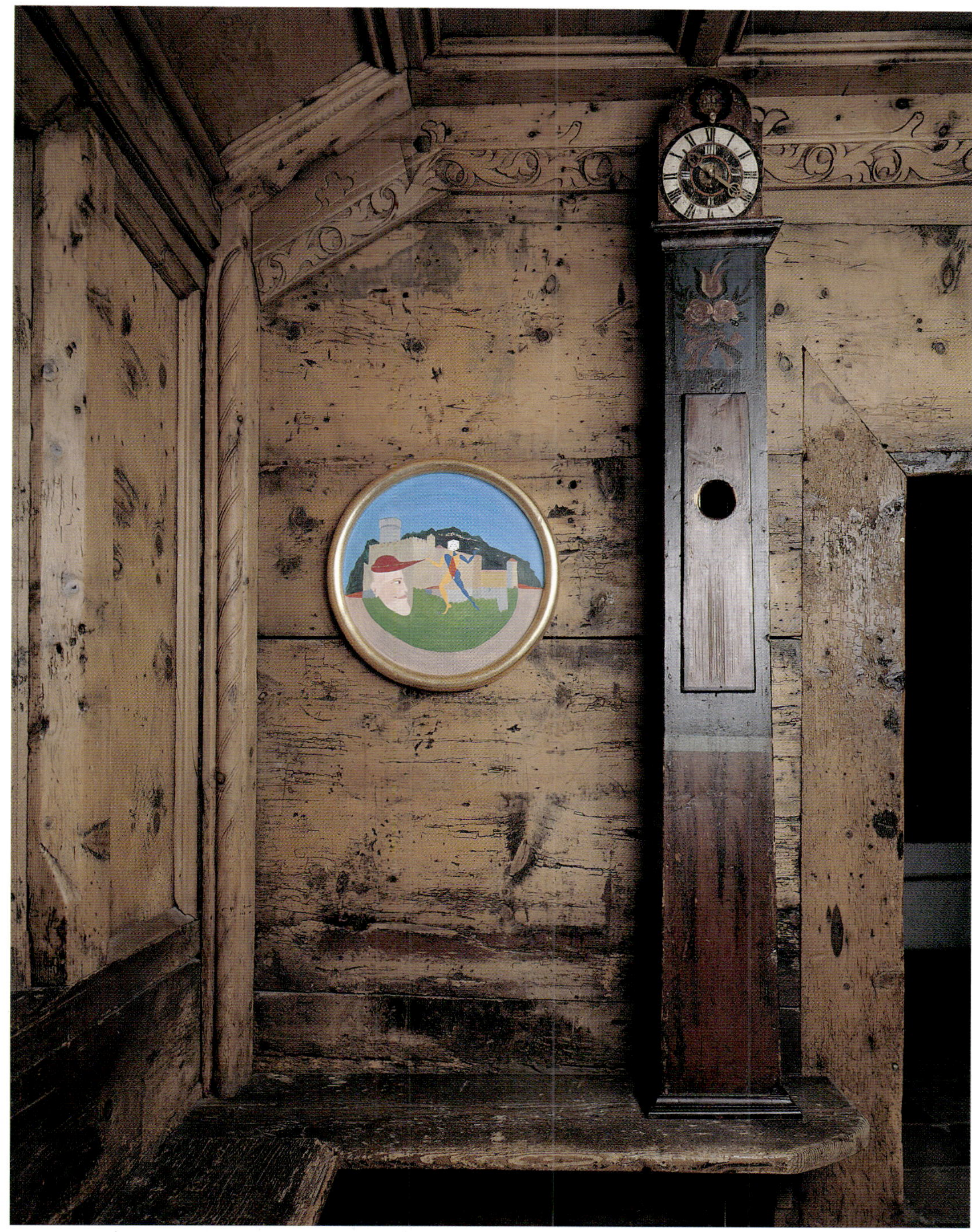

Installation mit

Trento 3 30 33, 1993

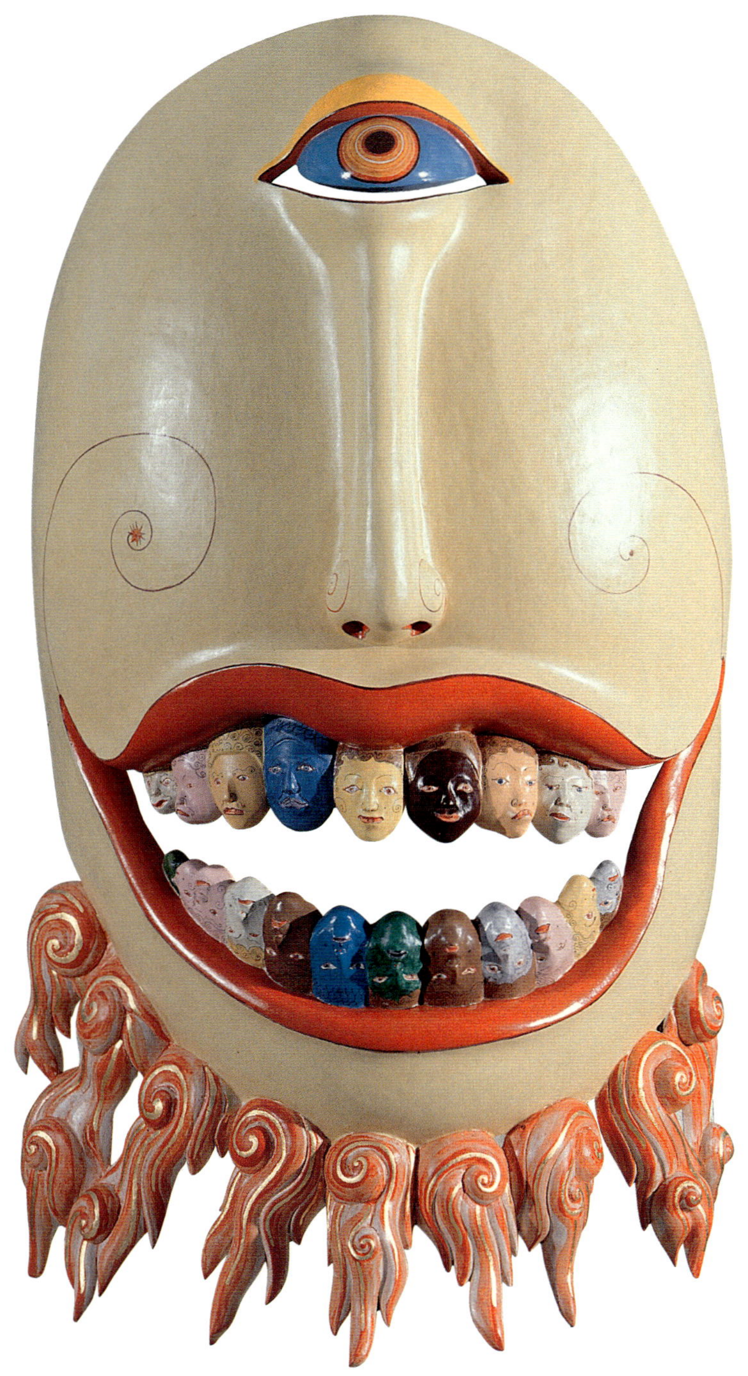

CiclopOrcOvo, 1996

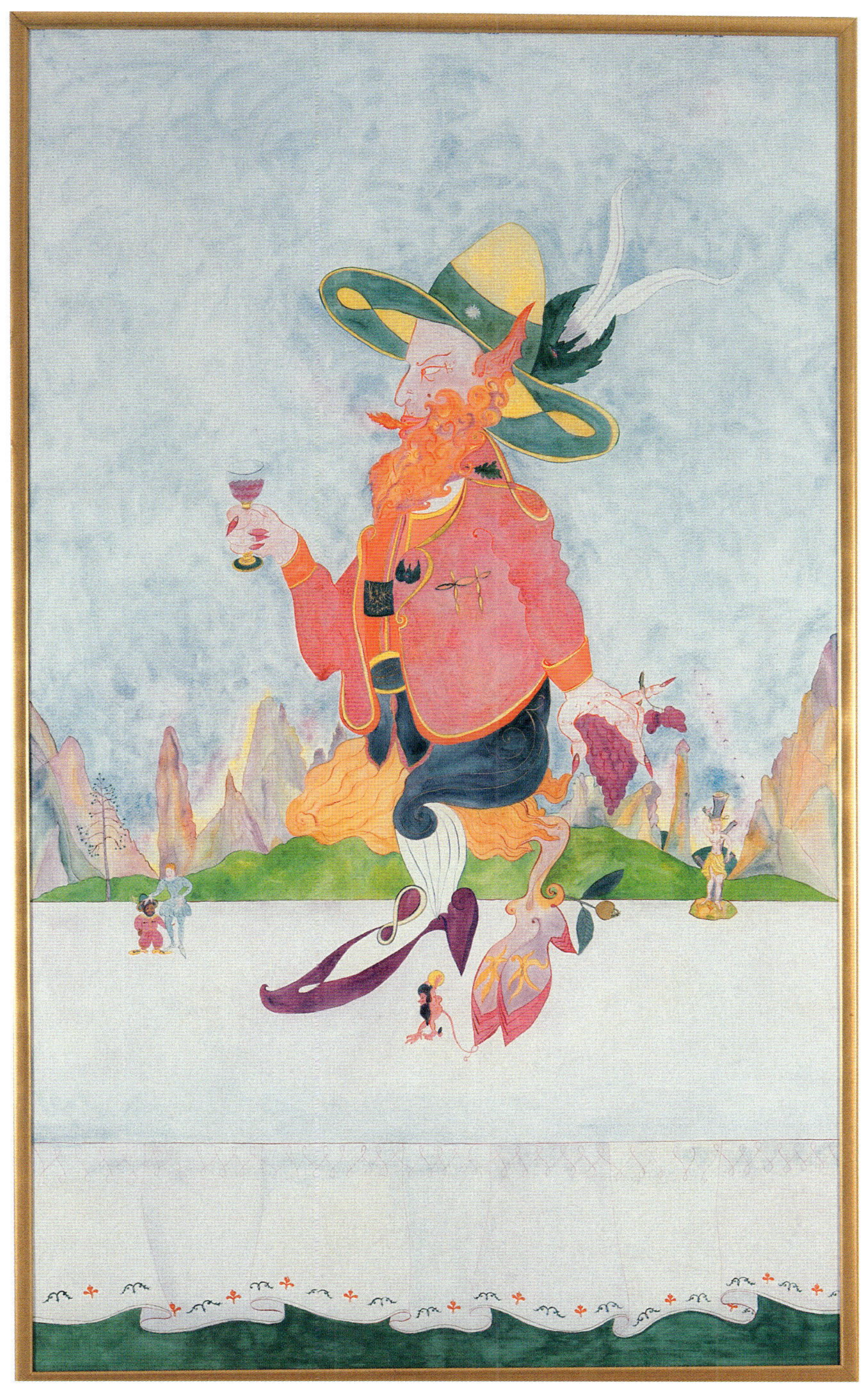

GrillAlpino Adoratore diVino, 1996

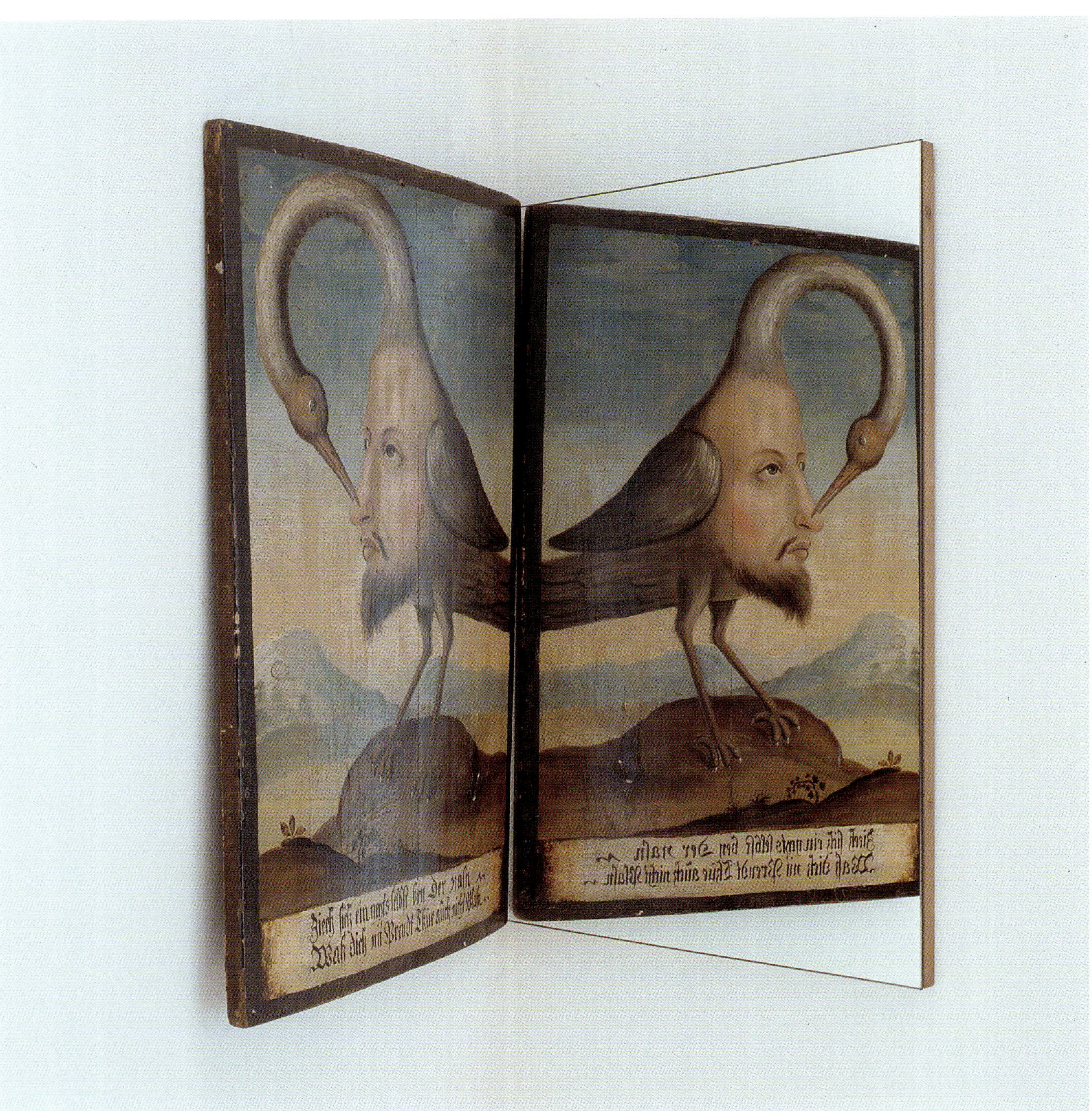

L'uccello che guarda se stesso, 1998

Ricordo negli occhi dello scriba di Saqqara
al Louvre, riflesse nelle sue pupille
di cristallo, d'aver visto un giorno
passare nuvole bianche del cielo di Parigi.
Al di là delle nuvole occhi,
dentro gli occhi millenni —

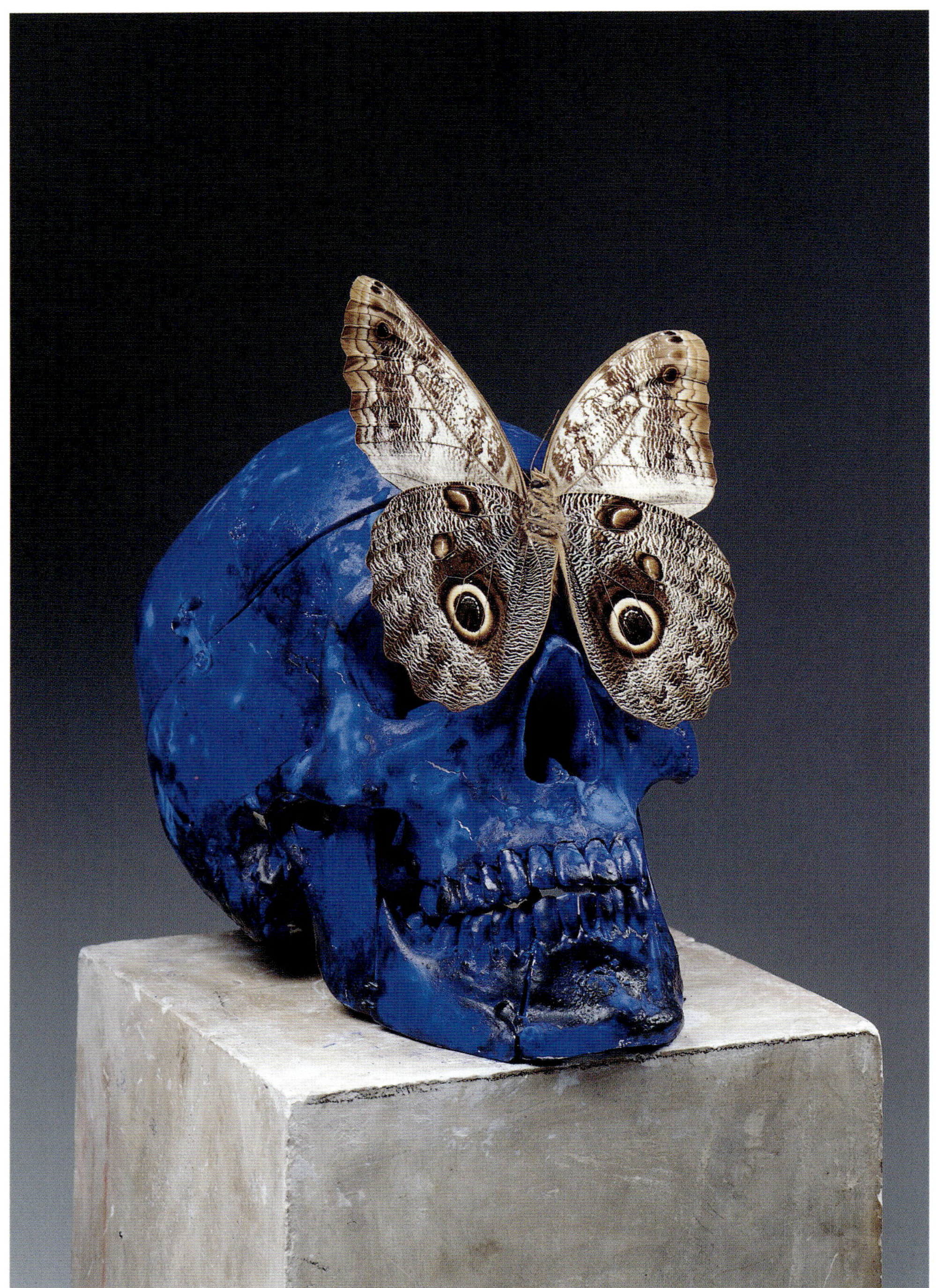

Senza titolo, 1997

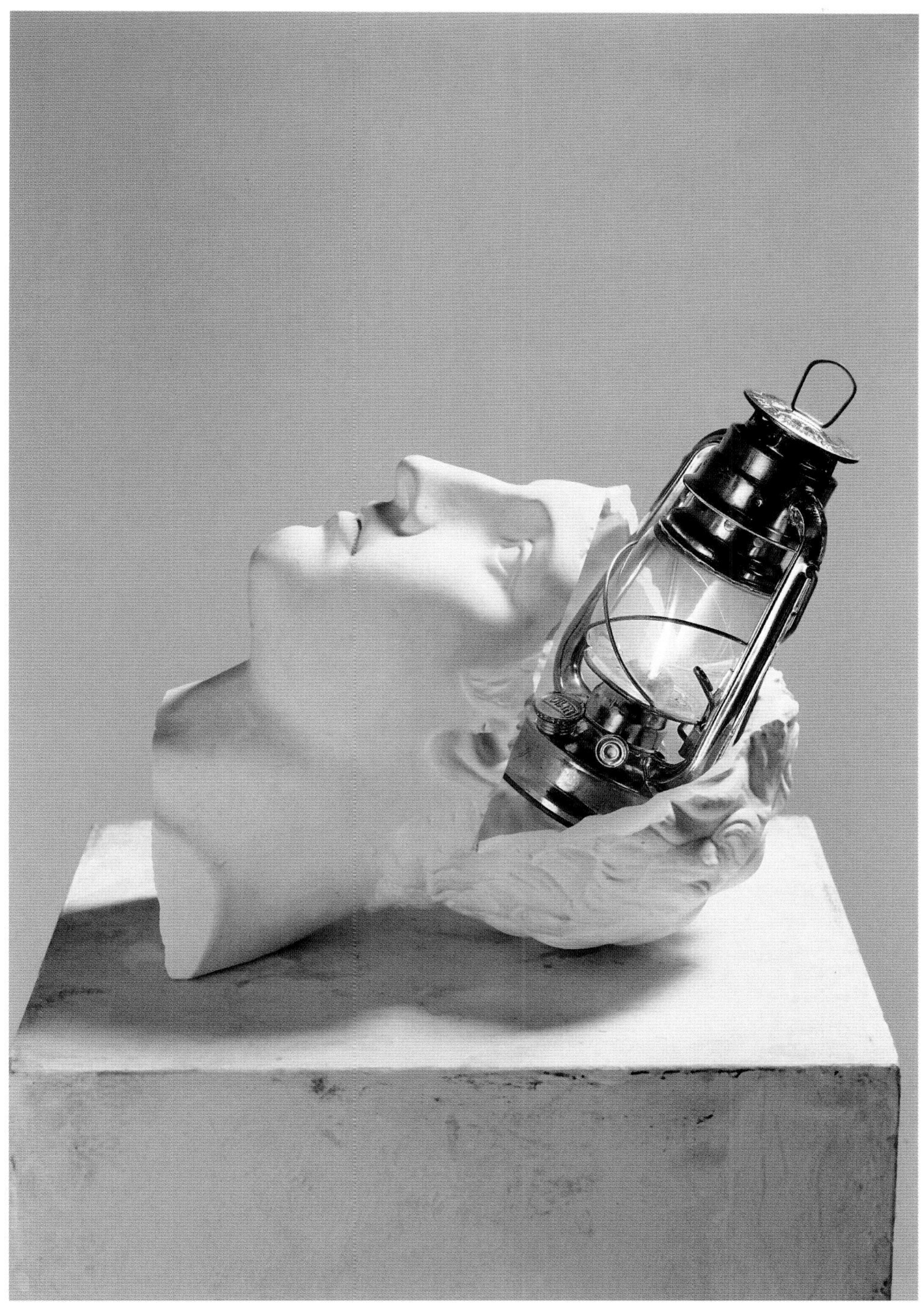

Senza titolo, 1995
Courtesy Christian Stein, Milano

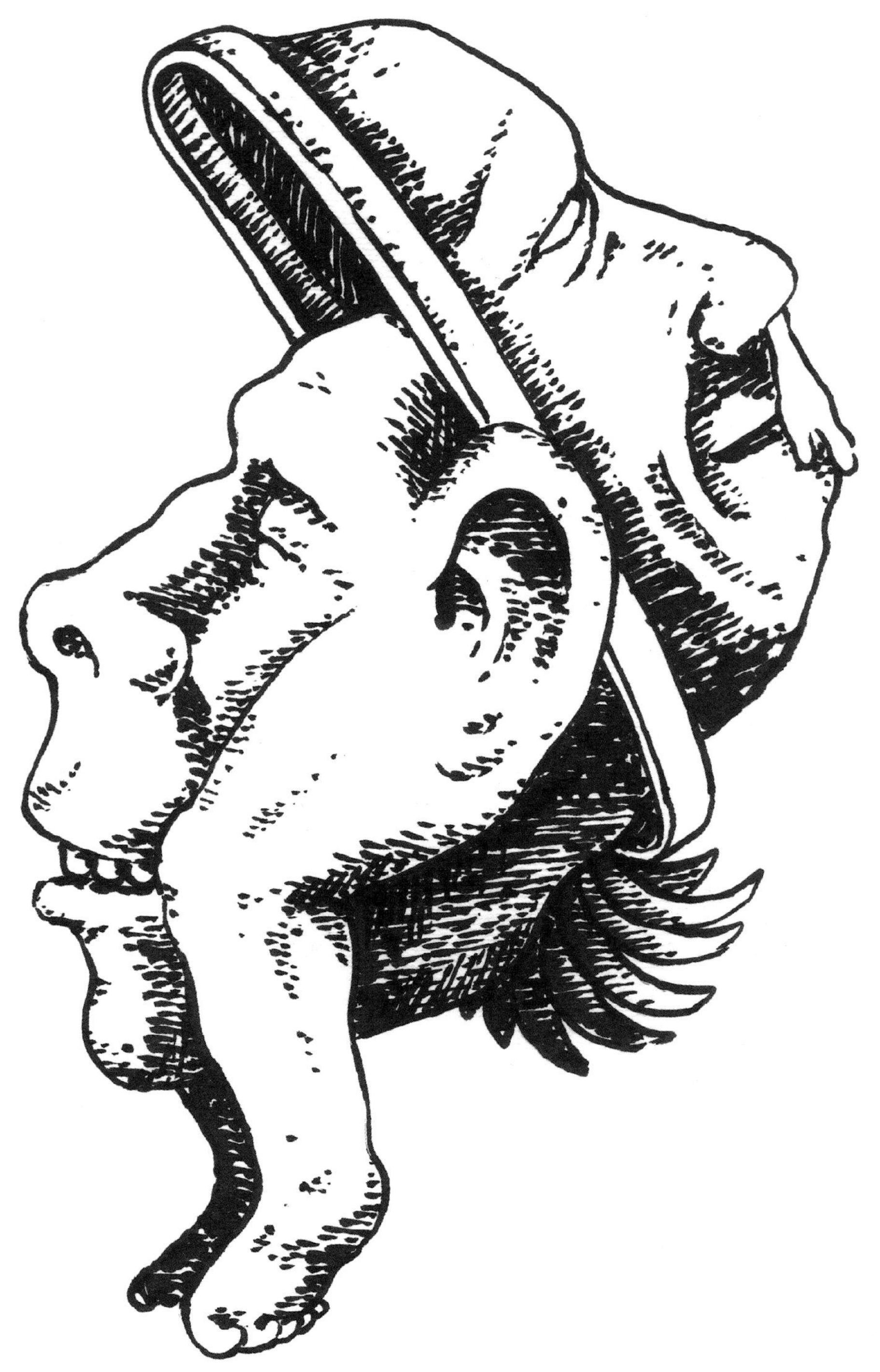

The Sense of Imperfection, 1998

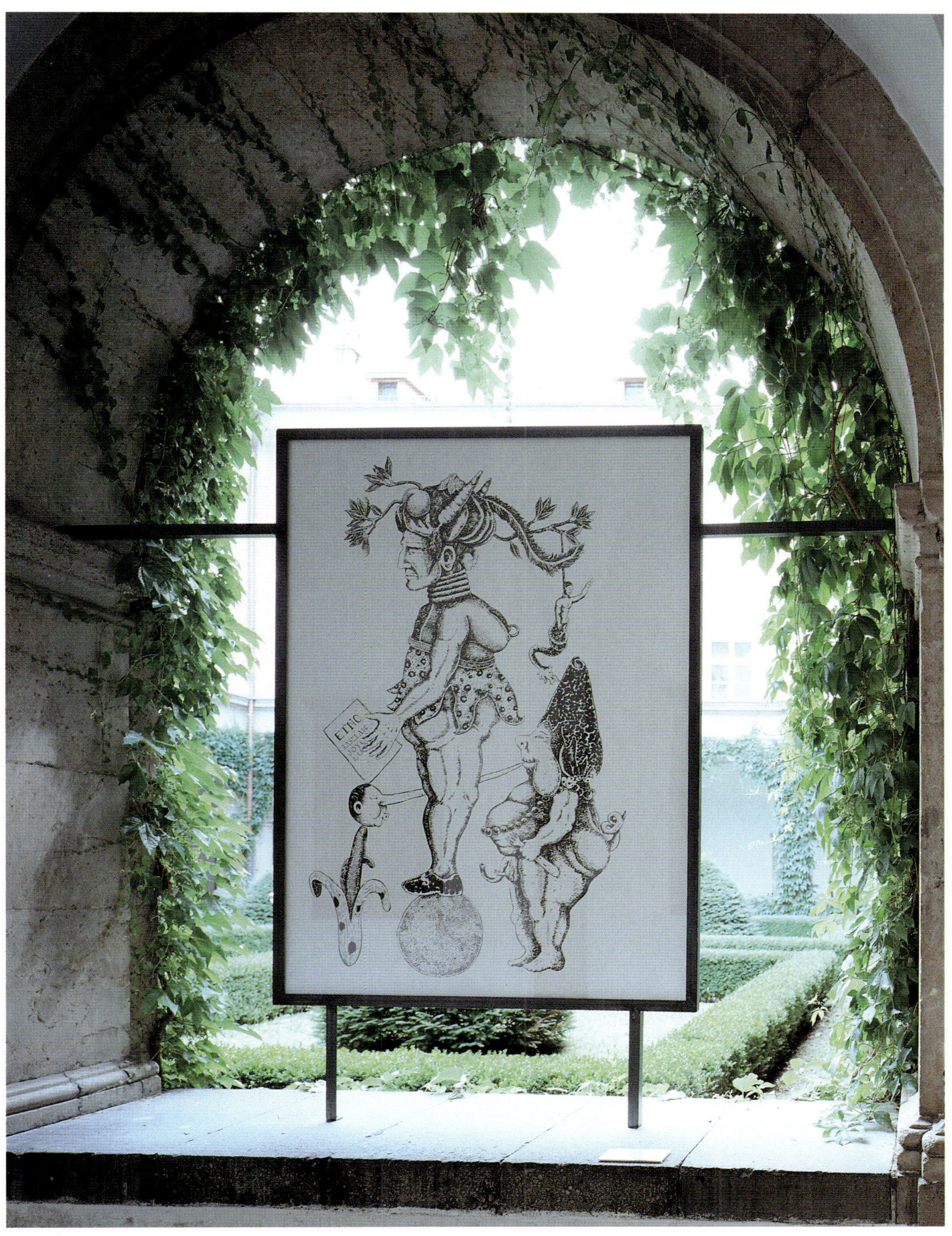
ETIC

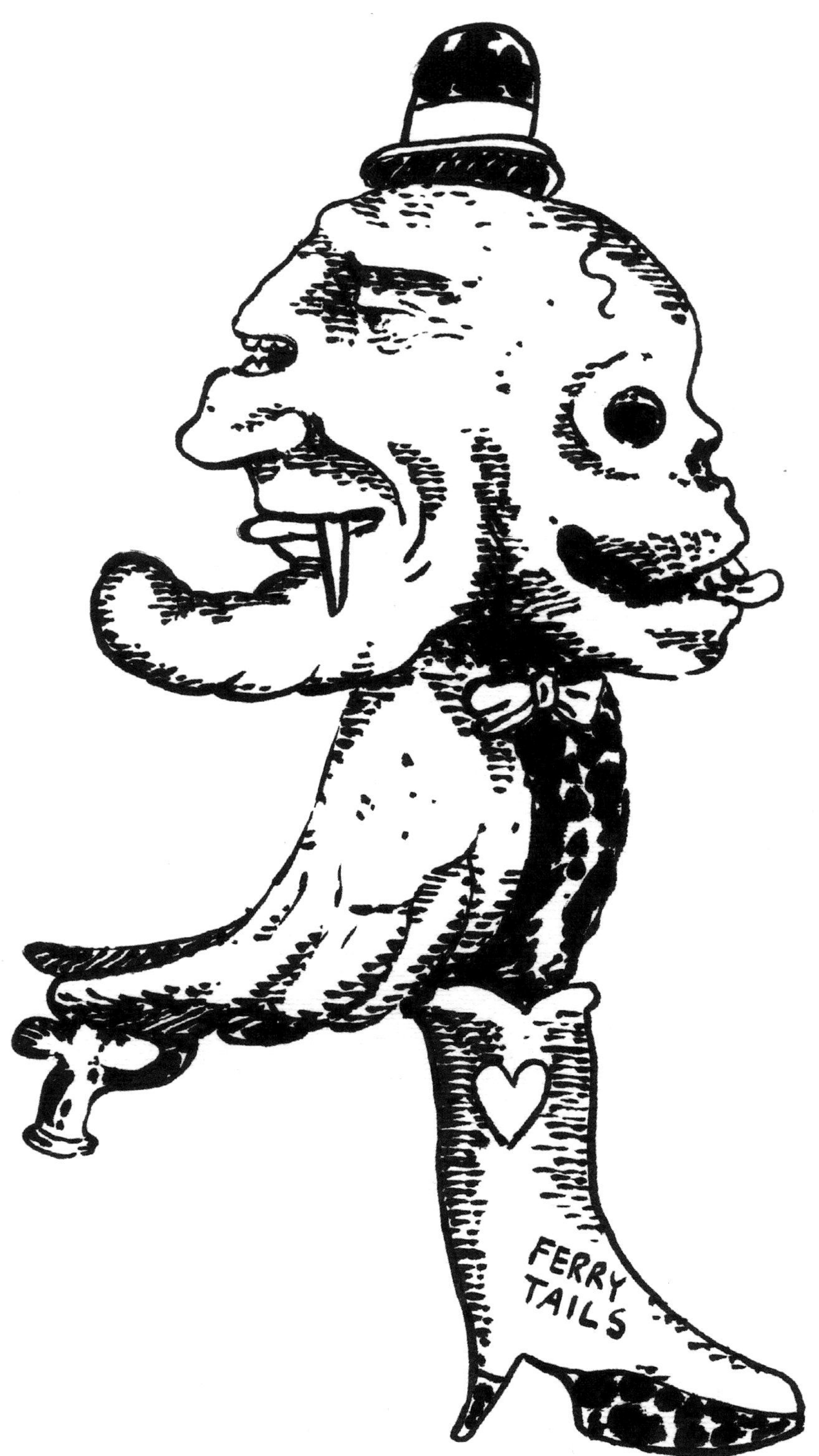

The Sense of Imperfection, 1998

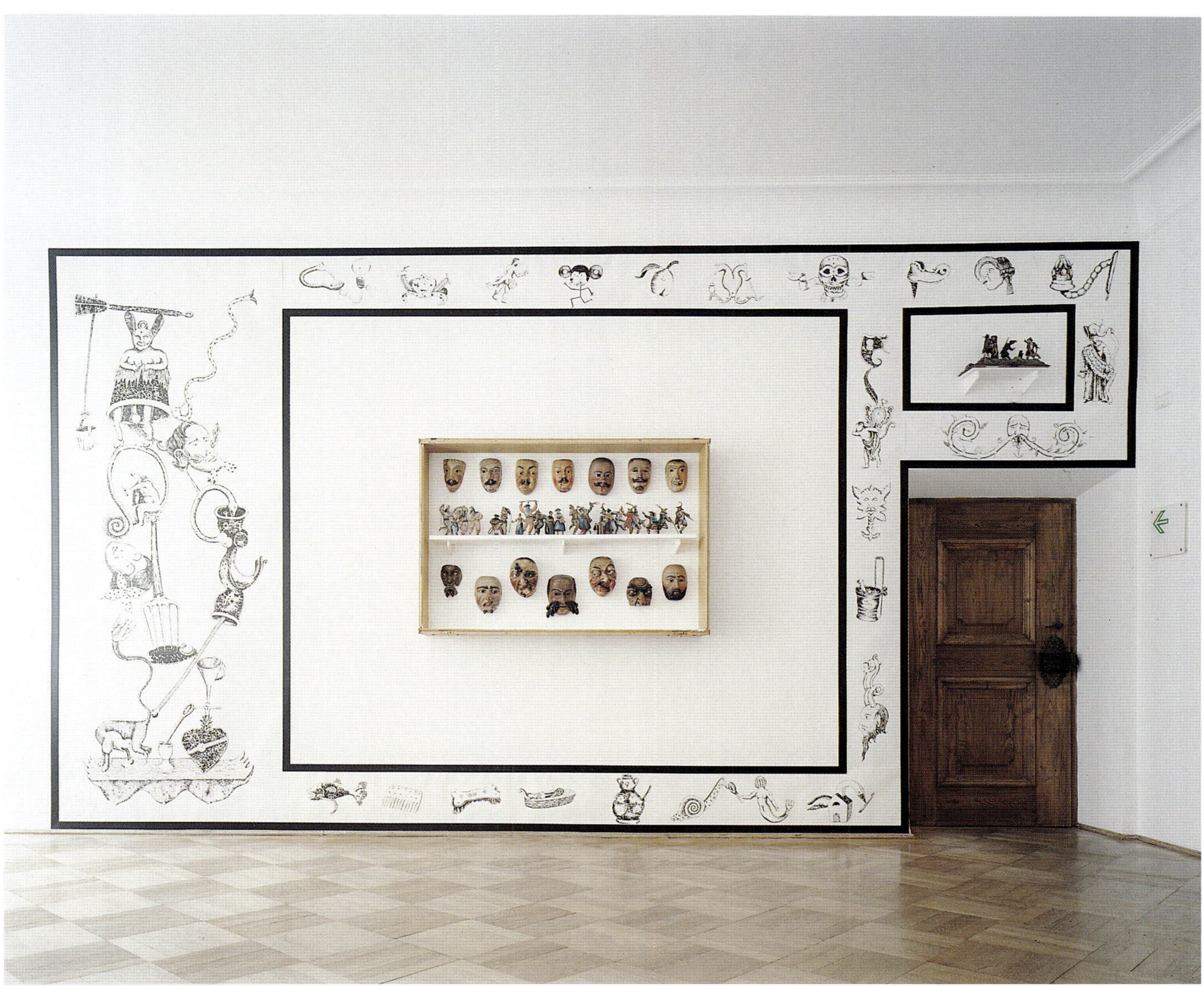

La pieza «Der Handtuchhalter» es una pieza simbolicamente completa
para la intención de esta instalación, pues en si es un espejo
de la condición humana natural y por otro lado yo encuentro en ella también
los elementos duales que construyen la cultura, el reto de el hombre
desde el punto de vista de desarrollar y elevar sus percepciones espirituales,
sus valores éticos y sus planteamientos conceptuales ante
los indecifrables misterios por ejemplo como el de la transformación
de la materia y el cambio natural de todas las cosas,
somos un resultado cultural, aunque no nos demos cuenta,
entre las fronteras del presente y el futuro solo existe
un instante, es este instante, el que quiero hacer sentir en esta obra.

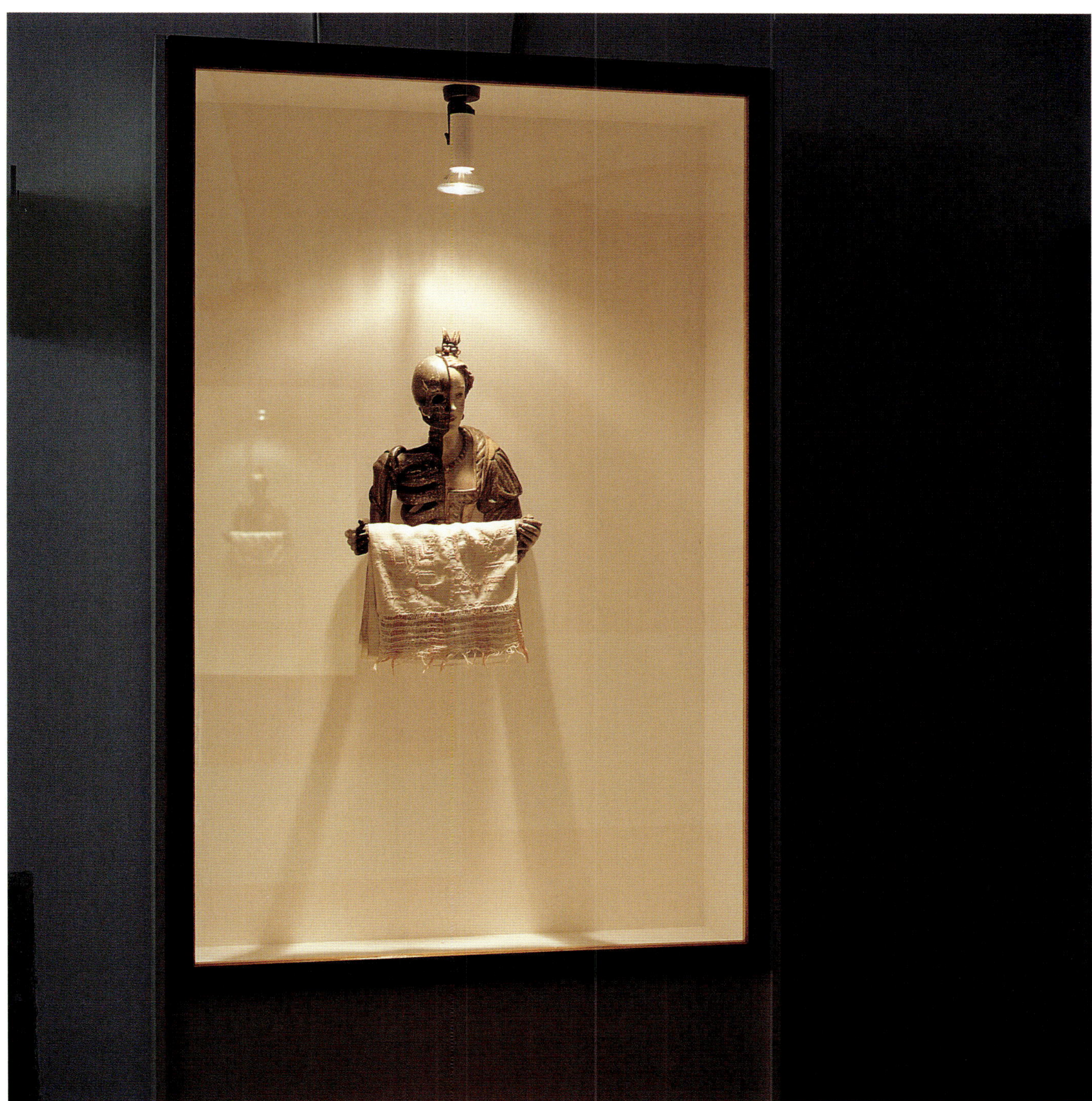

Der Handtuchhalter, 1998

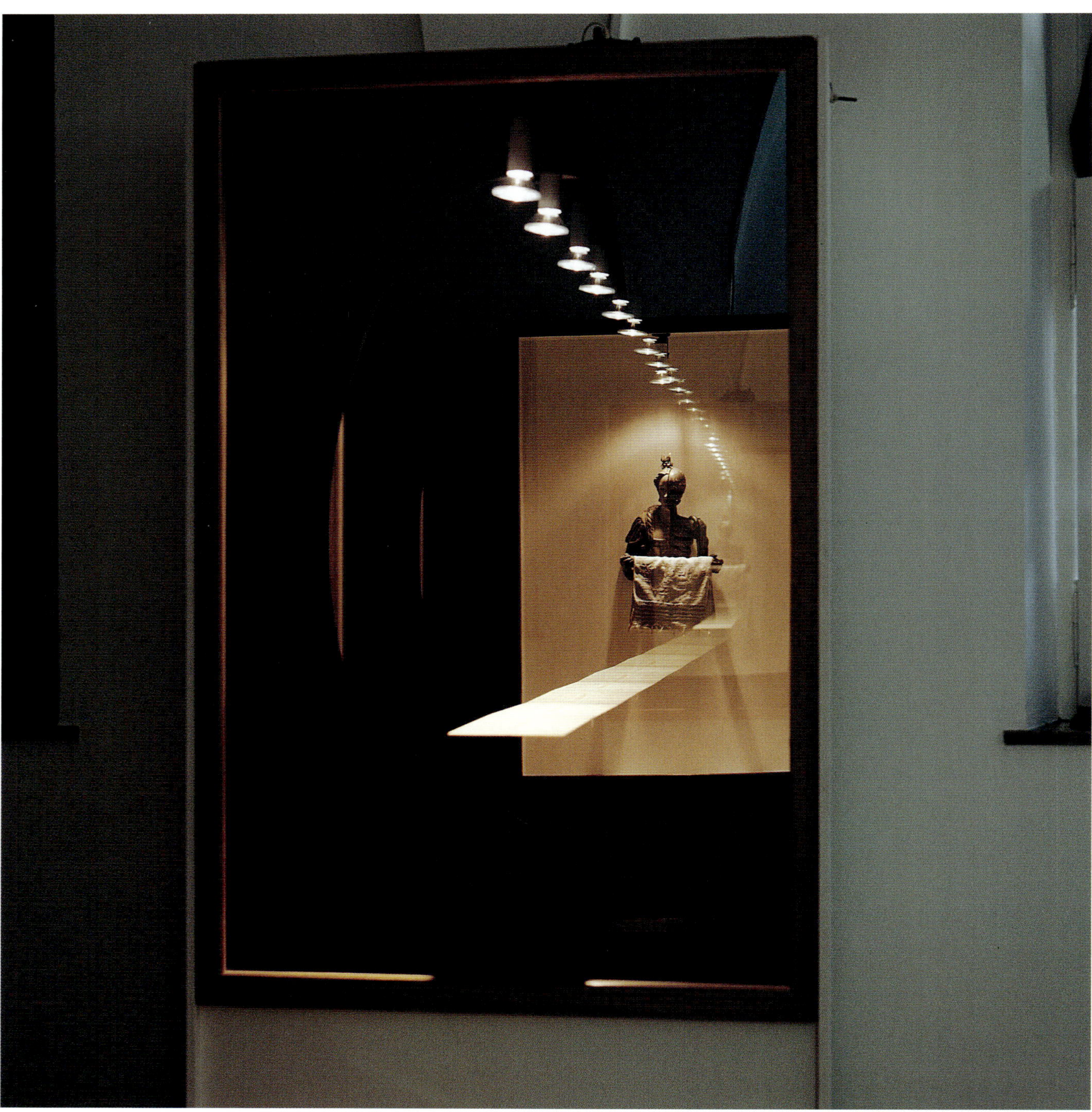

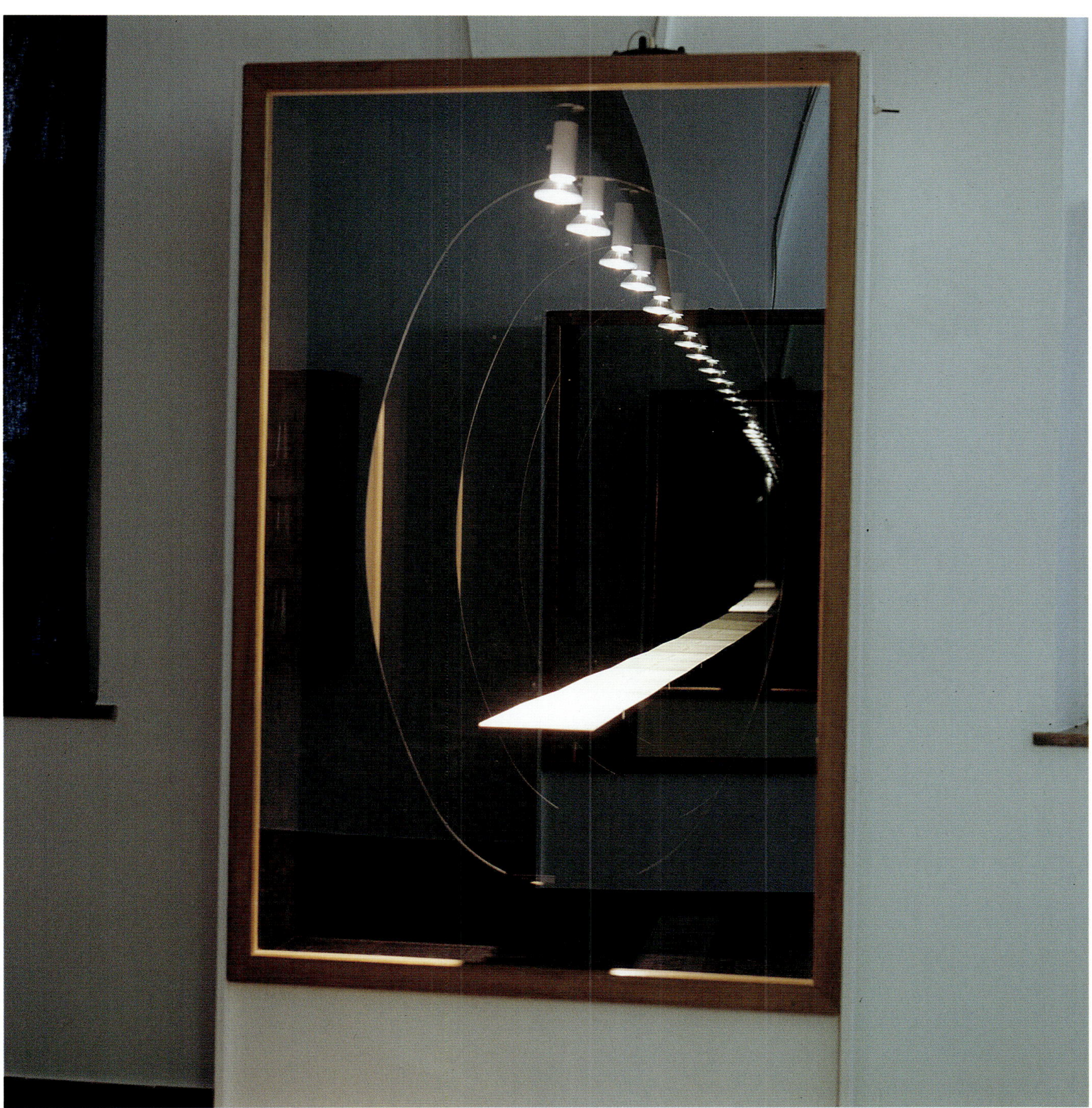

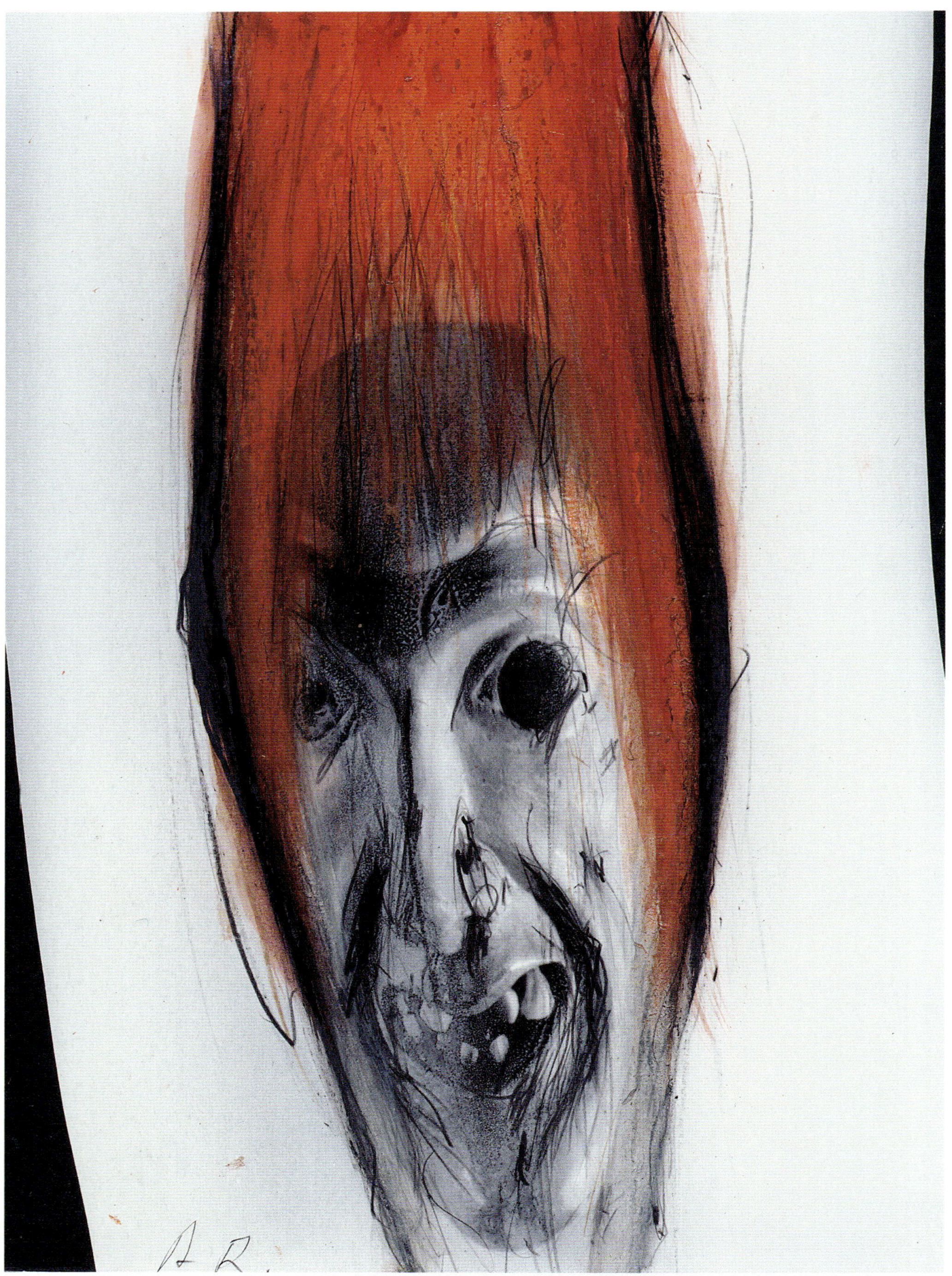

Maskenvariationen, 1998

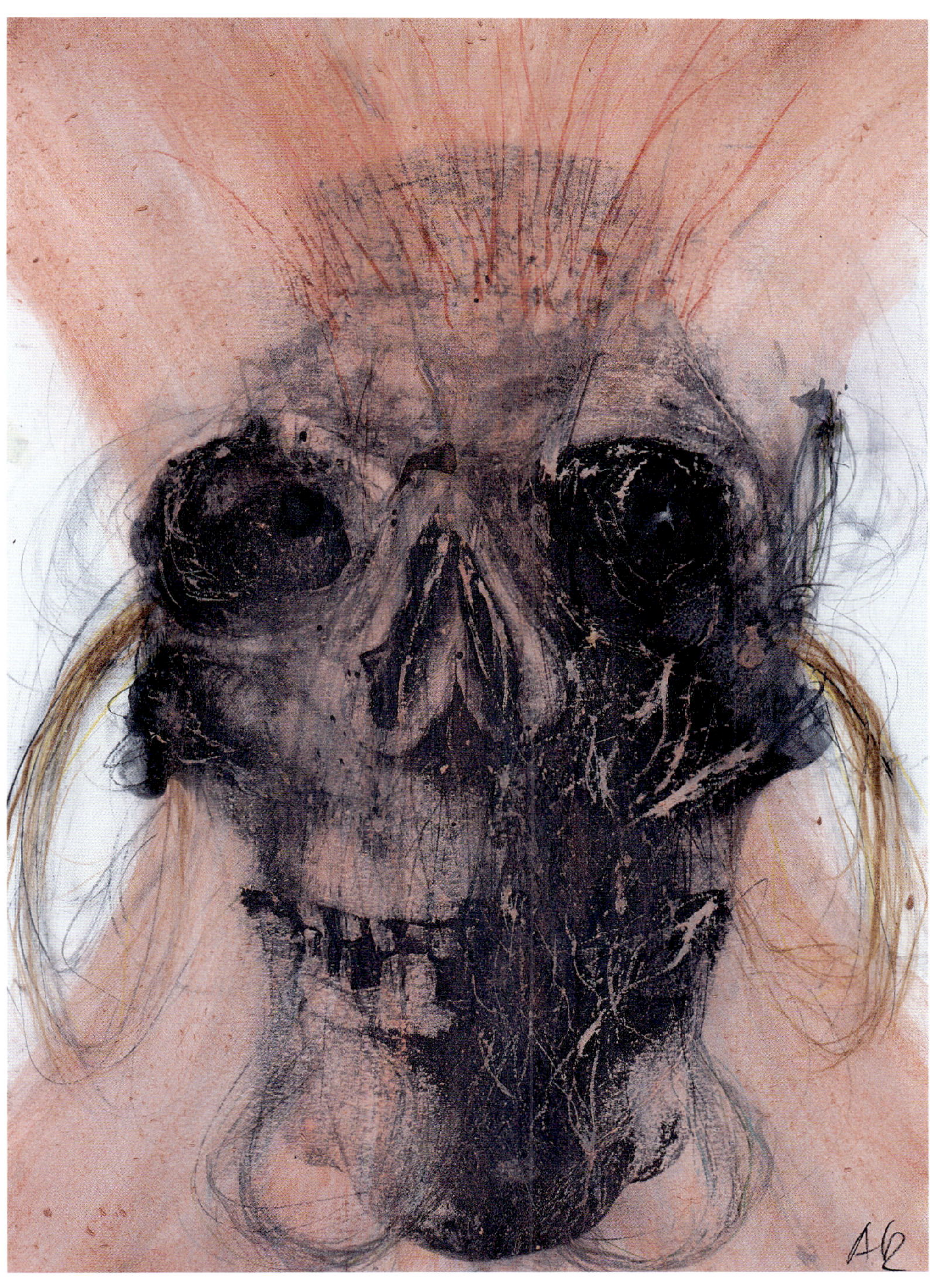

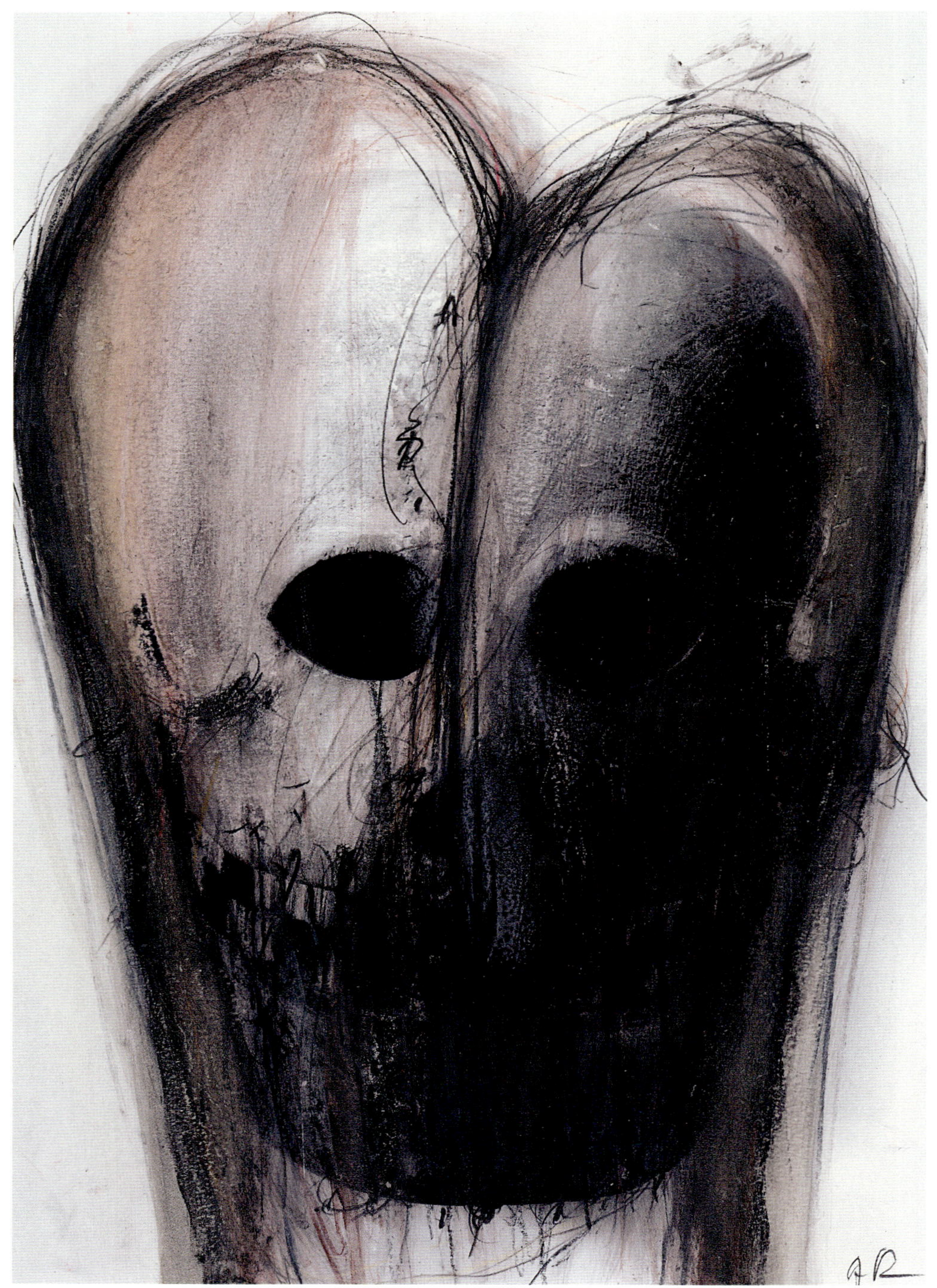

Maskenvariationen, 1998

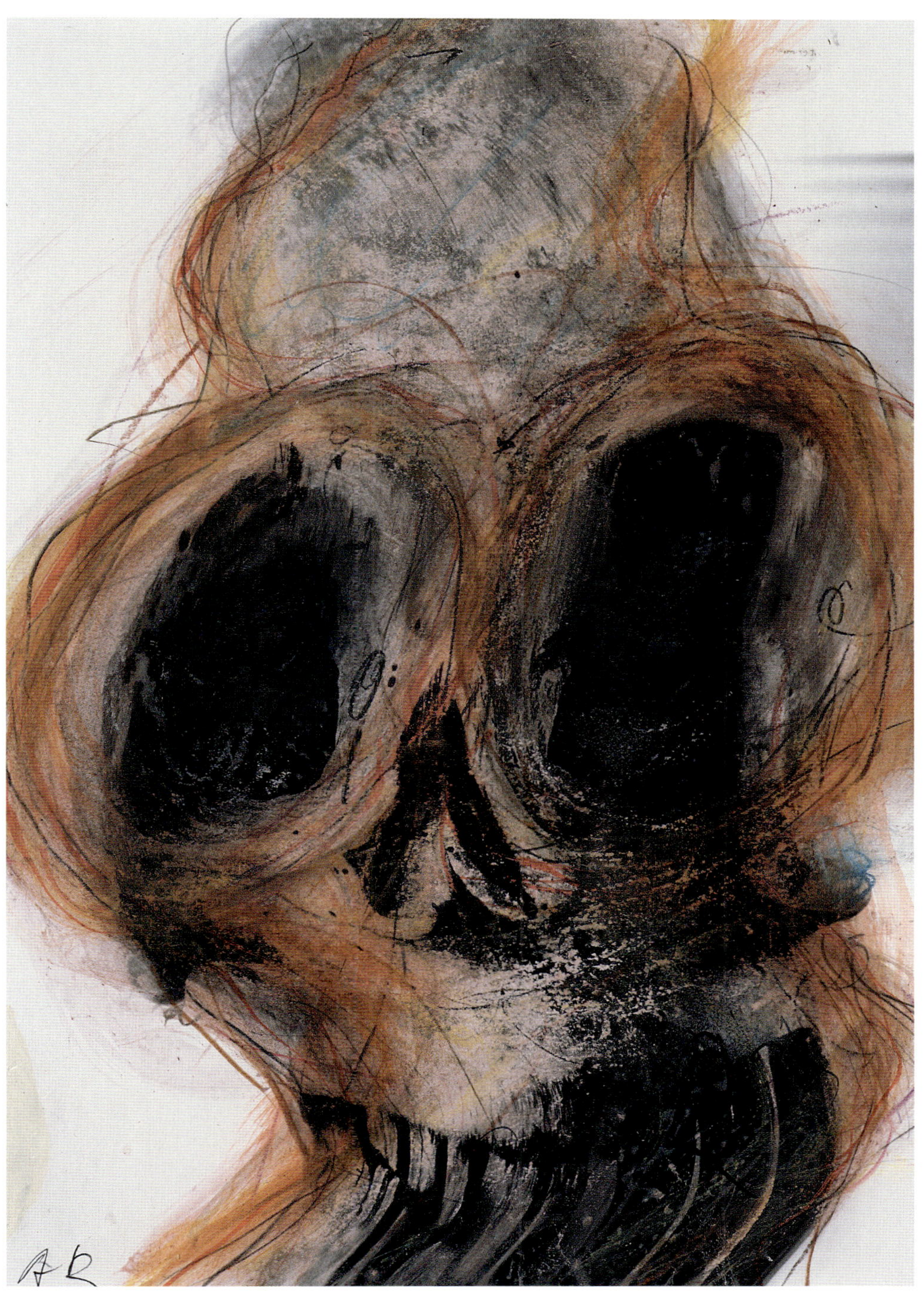

Das Sowohl begegnet dem Wie-auch-immer

Die Werkgruppe ist ein Versuch, Beziehungen zu schaffen zwischen den vorhandenen musealen Sammlungsgegenständen und den ausgewählten Gesichtspunkten des künstlerischen Eingriffs. Die Sammlungsgegenstände sind ihrer Funktionalität als auch ihrer rituellen Gebräuchlichkeit enthoben. Indem sie in den Räumen an den Wänden plaziert sind oder sich in den Vitrinen befinden, stellen sie gewissermaßen eine Entfernung von ihrer ursprünglichen Bestimmung dar sowie gleichzeitig eine Art Nähe zum mehr oder weniger oder gar nicht eingeweihten Betrachter und Museumsbesucher.

Was ihnen geblieben ist, ist ihre prägende wie eigenartige Erscheinung, die teilweise Zeugnis abzugeben vermag über ihren spezifischen Symbolgehalt einerseits und über ihre faszinierende Aura in der kultischen Handlung andererseits. Beide wissen und erahnen wir sehr tief im religiösen Glauben verwurzelt, der stark mit dem örtlichen Volks- und Aberglauben verwachsen ist. Daß sich dieser mitsamt der Volkskunst zu erhalten vermochte – zum Trotz des ständigen Fremdeinflusses, des regen Durchgangsverkehrs, der wechselnden politischen Entwicklungen und nationalen Zugehörigkeiten –, bleibt eine erstaunliche, bewundernswerte und anregende Tatsache.

Tirol, vor allem mit dem Brennerpaß eine der wichtigsten und ältesten Nord-Süd-Passagen der Alpen, gehört zu jenen besonderen Gebieten (ähnlich wie Splügen, Gotthard, Simplon, Großer St. Bernhard und andere Pässe), in welchen sich Kulturen begegnen und zum Teil auch vermischen. Die mediterrane Kultur trifft auf die alpine, beziehungsweise auf die nördlich der Alpen gelegenen Kulturkreise – beide mit ihren jeweiligen Mythologien. Stellvertretend abgeleitet trifft die Venus auf den Gartenzwerg (als nur eine mögliche Begegnung der Mythologien).

Weiter stark vereinfacht, geht es hier um die Gegend des Aufeinanderpralls und des Zusammenlebens von Weinkultur und Bierkultur ... oder Weinmythos -topos mit Biermythos -topos ...

Die künstlerische Intervention, bestehend aus vier Objektfiguren oder Versatzstücken, sucht in der Begegnung eine Ergänzung des (im Museum) Gegebenen. Diese Erweiterung soll auch eine Ebene erreichen, auf der die Autonomie wie auch das Vorhandensein der beiden (d. h. des Sammlungsstücks und des Kunstwerks) zwar gewahrt bleiben, darüber hinaus jedoch eine «Vermählung auf Zeit» stattfinden kann.

So bekommt der Saltner nach Jahren seines Ausgestelltseins eine Dame als Begleiterin ...

Die wunderbar geschnitzten und bemalten Betten werden für eine Weile von einem Paar beseelt ...

Die einmaligen Werkzeuge, geschaffen mit besonders heute spürbarer Achtung vor dem Handwerk, erhalten neidischen Besuch von ihren Nachkommen aus den europäischen Baumärkten.

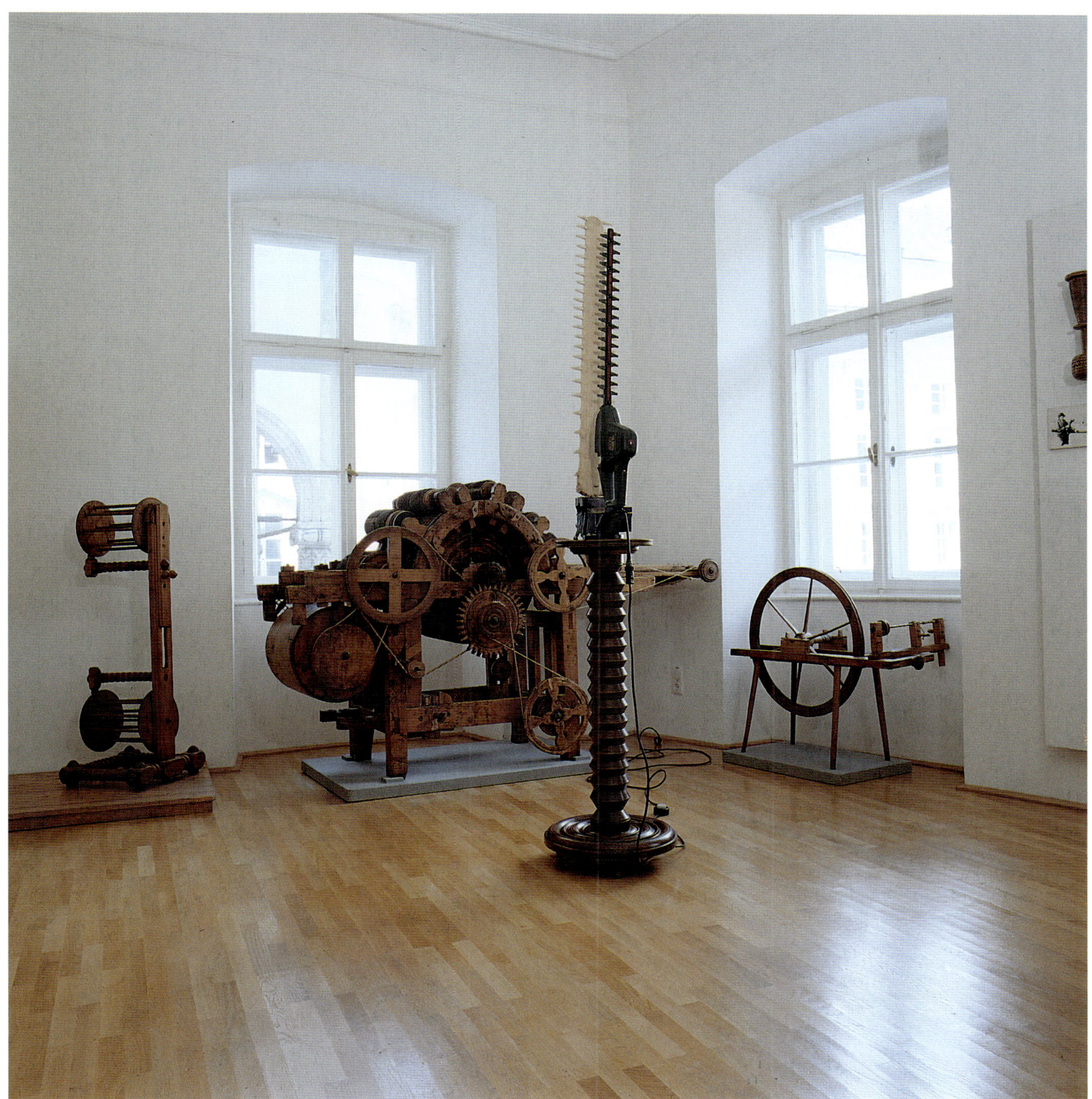

Decker & Black, 1995

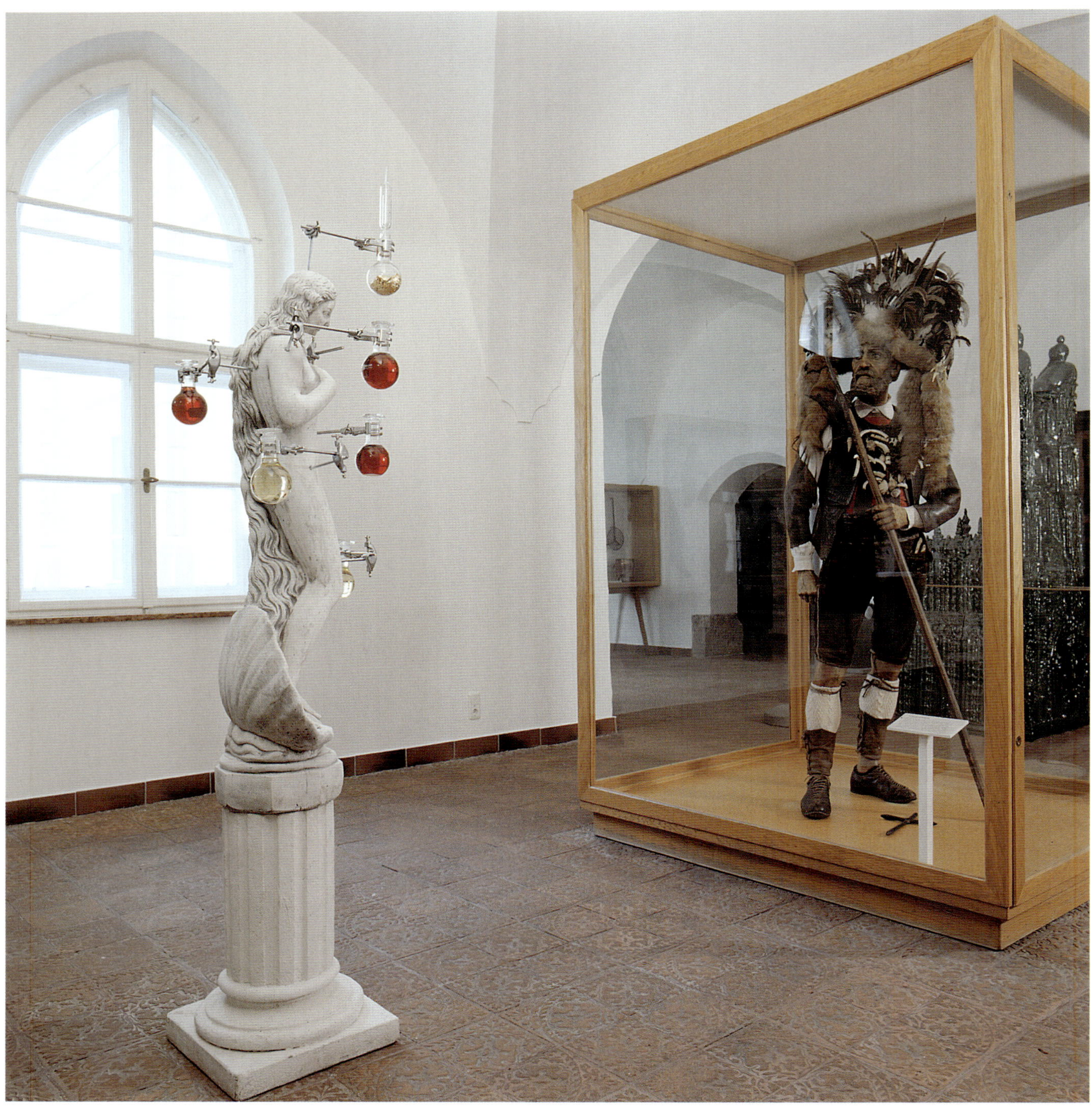

Saltners Traum, 1998

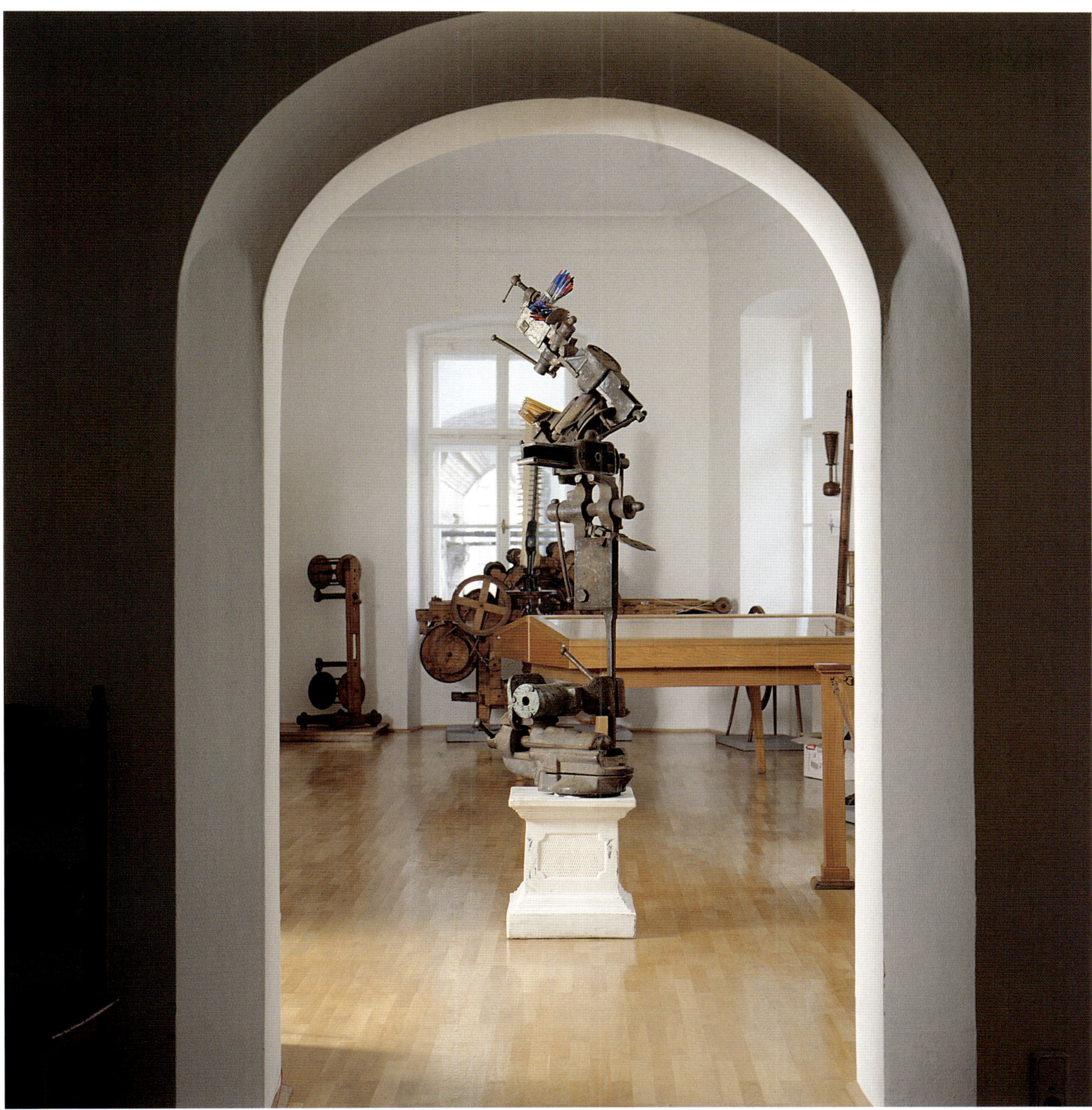

Schraubstöcke und Schreibstifte, 1996

Am Anfang steht die Wiege. Als Chilene ringe ich um die Vereinbarung meiner europäischen Wurzeln mit der Mystik Lateinamerikas. Meine Innsbrucker Installation ist eine Momentaufnahme dieser Spannung: Aus den sieben Tiroler Wiegen ragen die Holzstelen, auf denen sich meine Wahrnehmung der Welt spiegelt.

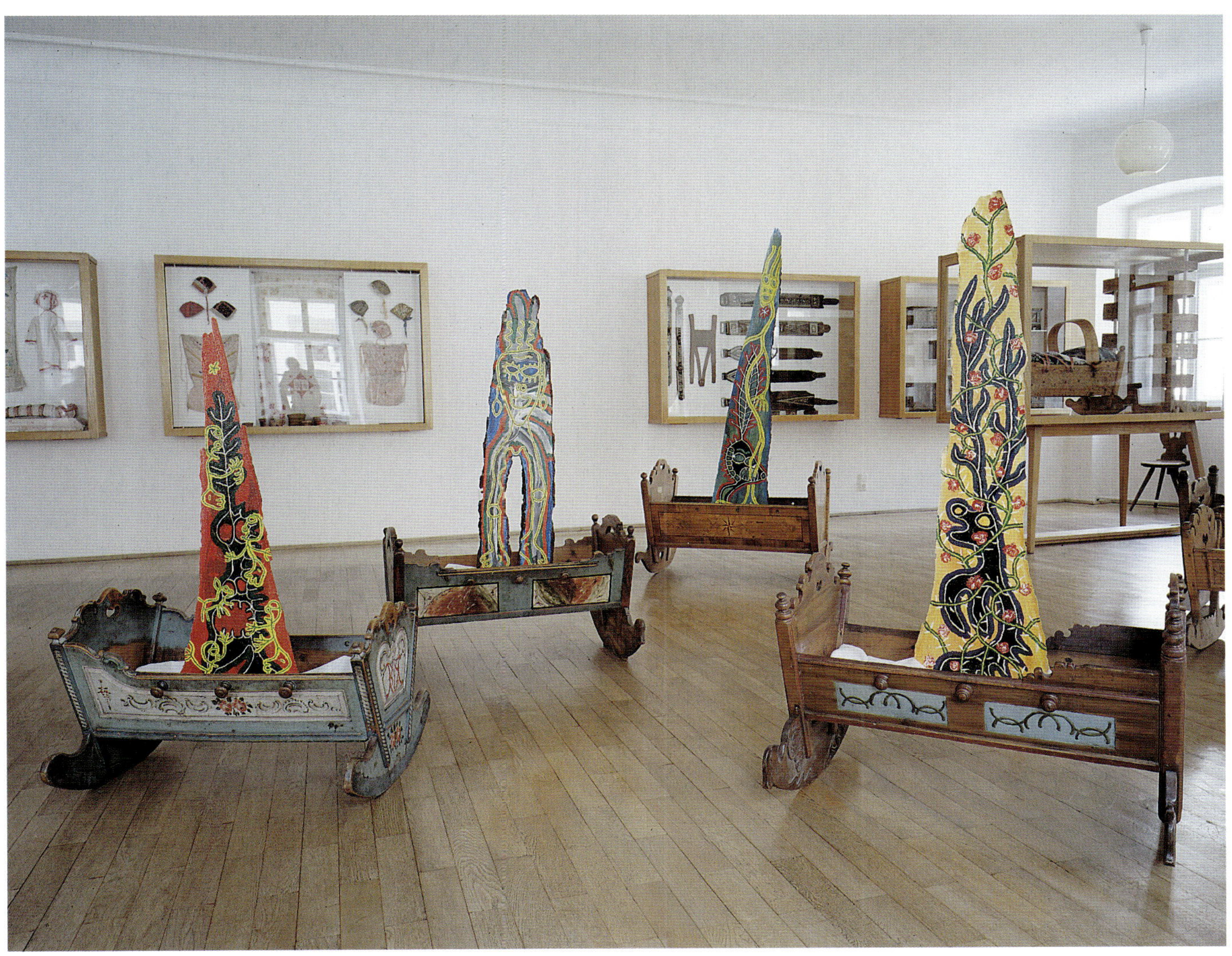

Kinderwald, 1998

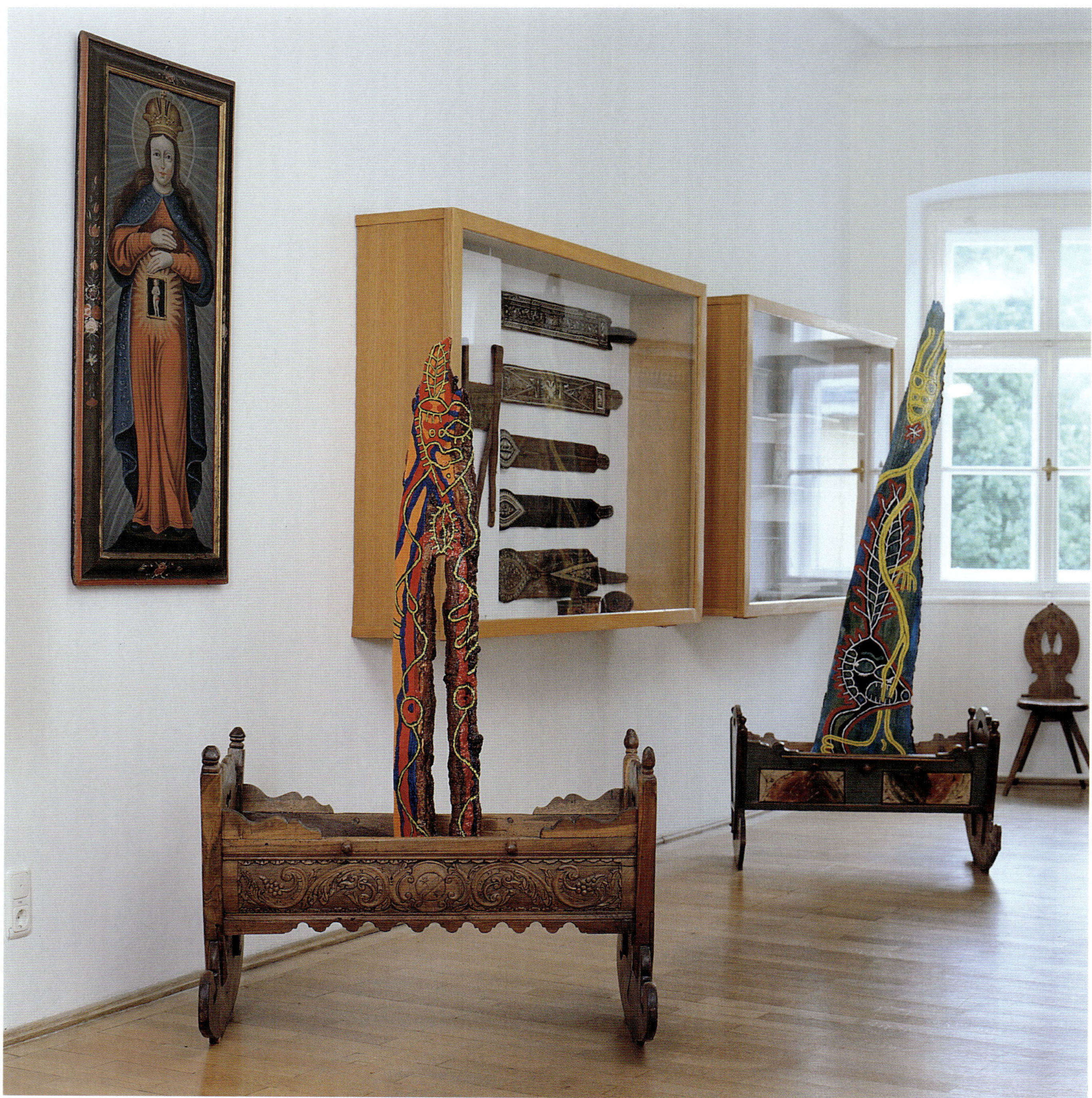

Kinderwald, 1998

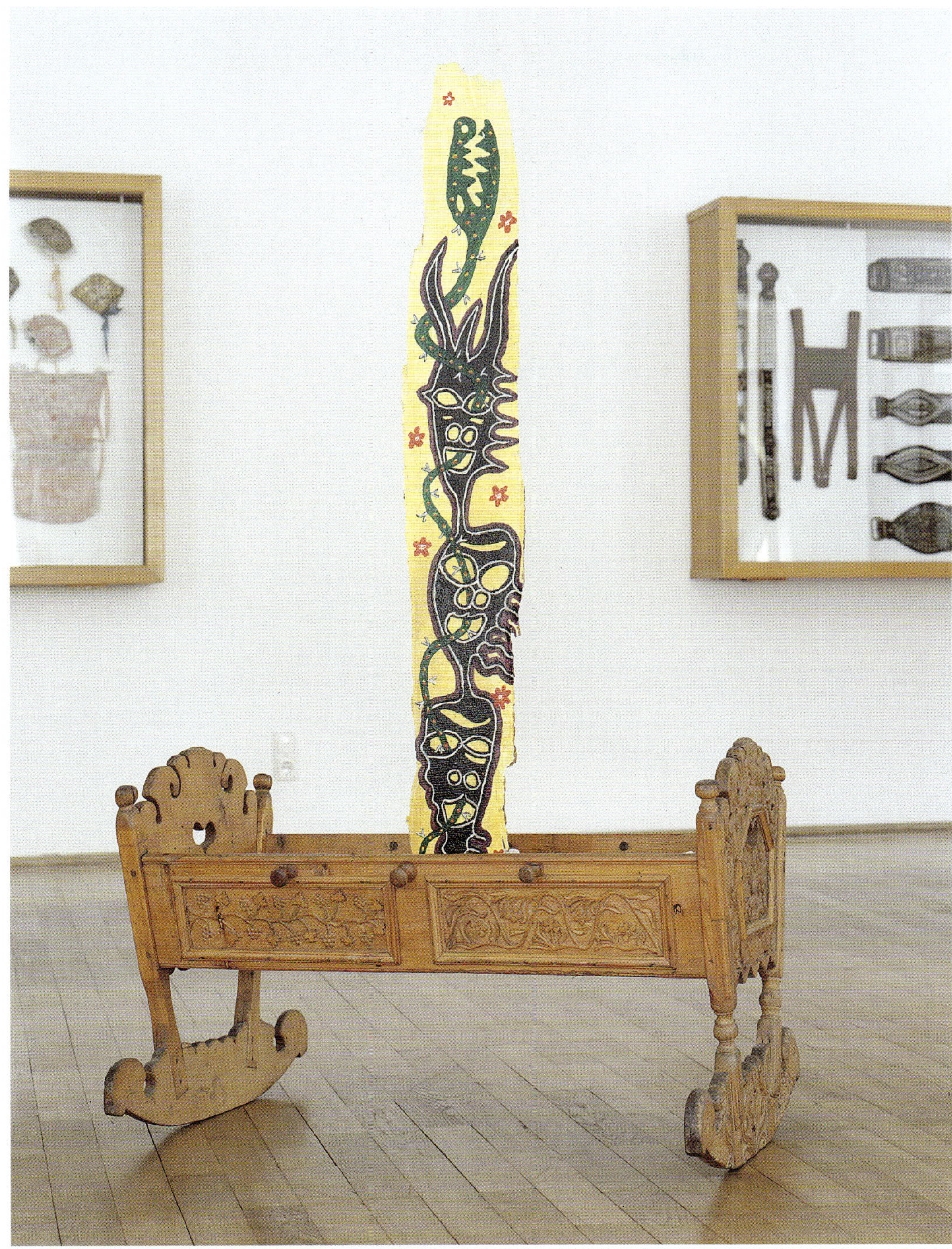

Kinderwald, 1998

OLD NEW BLACK WHITE IRON PAPER OPEN CLOSED PLAIN ORNATE
EXPENSIVE CHEAP DEAD ALIVE OLD NEW BLACK WHITE IRON PAPER
OPEN CLOSED ORNATE PLAIN EXPENSIVE CHEAP DEAD ALIVE OLD NEW
BLACK WHITE IRON PAPER OPEN CLOSED ORNATE PLAIN EXPENSIVE
CHEAP DEAD ALIVE OLD NEW BLACK WHITE IRON PAPER OPEN CLOSED
ORNATE PLAIN EXPENSIVE CHEAP DEAD ALIVE OLD NEW BLACK WHITE
IRON PAPER OPEN CLOSED ORNATE PLAIN EXPENSIVE CHEAP DEAD
ALIVE OLD NEW BLACK WHITE IRON PAPER OPEN CLOSED ORNATE
PLAIN EXPENSIVE CHEAP DEAD ALIVE OLD NEW BLACK WHITE IRON
PAPER OPEN CLOSED ORNATE PLAIN EXPENSIVE CHEAP DEAD ALIVE
OLD NEW BLACK WHITE IRON PAPER OPEN CLOSED ORNATE PLAIN
EXPENSIVE CHEAP DEAD ALIVE OLD NEW BLACK WHITE IRON PAPER
OPEN CLOSED ORNATE PLAIN EXPENSIVE CHEAP DEAD ALIVE OLD NEW
BLACK WHITE IRON PAPER OPEN CLOSED PLAIN ORNATE EXPENSIVE
CHEAP DEAD ALIVE OLD NEW BLACK WHITE IRON PAPER OPEN CLOSED
PLAIN ORNATE EXPENSIVE CHEAP DEAD ALIVE OLD NEW BLACK WHITE
IRON PAPER OPEN CLOSED PLAIN ORNATE EXPENSIVE CHEAP DEAD
ALIVE OLD NEW BLACK WHITE IRON PAPER OPEN CLOSED PLAIN
ORNATE EXPENSIVE CHEAP DEAD ALIVE OLD NEW BLACK WHITE IRON
PAPER OPEN CLOSED PLAIN ORNATE EXPENSIVE CHEAP DEAD ALIVE
OLD NEW BLACK WHITE IRON PAPER OPEN CLOSED PLAIN ORNATE
EXPENSIVE CHEAP DEAD ALIVE OLD NEW BLACK WHITE IRON PAPER
OPEN CLOSED PLAIN ORNATE EXPENSIVE CHEAP DEAD ALIVE OLD NEW
BLACK WHITE IRON PAPER OPEN CLOSED PLAIN ORNATE EXPENSIVE
CHEAP DEAD ALIVE OLD NEW BLACK WHITE IRON PAPER OPEN CLOSED
PLAIN ORNATE EXPENSIVE CHEAP DEAD ALIVE OLD NEW BLACK WHITE
IRON PAPER OPEN CLOSED PLAIN ORNATE EXPENSIVE CHEAP DEAD
ALIVE OLD NEW BLACK WHITE IRON PAPER OPEN CLOSED PLAIN
ORNATE EXPENSIVE CHEAP DEAD ALIVE OLD NEW BLACK WHITE IRON
PAPER OPEN CLOSED PLAIN ORNATE EXPENSIVE CHEAP DEAD ALIVE
OLD NEW BLACK WHITE IRON PAPER OPEN CLOSED PLAIN ORNATE
EXPENSIVE CHEAP DEAD ALIVE OLD NEW BLACK WHITE IRON PAPER

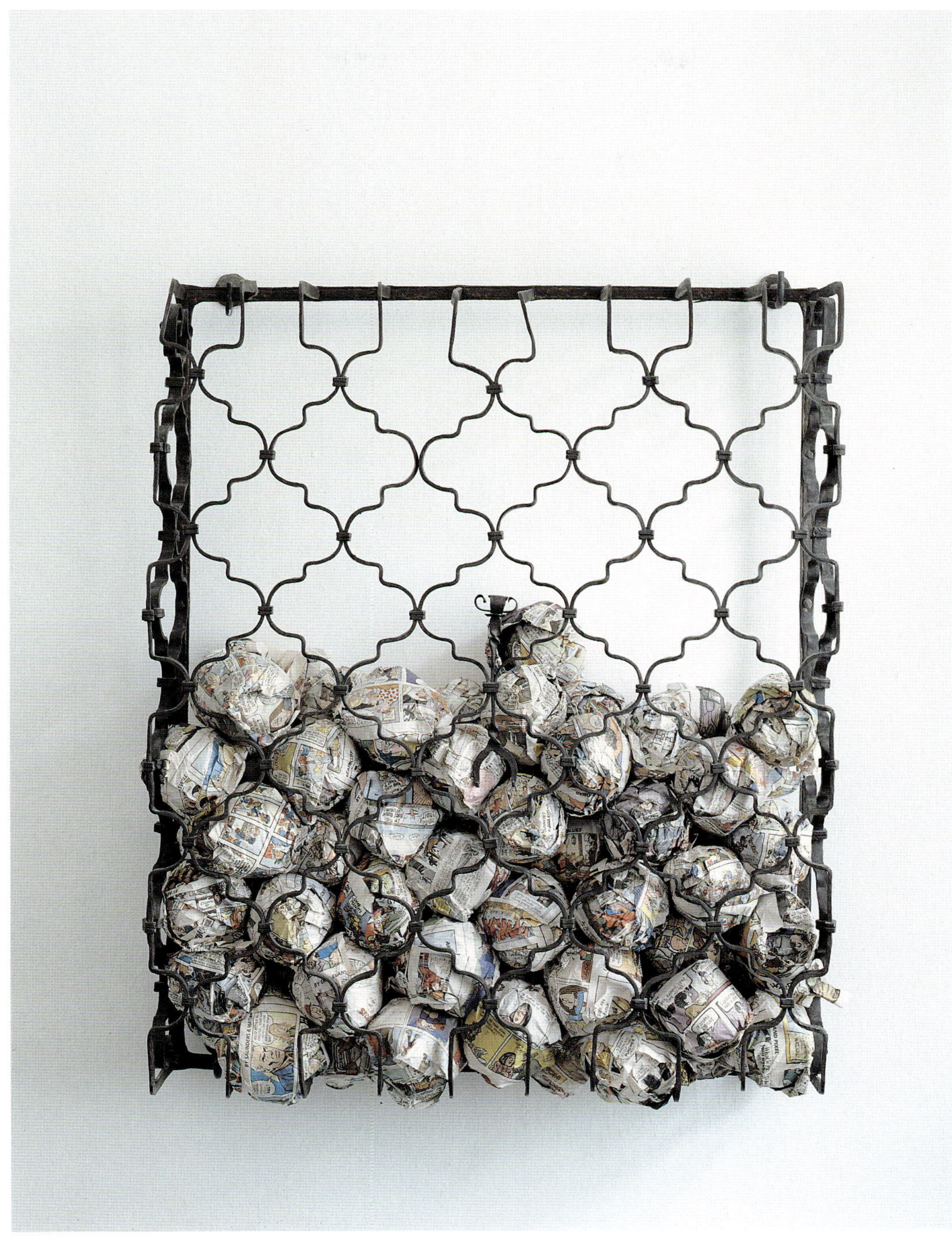

Austrian News Wads, 1998

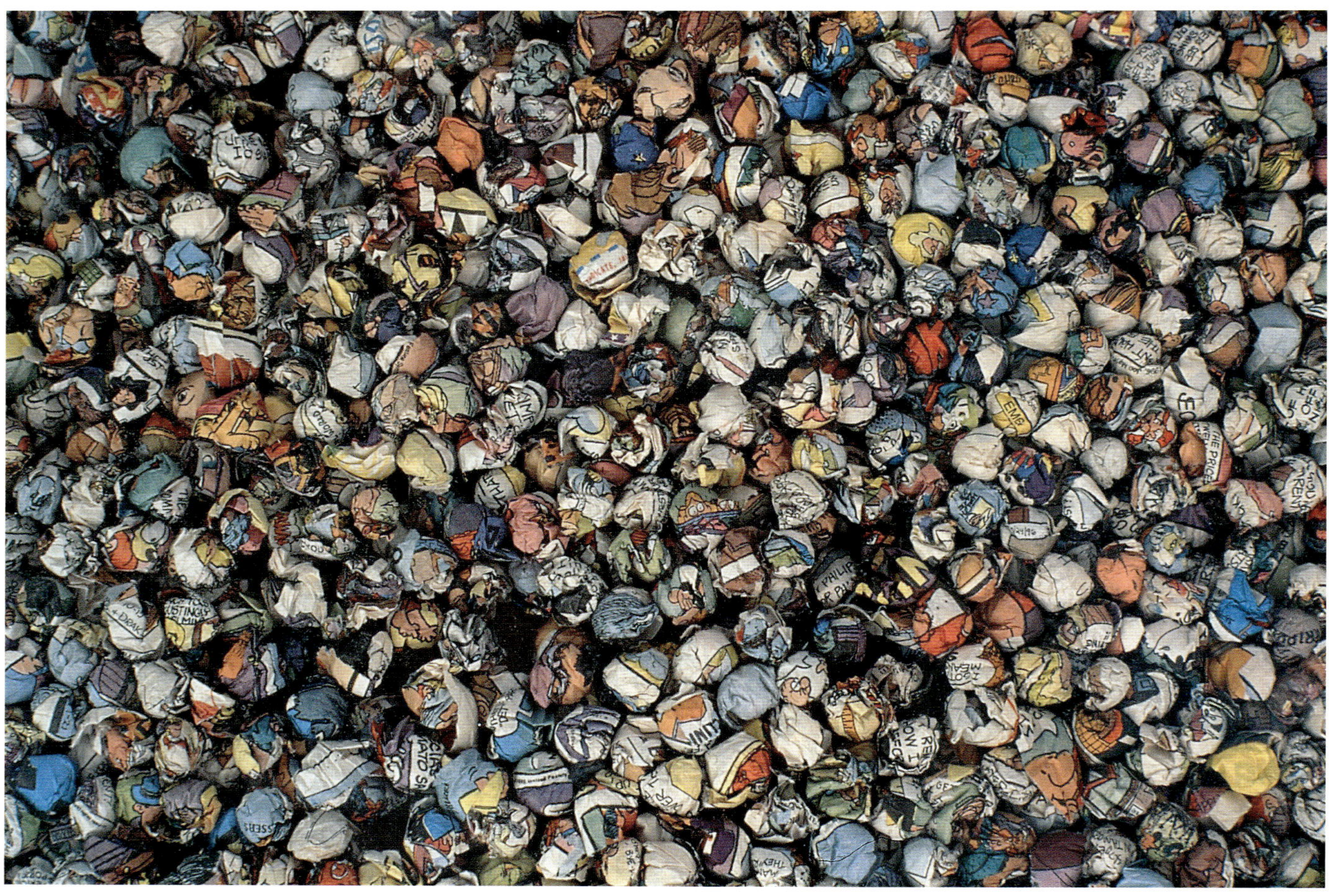

Comic Wads, 1997 (Detail)

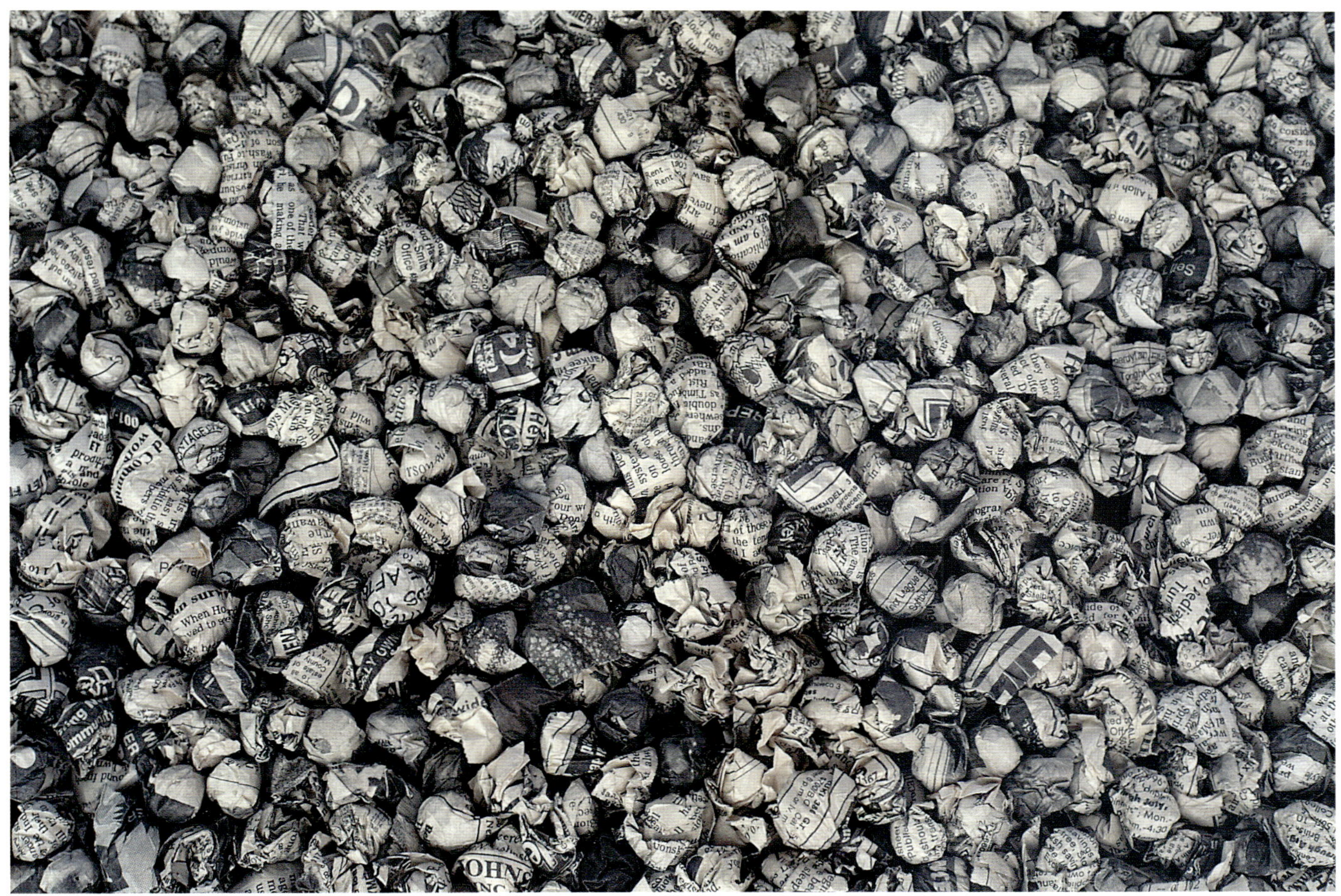

News Wads, 1997 (Detail)

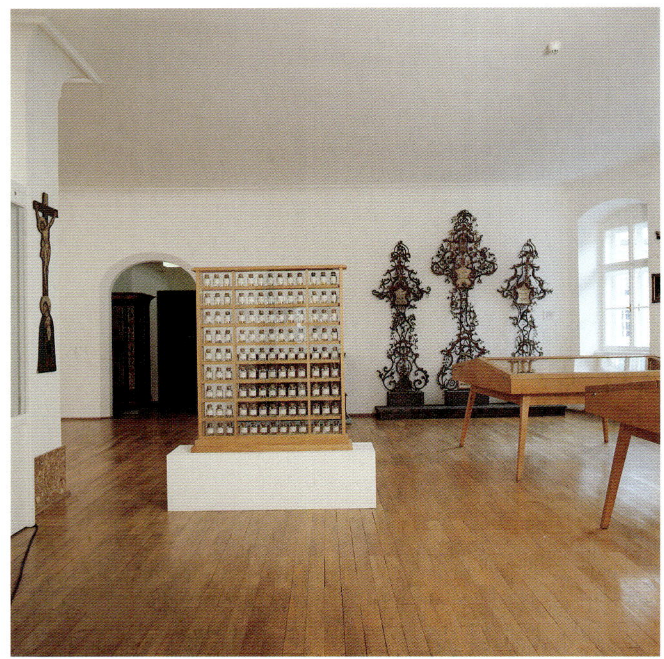

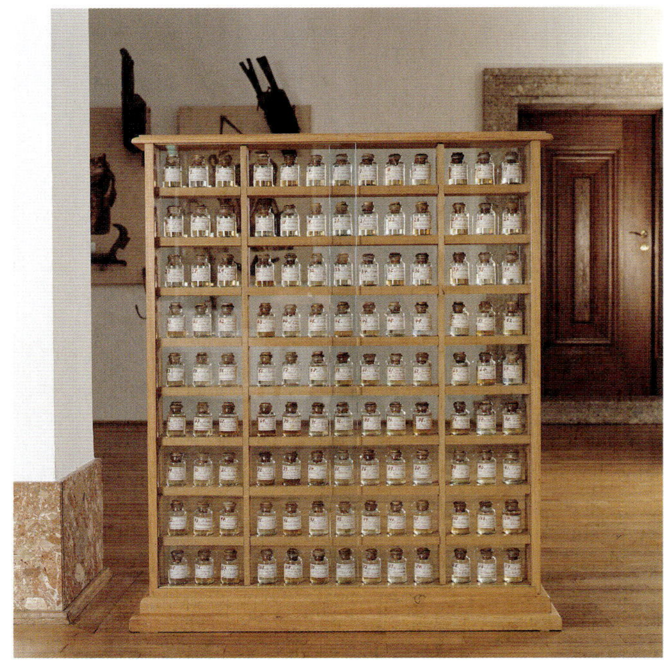

Pharmacie Bretonne, 1970–77

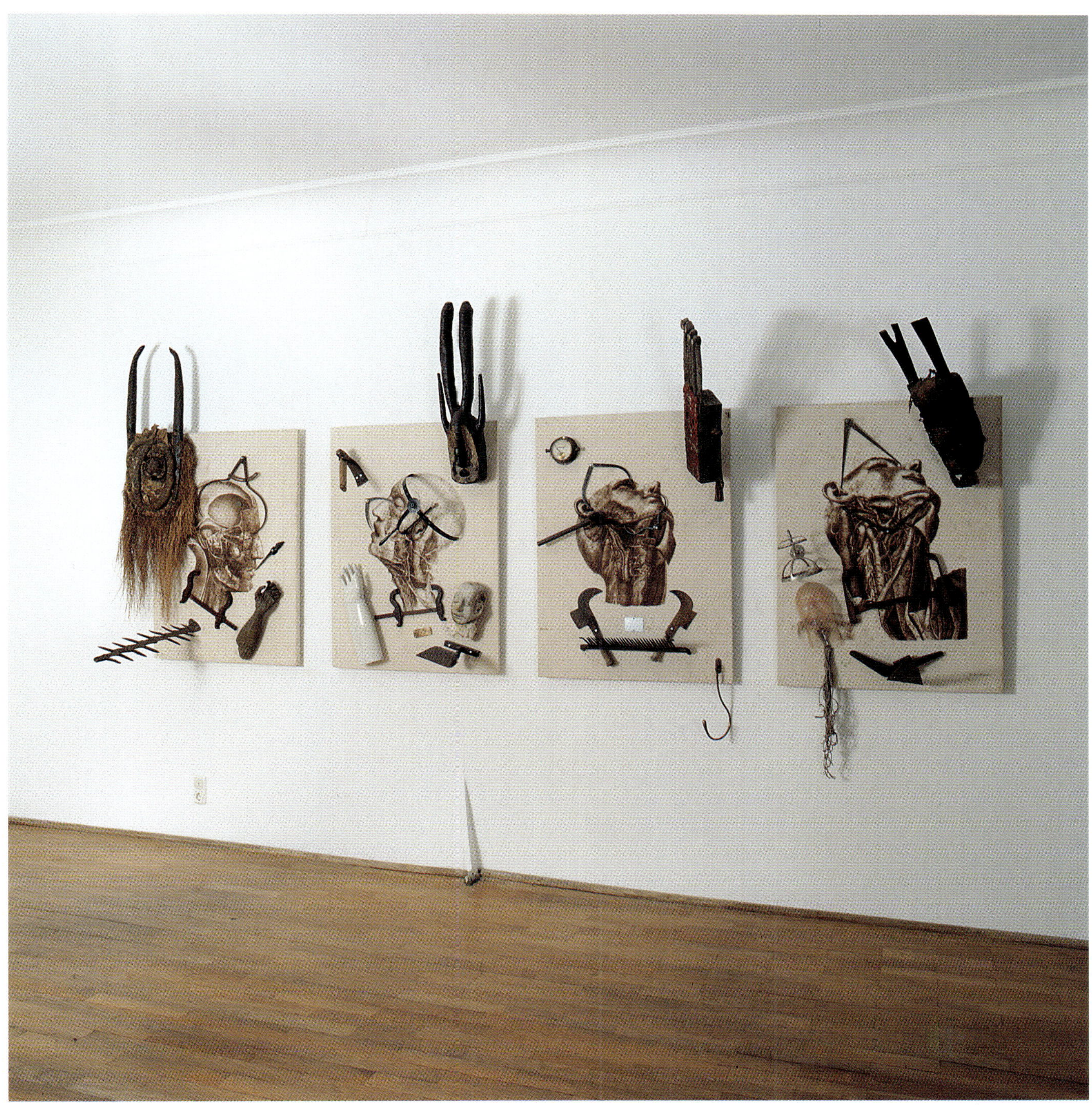

Requiem für Orlando Topor, 1997 (4teilig)

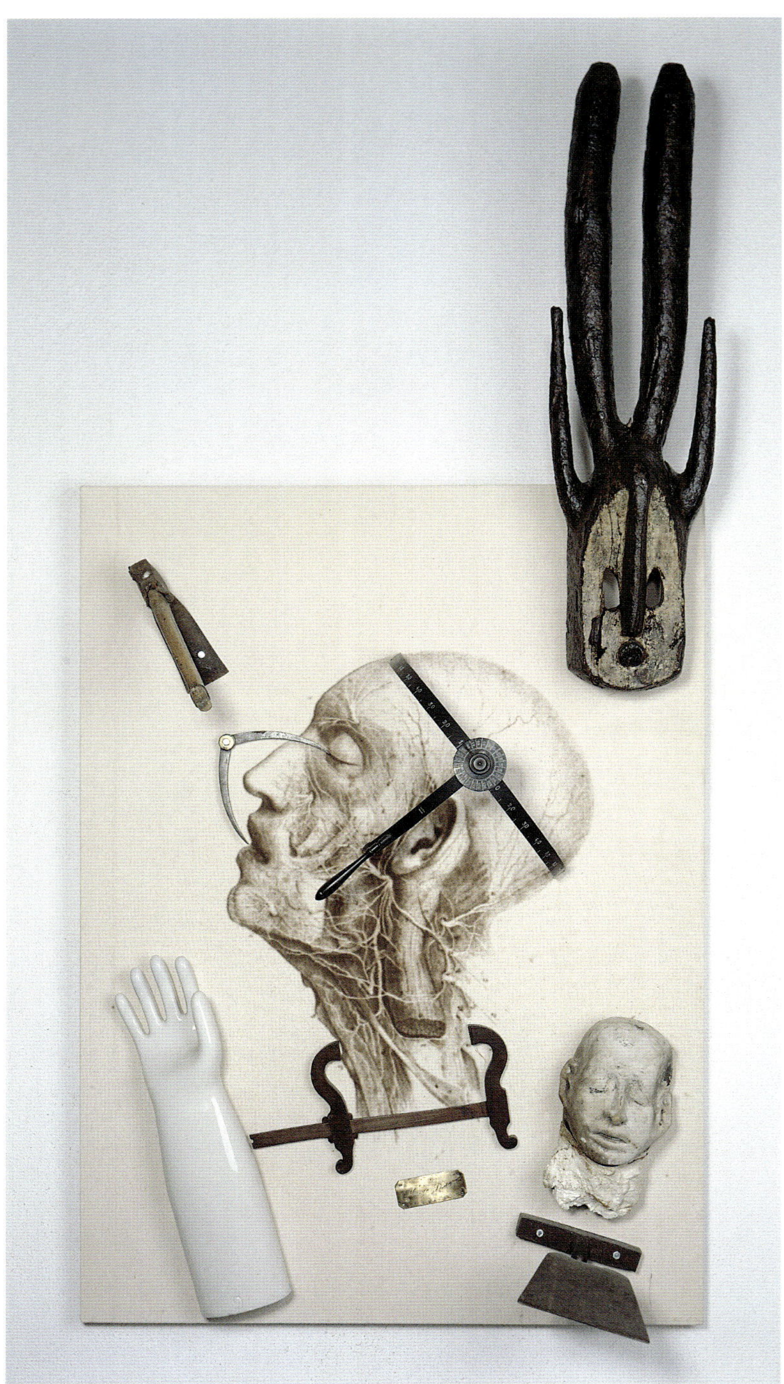

Requiem für Orlando Topor, 1997 (4teilig, Detail)

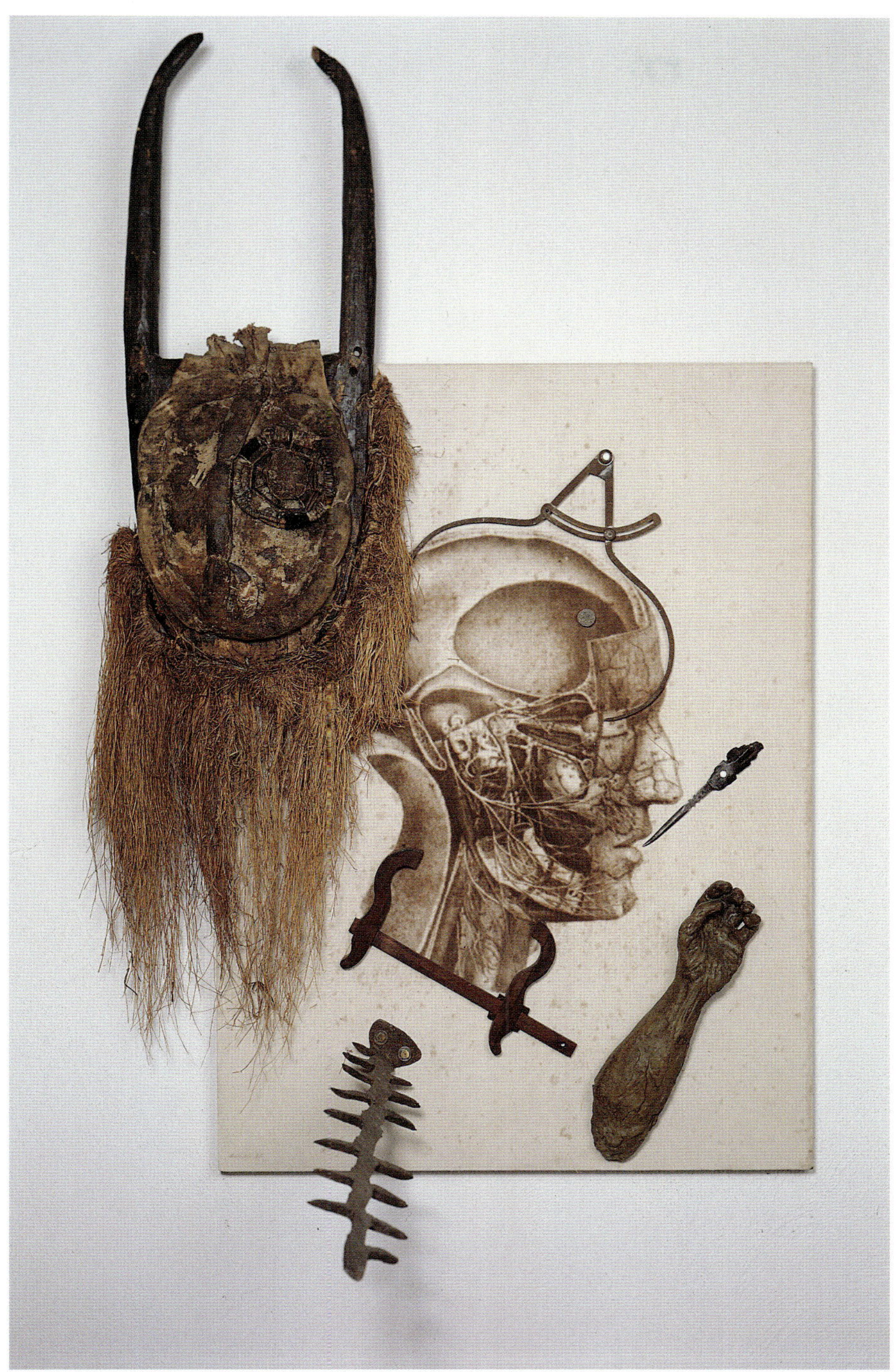

Requiem für Orlando Topor, 1997 (4teilig, Detail)

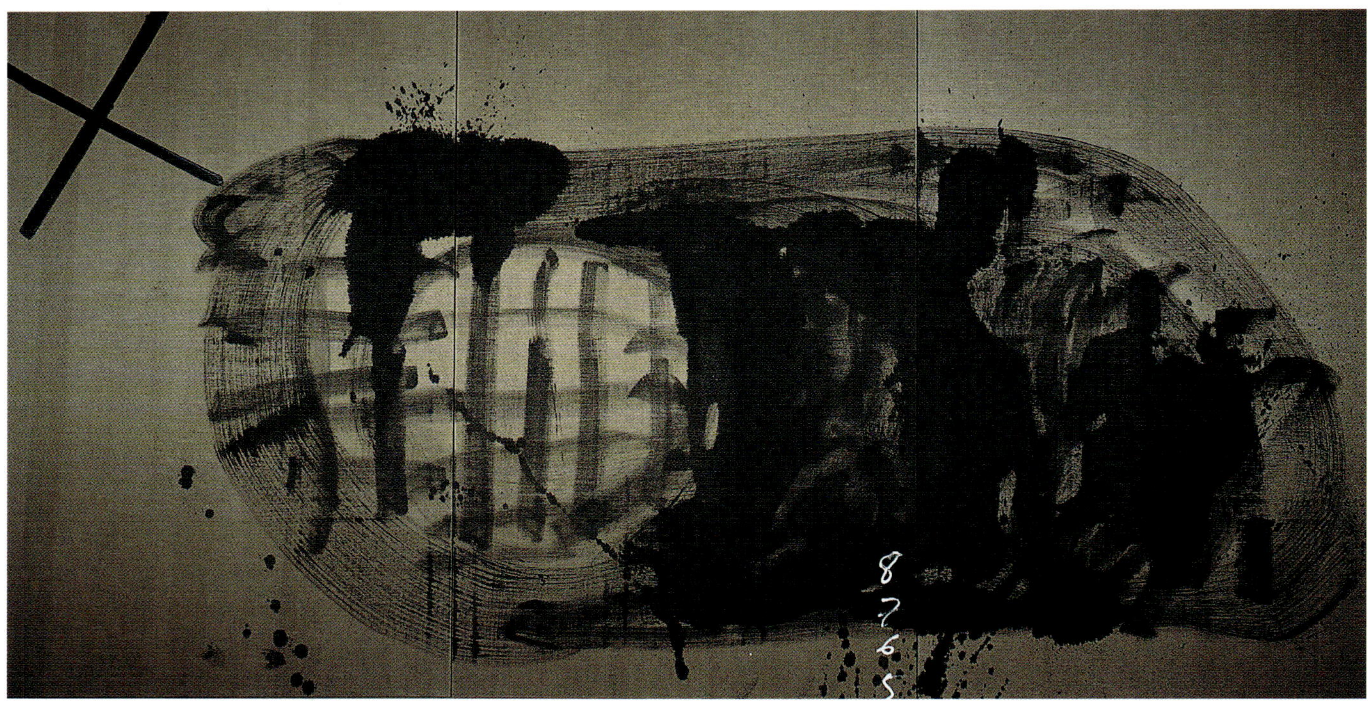

Triptyque, 1985
Courtesy Galerie Lelong Zürich

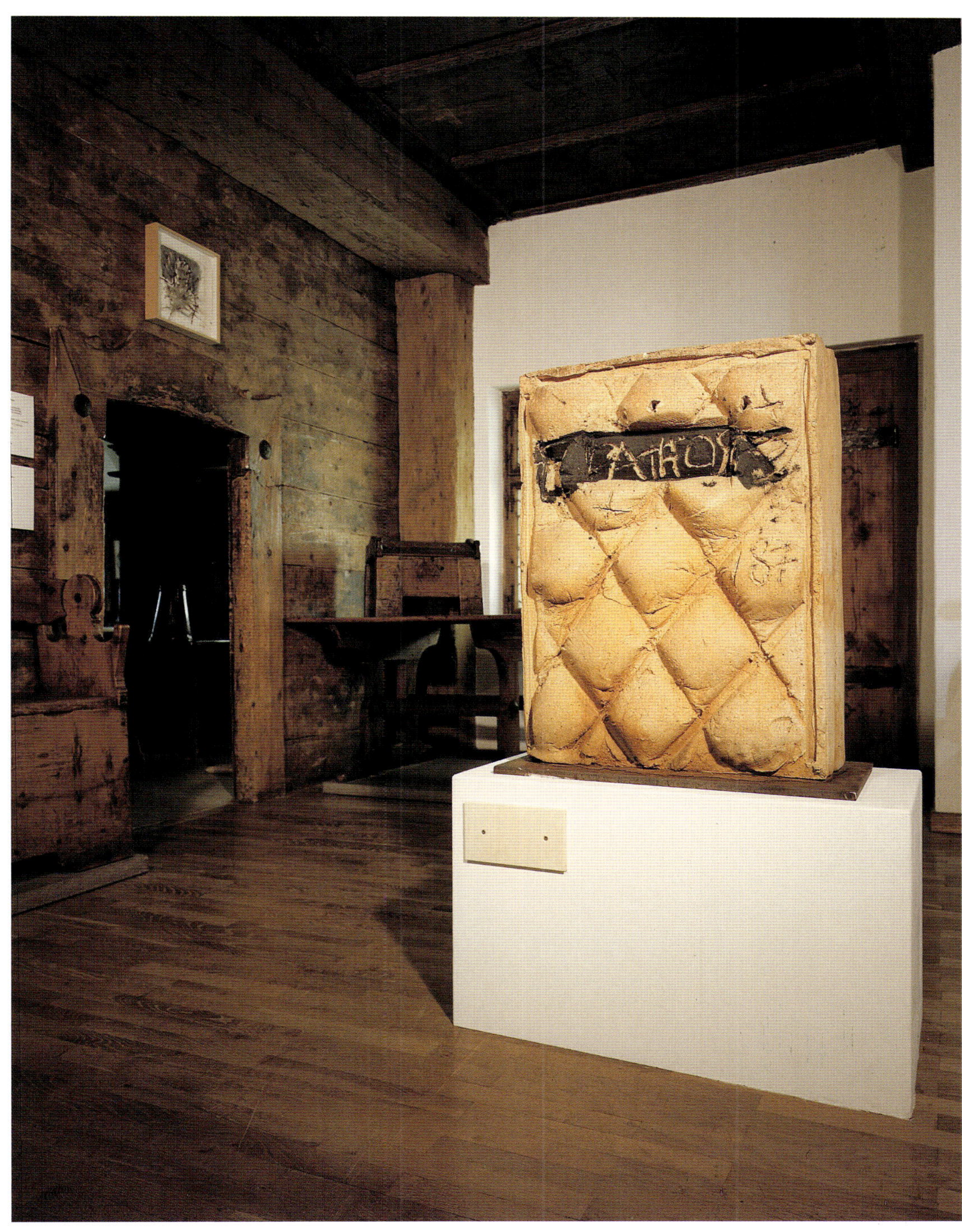

Installation mit

Dossier, 1988

Chaussure, 1988
Courtesy Galerie Lelong Zürich

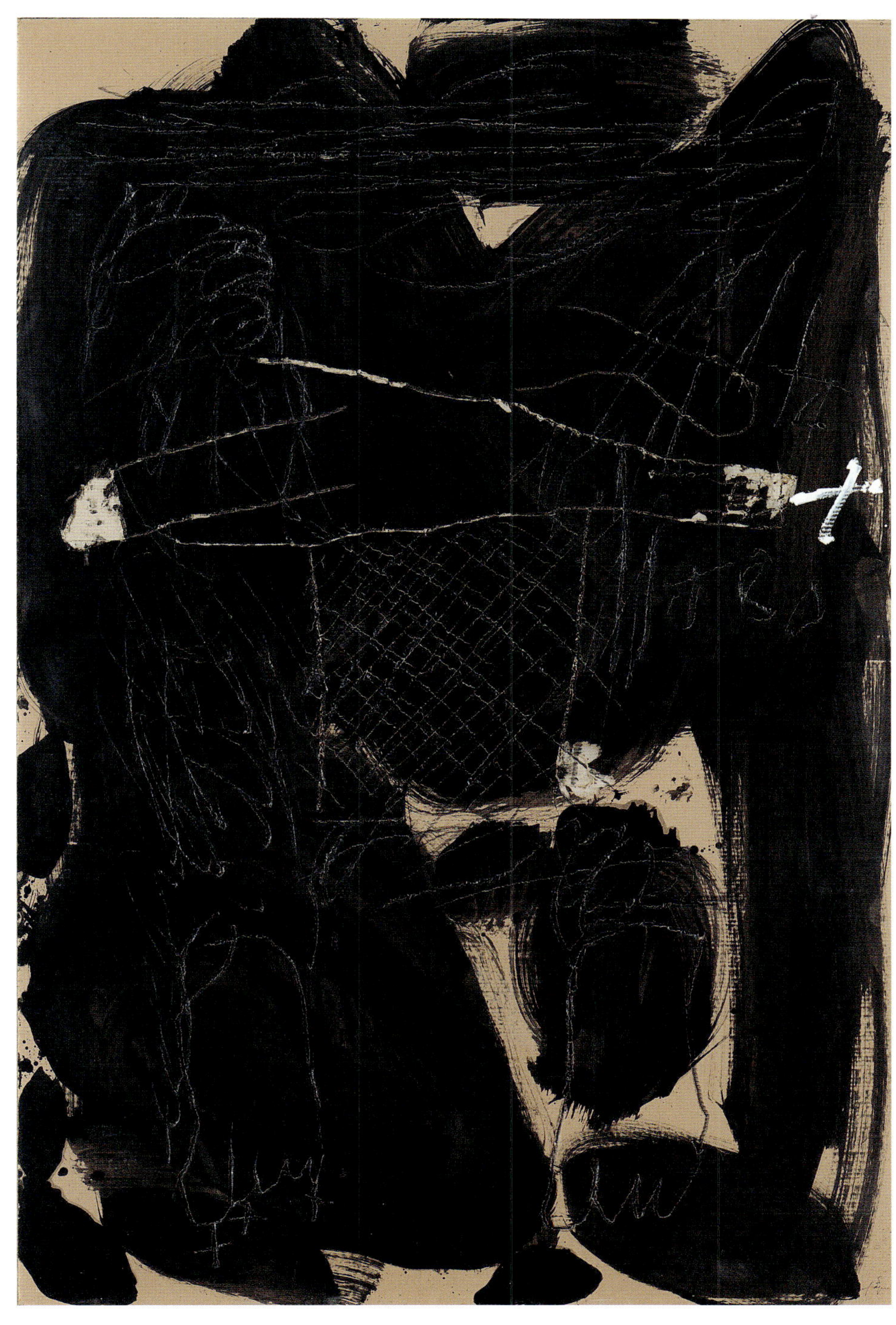

Graphismes sur noir, 1988
Courtesy Galerie Lelong Zürich

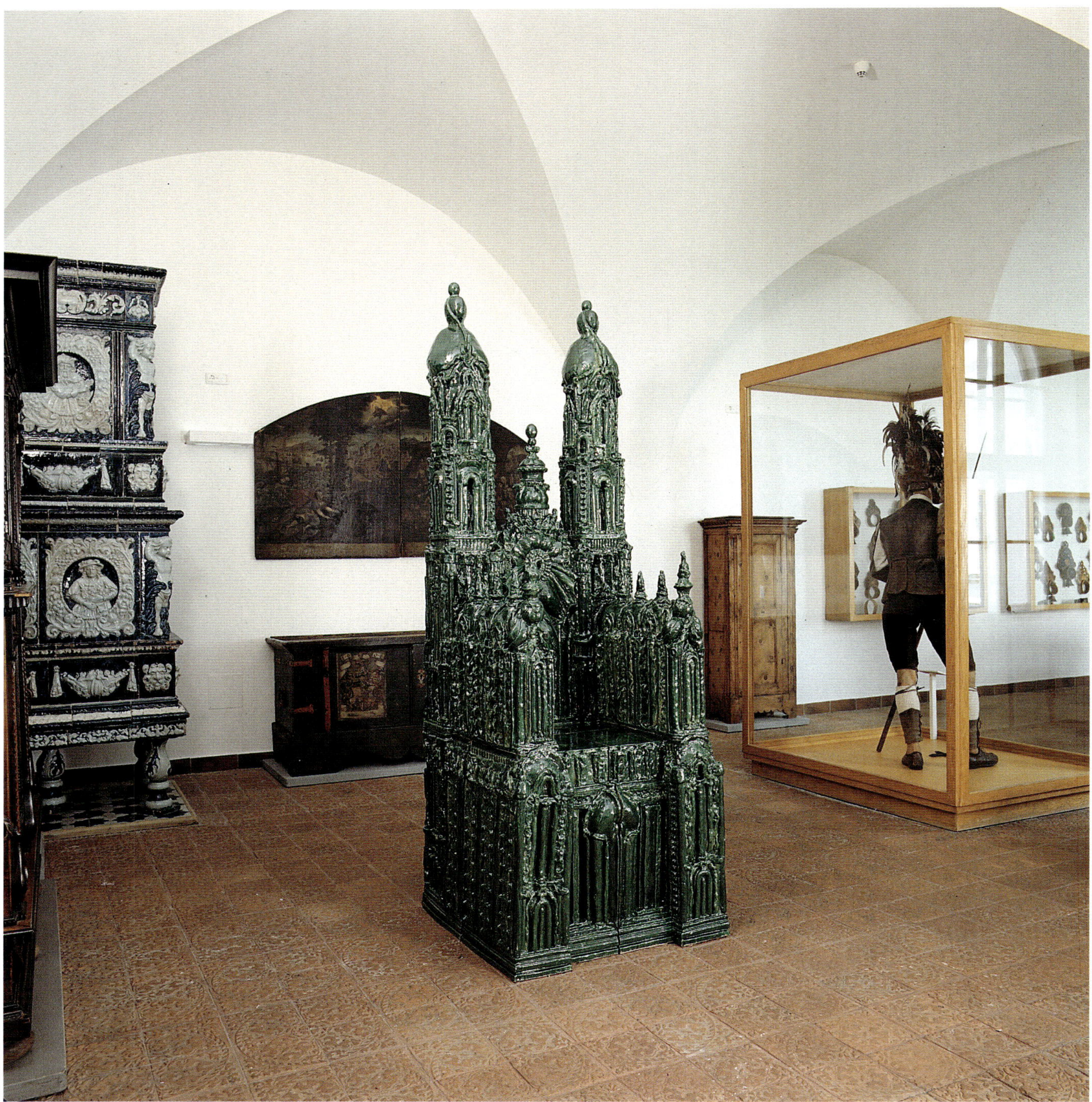

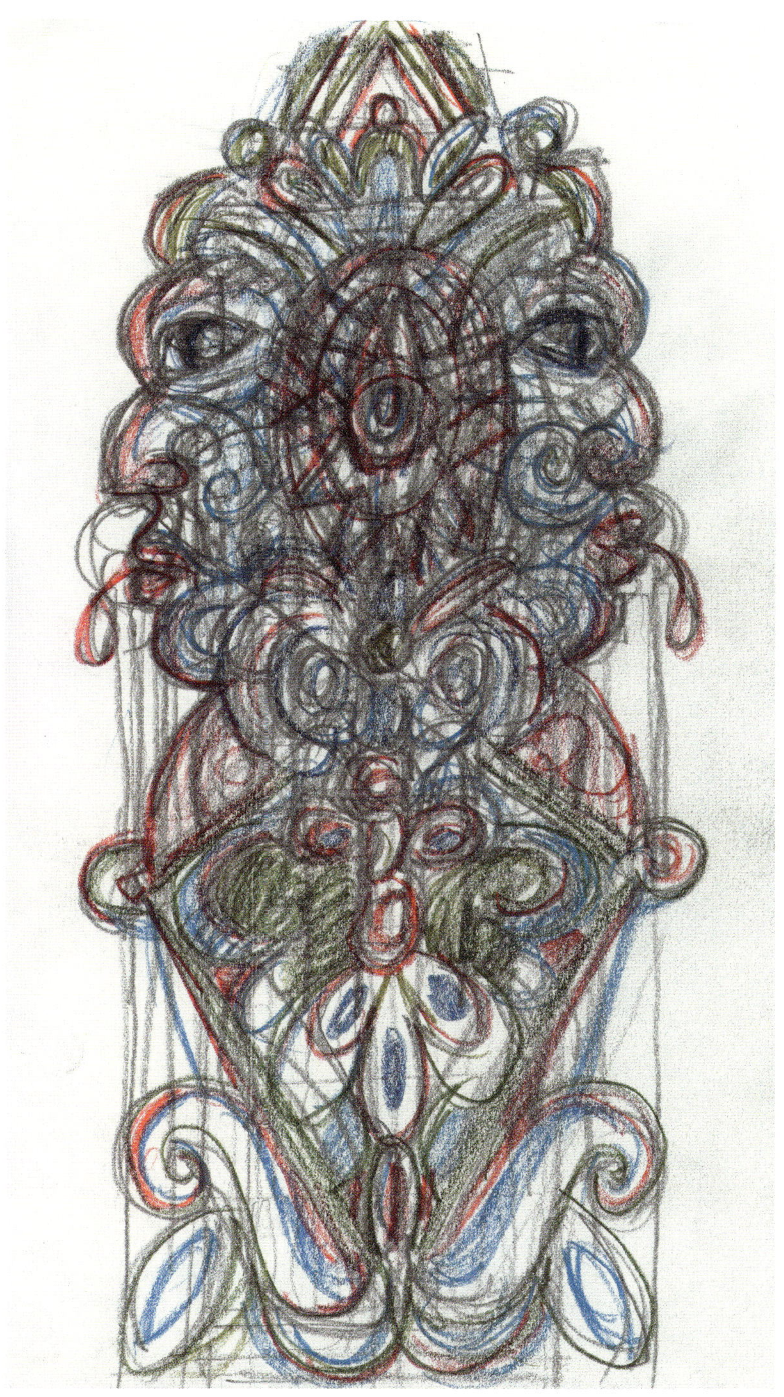

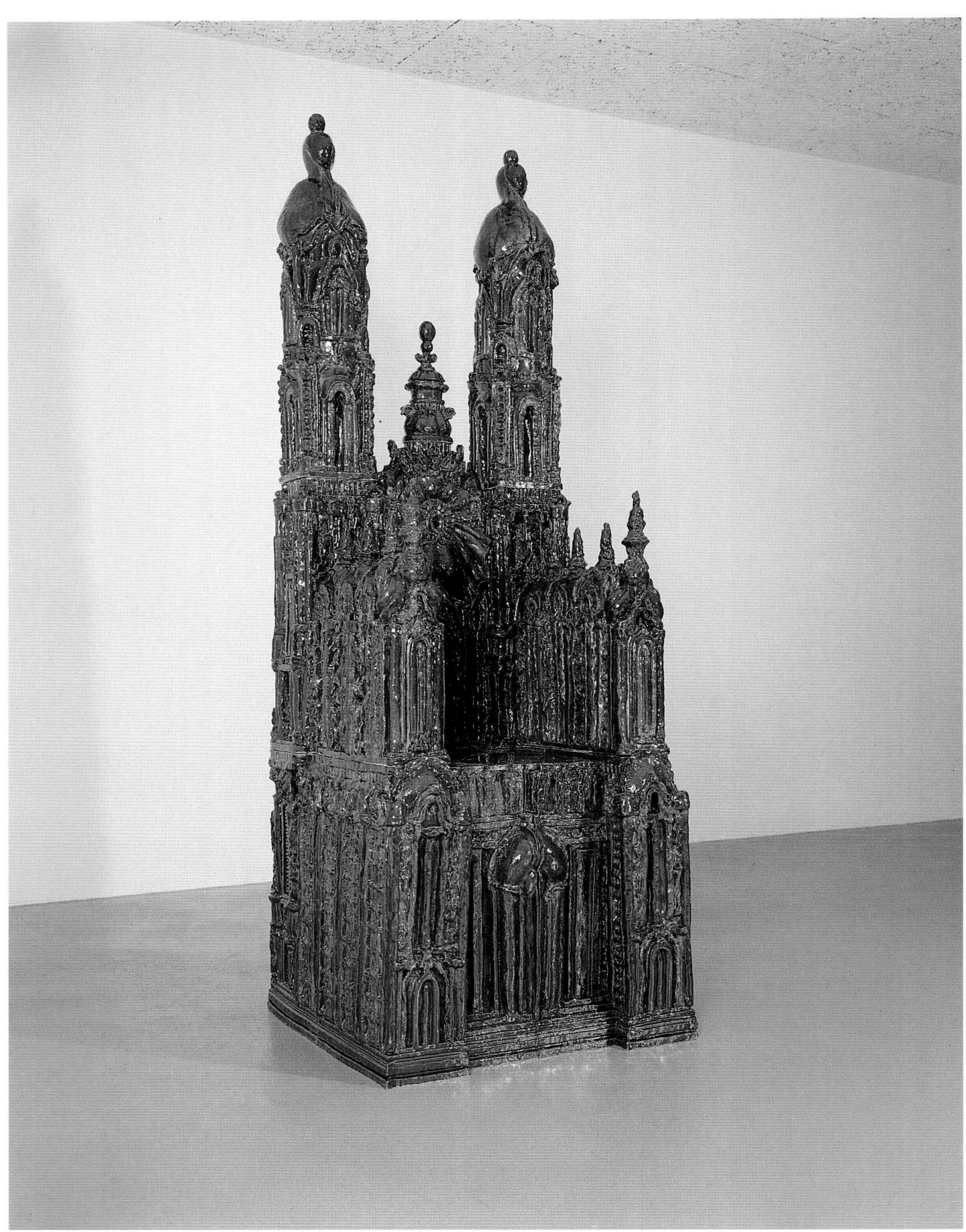

Ton gebrannt, grün glasiert, 1998 (9teilig)

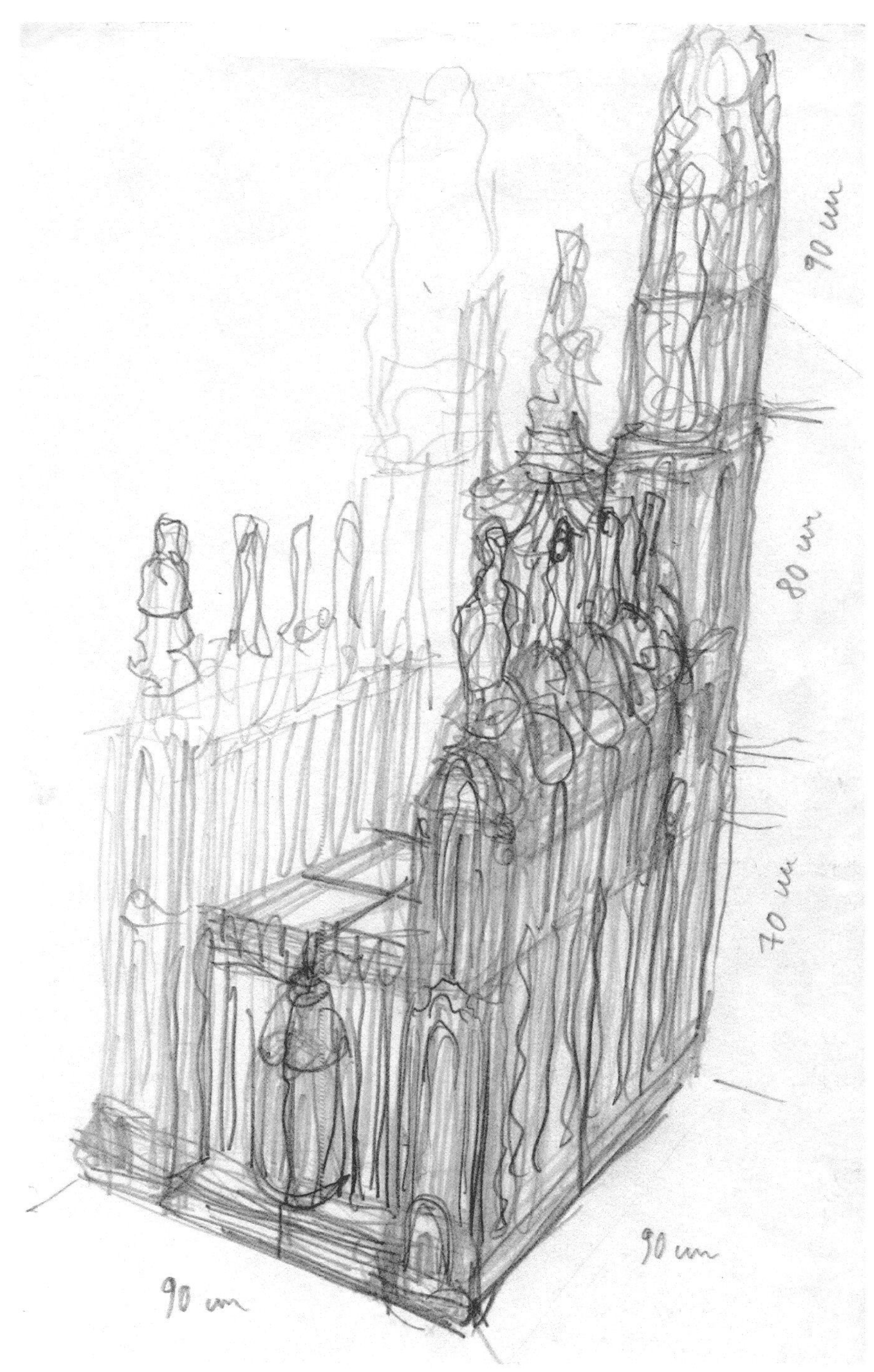
90 cm
80 cm
70 cm
90 cm
90 cm

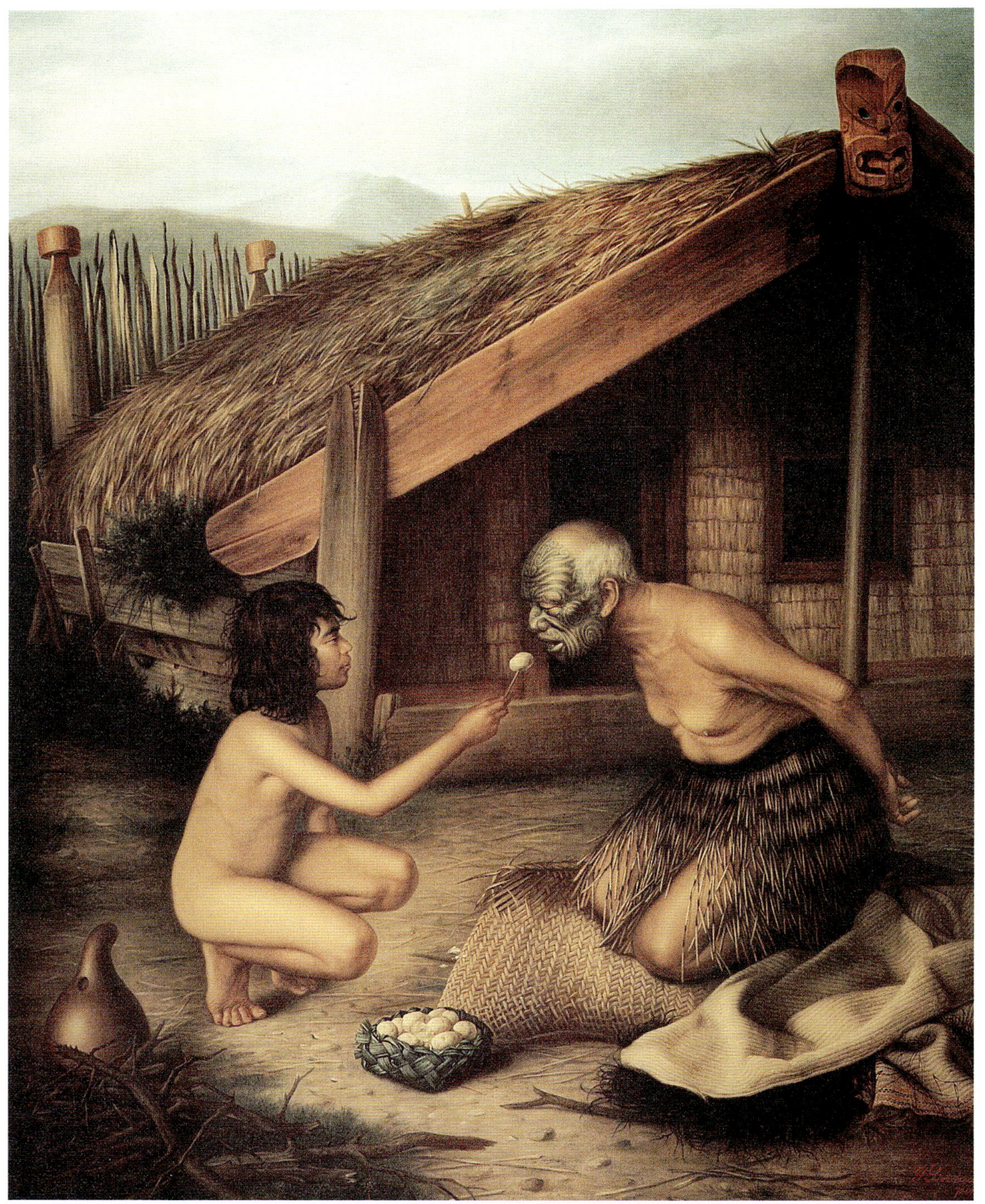

Ahakoa kai tahi, térà a roto te hahae ké rà.

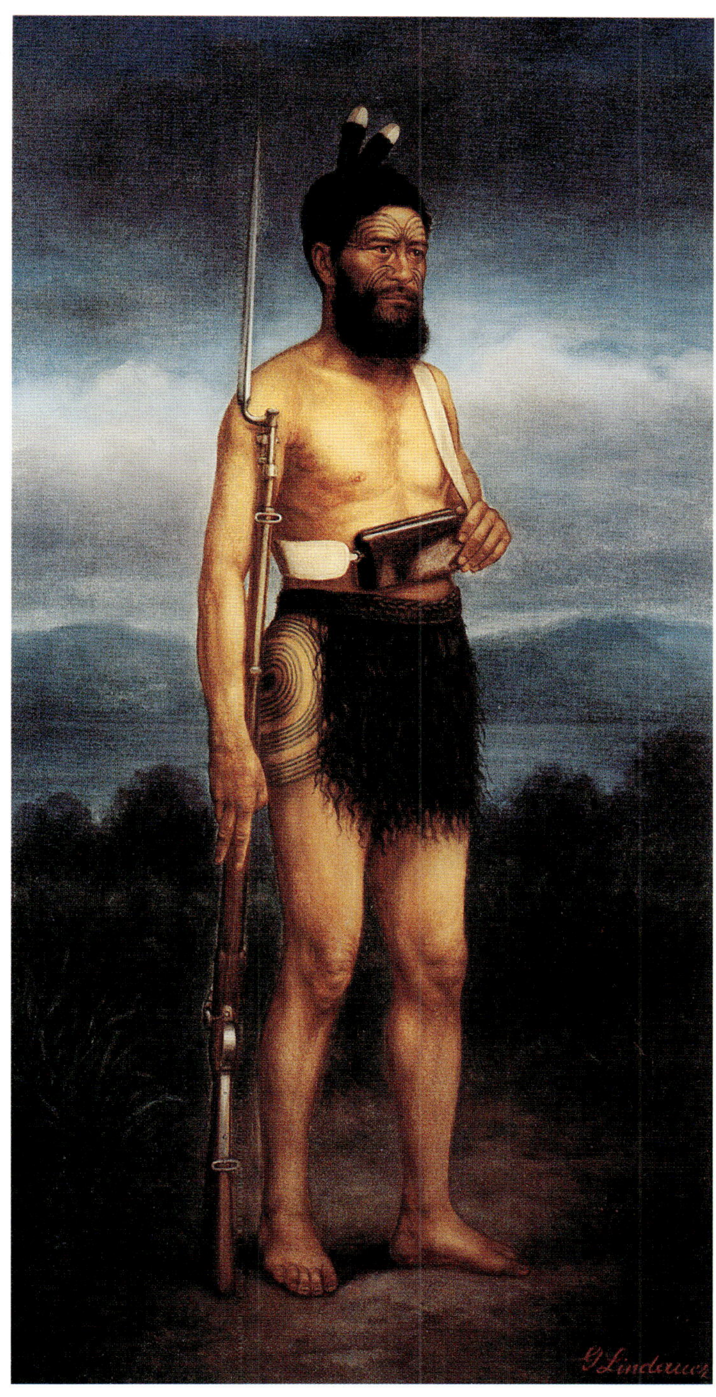

Kotahi te kóhao o te ngira e kuhuna ai te miro mà, te miro pangc, te miro whero.
I muri, kia mau ki te aroha, ki te ture, me te whakapono.

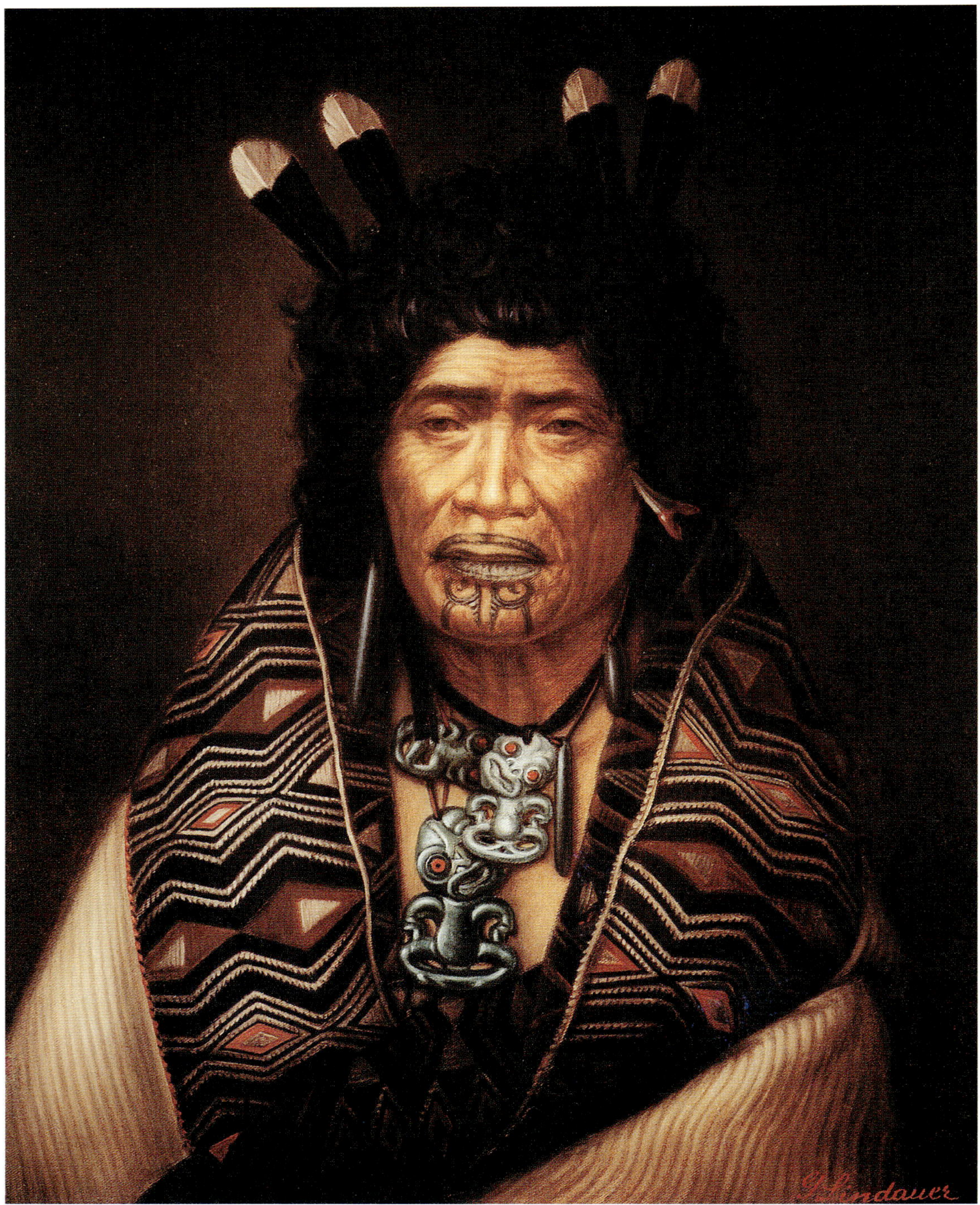

Toitù he kàinga, whatu ngarongaro he tangata.

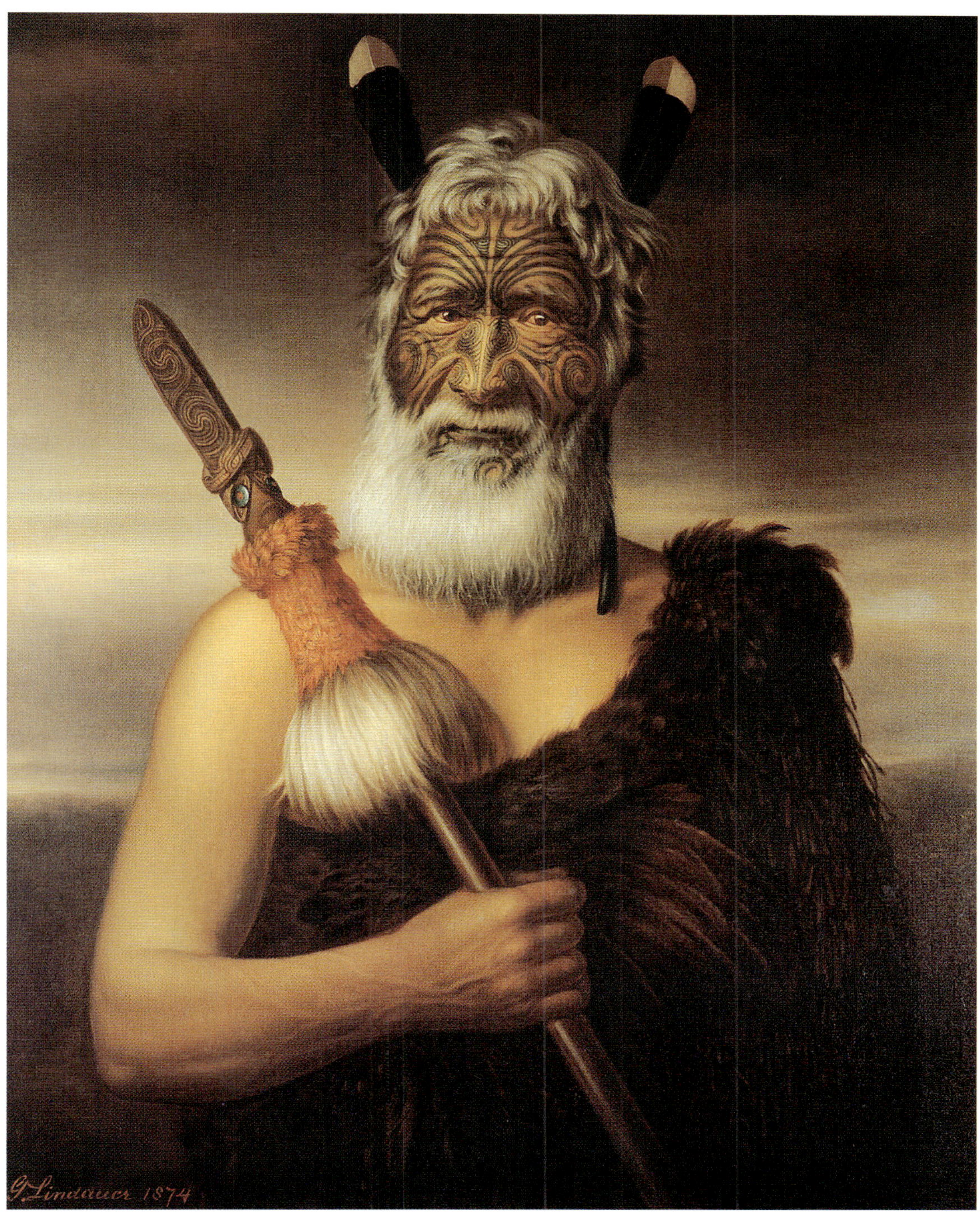

Ehara tá te tangata kai, he kai titongi kau;
engari mahi ai ia ki te whenua tino kai, tino mákona.

Folk Art and Modernism

Wolfgang Brückner

"Folk art" – both the term and the phenomenon itself – has existed for barely a hundred years. Near the end of what is known as the Historicist era, an awareness emerged of structures and decorative forms that appeared to express an autonomous stylistic sensibility of their own. Fascination with the unfamiliar from other cultures was joined by the discovery of quasi exotic peculiarities in our own culture as well, particularly as they were manifested in rural areas. As early as the 1860s it was possible to speak, albeit only with reference to an exhibition of commercial handicrafts in Munich, of the "peasant style" as a historical decorative form. The once arrogant and disdaining view entertained by middle-class city-dwellers of the supposed lack of education and even the artistic incapacity of the peasantry was transformed with respect to certain aesthetic preferences and creations into new, positive visual experiences – in much the same way as had occurred a century before, as literary figures of the Late Enlightenment and Romantic periods turned their attention to linguistic traditions.

The latter case had involved the discovery and heightened appreciation of phenomena that were also given new names, so-called folk songs, fairy tales and other forms comprised within the oral tradition. Now it was civilization-minded patrons of local culture and visual artists of the modern period who began, around 1900, to direct public attention towards things that had previously been ignored or even condemned by shapers of opinion within the art scene. Both aspects of this new, positive approach to so-called folk art had also accompanied the discovery of "folk poetry" around 1800: on the one hand, the concept of rescue, which implied the idea of preservation in the interest of the national cultural identity; on the other, the belief in the value of the discovered items or texts as models to be used in a renewal of high art, as they were now seen as particularly healthy – that is, original and creative. The view into the past uncovered long-forgotten traditional values for a cultural consciousness; the gaze forward into the future saw them as models for future innovations as well. Thus there was, in both cases, a close link between artistic and social modernism, despite the fact that such conservation-oriented excursions into the past may strike us today as nostalgic, conservative and thus essentially anti-modern.

New was the stimulating discovery of something old, in the same way that the experiments of Historicism brought forth not only repetition but an amalgamation of past epochal styles. They represented a deliberate, probing exploration of history in search of utilitarian patterns that could be converted for use in the present. As a successor to Byzantinism and Romanticism, to Gothic and Renaissance art, to the baroque and rococo styles, folk and ethnic art emerged as fields of exemplary models. They in turn represented logically consistent rediscoveries of a segment of local folk history or of a foreign culture in the colonies. What was truly new about this, however, was the discovery of primitiveness or simplicity in these regions far from the pale of intellectualism. It was here that the truly modern character of early modernism, or of what we regard today as modernism, was kindled – the essentially revolutionary protest against prevailing conditions, specifically as they related to art, implicit in the categorical rejection of 19th-century academism, of the official concept of art grounded in classicist aesthetics since the French Revolution.

Today, one hundred years later, this has long since come to be seen as "classical modernism," and everything that has followed it bears the mark of its aesthetic, indeed its political orientation, except that there have been museums of modern art for many years – like the Neue Pinakothek once dedicated to the new art of the 19th century as it emerged, sponsored by the academies, as is still the case today – museums that have room for nothing but that which views itself as revolutionary but which, by virtue of its accord with the culture pages, with commerce and with the institutions of culture can no longer be revolutionary at all. Established, sponsored contemporary art has become market-oriented convention.

In the beginning, what we look upon as modern art had at least two faces: one gazing ahead and intent upon overcoming what had been – a revolutionary impulse – and one that looked back upon a previously misunderstood ancestry in search of models capable of pointing the way to new horizons. The term "modern" denotes not only modernism in art, however, but also refers to social, and in particular to economic and political progress. This modern character of our "modern times," to which the title of the famous satirical silent film by Charlie Chaplin characteristically alludes, was not questioned from the standpoint of a critical view of civilization alone. Paradoxically, both the advancement and the rejection of modernism originated in the same minds. Thus, with reference to mid-19th-century France, science historian Wolf Lepenies states, "Modernism, in the arts as well as the social sciences, is the anticipatory criticism of modernization."

The end of the century witnessed the emergence of the anti-modernist movements, as they have been called with a certain lack of precision, that grew forth from a closely related triad – conservationism, monument protection and the preservation of local culture – whose influence is still present and indeed has become significantly more potent in the public eye in our time. These movements are not mere reactions, in the sense of corrective or ideological fields of retreat, but are entirely contemporary manifestations and conceptual constructions of an explicitly revolutionary modernism. Thus that term is associated with the ideological seal of quality of a "project modernism" (Jürgen Habermas), a child of the Age of Enlightenment. For the so-called progressives from the fields of philosophy, sociology, political science and related arts committed to similar objectives who see themselves within this context, the term post-modernism therefore has only pejorative meaning and is associated with betrayal of modernism and its supposedly exclusive claim to moral validity.

What has all of this to do with folk art? Or, more precisely, with "museums of folk art" in our century? The problem is related to the terms themselves. In the view of the folklorist who thinks within the framework of social history, the difficulty arises in the multiplicity of meanings associated with the German concept of *Volk,* which in our context continues to perpetuate the false connotation of peasant life. To the art historian, the modern concept of quality standards in art obscures paths of access to aesthetic premises that would be amenable to change. Painstakingly collected and monumentalized in museums during the fifty-year period between 1890 and 1940, the "products of household industry," as they were originally and quite rightly called, were generally declared as "folk art" after World War I. Museums and departments were renamed accordingly, and a restrictive distinction between "folklore" and "folk art" was constructed. Following in the footsteps of artists' manifestos, the approaches of art historians had irreversibly culminated in the invention of a new field of national art production, conceived within the framework of its own laws, alongside international developments in style.

They clothe it (as was still the case, for example, at the first post-war exhibition of so-called folk art at the Bayerisches Nationalmuseum in Munich in 1950) in the dedicatory language of cultural criticism and scholarship familiar to us from culture pages since the 1920s, forming finely-carved essays as literary works of art.

Arno Schönberger, a noteworthy specialist in handicrafts who originally worked in Munich and later in Berlin and Nürnberg, formulated the idea quite in keeping with contemporary reflections following the populist distortions of Nazism and even older theoretical interests in those objects. He rejected the concept of mere "cultural heritage sinking down" from the upper classes (a major thesis underlying sober research undertaken at the beginning of our century). That was, he said, as "one-sided" as the "exaggerated value" placed upon "primitiveness" as "aesthetic quality" (a tendency observed at the same time among the Expressionists during the first two decades of the century). The recognition of certain realms of things as merely "a rich field for research in the psychology of religion" also struck him as inadequate (as it applied to the interpretation of the real objects of popular piety discovered after 1900). Indeed, Schönberger saw folk art as "the formal manifestation of the view of life of a tribal-style class community. Ancient wisdom preserved in mores and customs, received as a legacy and passed down from generation to generation, gives human life its place within the great rhythms of nature, in the field of forces between birth and death. Folk art is above all peasant art."

This last statement brings us back to the familiar older tendency to restrict the concept to a particular social class and thus, historically speaking, to a specific stage of development, namely the era of rapid transition from the post-medieval period to the industrial age, the period between 1750 and 1850. Such an observation gives way to analytical phenomenological descriptions. These are apparent in the items exhibited in our collections and exhibitions of folk art, and they prompt us to ask what really took place in the country as the early modern world began to replace rural class society – what special forms and mass-produced cheap versions of luxury-good surrogates were made available to an expanding consumer class?

Today we know that "peasant art," defined as the production of objects by a clearly definable professional class, did not exist. What did exist during that late period were a free rural handicraft industry operating beyond the pale of the restrictions imposed by urban guilds and a wandering population of disrupters representing a number of different crafts. And there were monastic craftsmen condemned in the wake of secularization to work in local carpentry shops, for example, who fabricated the so-called "peasant baroque" creations of the Biedermeier period. In existence alongside these were a commission-based domestic woodworking industry that produced toys, devotional items and small utility objects in distant mountain and forest regions as well as a family-based cottage industry located in the vicinity of proto-industrial manufacturing operations, such as glassworks. Most noteworthy, however, were concessioned special markets and fairs and the wandering population of door-to-door traders who performed a central distribution function.

What we know thanks to research about this small, barely one-hundred-year period in the cultural history of the rural population of Central Europe is not immediately evident in the objects produced during those years. Exhibited in museums, they remain "consumable" in only an aesthetic sense, as is true of all of the intellectual goods generated by middle-class society during the past two hundred years. And this is due mainly to the reorientation in visual habits effected in the course of the past century by its companion phenomenon, modern art, which has done its part in placing things once regarded as worthless upon a pedestal of admiration. The expressive simplification of classical modernism in art and the spread of the same kind of visual approach promoted by practical exercises in art in schools have brought everyone closer to what was once contemporary art and, in the process, erased the memory of academic historicism and realism in advertising and household goods to the extent that the general approval of the infamous 1937 Munich exhibition of so-called "degenerate art" expressed by the broad masses at the time would be inconceivable today. At the risk of overgeneralization, one might say that the modern art produced up to about 1970 is widely accepted today.

This prompts me to ask how the exponents of the most recent artist generation of the past 30 years view the "folk art" that has accumulated in its dusty former modernity since the beginning of our century; or how much of it do they perceive at all today?

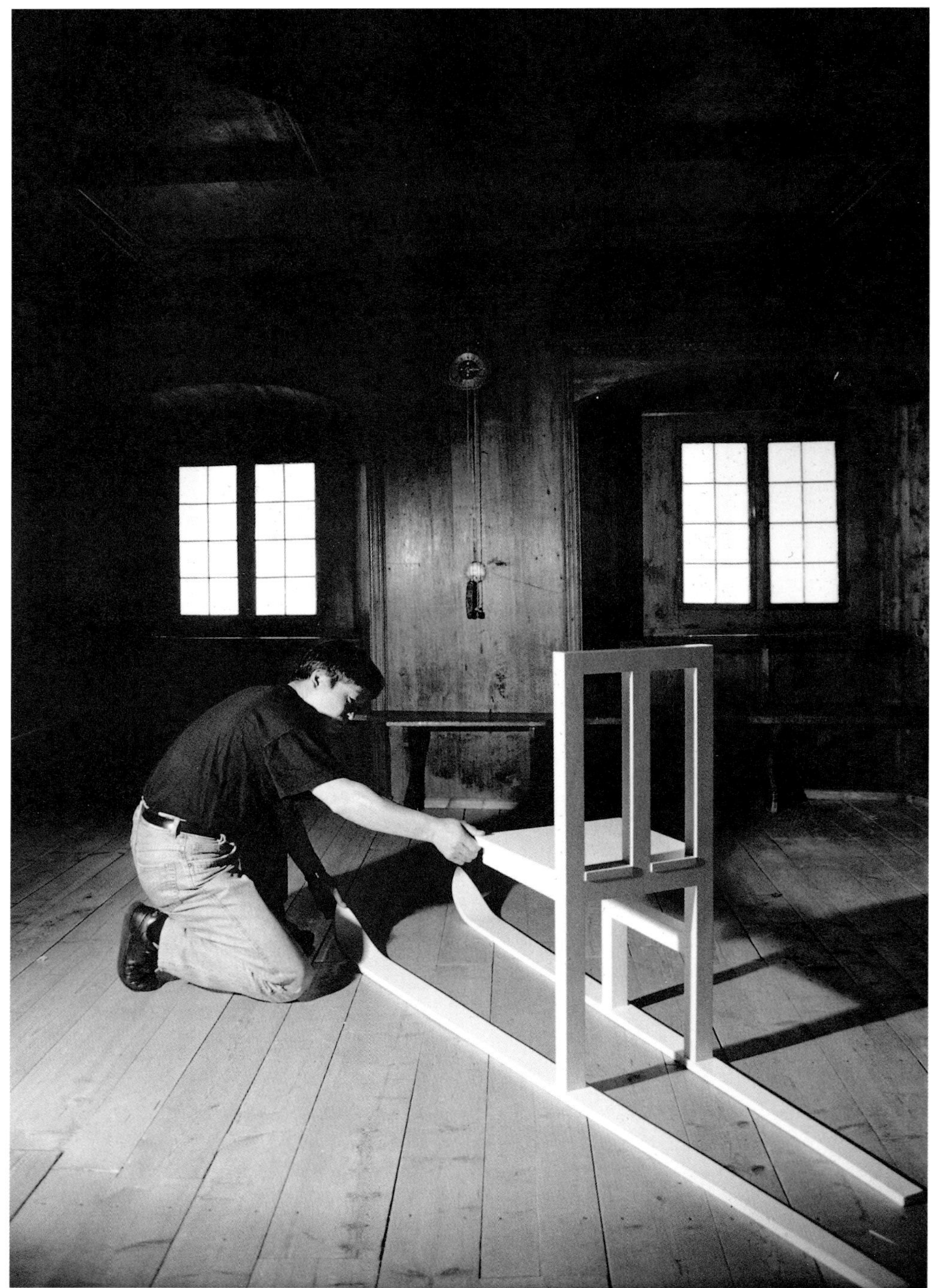

Kazuo Katase installing his work

Perspectives on the Past: Artists and Objects

Jean-Hubert Martin

Following the dissolution of the avant-garde in the early years of the 20th century, museums were first established for modern art and then, somewhat later, for contemporary art. These temples to an art that justified its existence on the basis of its own history sought to establish their autonomy and to defend aesthetic values liberated from the shackles of naturalistic representation which had dominated western art since the Renaissance. Once the values of modern art had been determined, the fundamental features of a stubbornly self-preserving artistic tradition began to assert themselves with increasing forcefulness. During the past twenty years or so, an increasing number of museum directors have sought ways to bring works of 20th-century art and those of earlier periods closer together. Given the dominance of art history and its chronological perspective, however, such undertakings have involved substantial risks.

Museum curators legitimize their work on the basis of a decidedly historical approach to art which favors classification by periods, styles and schools. Any attempt to escape this system of taxonomy, which prevails in virtually all museum institutions, is a perilous undertaking.

The system has grown rigid along with the profession. Royal collections were once managed by artists. Charles Le Brun, for example, was responsible for the collections of Louis XIV. Even the French Revolution did little to alter this basic pattern. The great provincial museums were founded during the revolution for the purpose of providing the academies and their students superior examples of the art of the past. As a rule, these decentralized museums were run by artist-curators who, in many cases, also served as directors of the respective local art schools. There can be no doubt that the artists in charge during those years arranged the presentation of works according to aesthetic criteria, that is, on the basis of considerations related to the creative process. It was not until very late in the 19th century that the historical perspective gained ascendancy and began to establish its unshakable framework in a chronological sequence of artists and movements. Even the contemporary art of the latter half of the 20th century has joined the ceaseless litany of movements giving way to new movements, a principle that continues to govern approaches to the presentation of contemporary art in most museums today.

The strategy employed in recent years – consciously or unconsciously – by curators attempting to break free of the bonds of historicist dogma and to develop modes of presentation that transcend regional and chronological boundaries has been to involve artists in the process. For the past twenty years, more and more curators have pursued such a course as a way of justifying unabashed violations of historicist principles and achieving a freer interaction among exhibited works. This has given rise to stimulating and often unexpected comparisons. Surprise – one of the ingredients of aesthetic pleasure – emerges from a juxtaposition of objects that generates different perspectives and new ideas.

Two basic types of examples have appeared. The first is the temporary exhibition conceived by an artist or artists and characterized by a creative approach to the presentation of objects and works of art. Here, the artists define the rules of exhibition, often daring to introduce conceptual innovations which a curator could scarcely justify.

The second form involves the intervention of artists in the presentation of permanent exhibitions at a museum. They may totally reorganize the arrangement of exhibits and the exhibition mode and introduce an entirely new system of classification; or they may incorporate their own works into museum exhibits as a kind of positive disruption and an appeal for visual reorientation on the part of the viewer.

"The eagle from the Oligocene to the present. Marcel Broodthaers shows an experimental exhibition of his Musée d'Art Moderne, Eagles Department, Figures Section." Thus reads the title of the famous exhibition presented at the Kunsthalle Düsseldorf in 1972. In his brief texts, the artist insistently emphasizes the blindness of the public, the weighty significance of the eagle as a symbol of power and authority and the role of the artist as the author of a definition which permits him to appropriate random objects for his own purposes. This exhibition gathered together a large number of eagles from different eras and made of different materials. They were indexed in the catalogue in alphabetical order by location of origin. Each eagle was presented with an inscription, setting things straight: "This is not ... This is not a work of art." Broodthaers explains in the catalogue that the eagles illustrate an idea developed by Marcel Duchamp and René Magritte.

In addition, he writes: "... the inscription has the appearance of pure nonsense – that is, it is not in keeping with the level of discussion about the validity of Duchamp's or Magritte's ideas – and then the exhibition returns to classical principles: the eagle in art, in history, in ethnology, in folklore.... I would undoubtedly have done just as well with the snake, the lion or the bull."

In 1977 Spoerri presented a "musée sentimental" at the Centre Georges Pompidou in a room furnished by Tinguely for the purpose in his Crocrodrome. With this presentation, Spoerri pursued his interest in the ideal value ascribed by collectors to their possessions as "collectors' items," quite apart from their rarity or commercial worth. He compiled a collection of relics and fetish objects from our history in an eclectic mix of things including Brancusi's nail-cutter, Talleyrand's orthopedic shoe, a tin containing hair from the head of Victor Hugo, cut on various different occasions, a coffee spoon that had once belonged to Marcel Duchamp, Magritte's bowler, furniture from van Gogh's room in Auvers-sur-Oise, Rimbaud's suitcase, the powder-puff used to apply Paul McCartney's makeup and, last but not least, Ingres' violin.

The artist recorded each object's history painstakingly and accurately in a small catalogue, making it quite clear how important it was that each object be supported by a history that would stir the imagination – much like the items shown in old exhibits of curiosities. Following this first experiment on a modest scale, Spoerri took up the idea once again at the Kölner Kunstverein in 1979. He called it "Le Musée sentimental. Model for a lexicon of relics and relicts from two millennia: Cologne incognito." Finally, in 1981, he presented his "Musée sentimental de Prusse" in cooperation with Marie-Louise von Plessen in Berlin.

These two last exhibitions were accompanied by comprehensive catalogues containing detailed scholarly commentaries. Unlike traditional historical exhibitions, each of the two events offered an opportunity to circumvent good aesthetic and historical taste. All in all, they gave preference – by presenting objects whose material and processed value were inversely proportionate to their ideal value as collectors' items – to an emphasis upon layers of history previously ignored or held in contempt by the prevailing historical view.

Let us return to works of art, which represent a defined category, even when exposed to the actions of artists whose intent is to alter the definition. I would like to discuss several other examples of the significant role of artists in this context.

An exhibition entitled "Bertrand Lavier présente la peinture des Martin de 1603 à 1984" (B.L. presents the painting of the Martins from 1603 to 1984) took place in Bern in 1984. Based upon the presumption that Martin is the most common surname in Europe, the goal of the exhibition was to show a kind of statistical cross section of western painting. In a presentation covering four centuries, a number of different nations and most subjects were featured, including, of course both high and low genres: history paintings, battle paintings, still lifes, nudes, landscapes and then abstract painting, comics and conceptual art as well. The question of arrangement turned out to be an essential one, since to employ the traditional chronological scheme would have been tantamount to a return to museum principles and a negation of the originality of the undertaking. The viewer would have recognized stylistic similarities with ease, like links whose chain structure is familiar to every museum visitor. Thus Lavier opted for an alphabetical classification by first name, which involved the added benefit of ensuring surprises.

Yet other classification systems would have been possible as well. At the opening of the exhibition we presented a slide show with Bertrand Lavier comprising the roughly thirty Martin paintings, in which each of them appeared in its own place in an overview of the history of the world.

In 1990, Kosuth presented an exhibition devoted to Wittgenstein, entitled "Das Spiel des Unsagbaren" (The Game of the Unspeakable), in Vienna. Most of the works shown were those of living, in many cases quite young artists, and their presentation was staged in a totally stimulating and unprecedented manner. Above a quotation from Wittgenstein running along the walls midway between floor and ceiling, the works were exhibited in an arrangement so free that we have virtually forgotten how it was, so persistent are the conventions governing the hanging of paintings. Works hung side by side often provoked contradictory formal comparisons, while others – without regard for the material composition or their value – evoked inspiring associations simply by virtue of their proximity. Kosuth had no qualms about using the entire wall space, from the floor to the ceiling. The tenuous balance – it was important to avoid the impression of flea-market junkiness, for many of the works were ready-mades – depended upon the proper placement in the room in order to trigger visual and mental associations in the viewer and otherwise stimulate his imagination.

One artist now quite well known for his interventions based upon museum pieces is Braco Dimitrijevic. He has produced diverse versions of his *Triptychos post historicus* since 1975. In these works he combines an image incorporated as a semantic block with objects from everyday life and popular culture as well as natural, animal or vegetable elements. The combination of these three categories in an unexpected concentration promotes a non-hierarchical view of the objects and a healthy sense of estrangement with respect to the work of art.

In an equally subtle but quite different approach, Christian Boltanski and Jean Le Gac exhibited a showcase containing a number of objects and works at the Musée municipal du Costume militaire (Municipal Museum of Military Uniforms) in Fontainebleau and later at four provincial museums. The showcases contained remains and objects left over from the lives of the two artists, items that tended to suggest their disappearance. The following text was printed on the invitation cards:

Our work is an attempt to discover ways to communicate and preserve our experience of an artistic activity in our present: a mental obstacle course full of relics (photos, objects, text fragments …), which we want to protect against the wear and tear of everyday life. Of course we considered showing this in museums, whose very purpose is to turn back the hands of time by classifying both the document and its history.

It also occurred to us that the elements of our work could be studied for the purpose of discovering an egalitarian mode that would make it possible to compare them with other documents of human activity. Thus it was interesting for us to seek this comparison in the context of authentic museums, whose function it is to preserve the memory of rediscovered things and the reasons for their origins.

Finally, in selecting this context for our work, we doubtlessly gain a head start on our own deaths. It was utterly exciting to set our activity in a museographic perspective; for this is ultimately and irrevocably the last trap.

In 1970, Andy Warhol undertook a museum intervention which offered a contemporary view of the past without any reference whatsoever to the methods and taxonomy of museum conservators. Commissioned by John and Dominique de Menil, he compiled a random selection of items from the storage rooms of the Rhode Island Museum of Art. First shown in Houston and later in New Orleans, the exhibition was entitled "Raid the Icebox." It was divided into two sections, each featuring individual works and series. The first section, consisting of drawings, paintings and sculptures, presented a striking mixture of genres. Works by Cézanne,

Seurat and Degas were shown in the company of numerous pieces by Americans, including a number of naive and anonymous works.

The second section featured five cabinets containing 194 shoes, which fascinated Warhol so greatly that he chose to incorporate them into the exhibition unchanged. In another spot he discovered a stack of about a half dozen pictures, which he presented exactly as he had found it. Without regard for the categories evident in the first section, the other series were comprised of hatboxes (Warhol apparently preferred containers instead of contents), baskets, Indian ceramics and textiles, chairs, umbrellas and parasols and finally carpets. Warhol demanded that all of the 404 exhibited objects be catalogued as precisely as possible. Daniel Robbins, the museum director, commented in this context: "Each object inevitably harbors its own associations, and the outcome is a strange kind of poetry. The mixture of pedantry and sentimentality in the inscriptions is the serial world of images of history."

There are countless other examples of artists who have been invited to intervene in museum collections: "Auf Bewährung – Ein Museum auf dem Prüfstand zeitgenössischer Kunst" at the Museum für das Fürstentum in Lüneburg in 1991, "Interventions sur collections. Des artistes de l'Hôpital Ephémère au musée de l'Assistance publique" in Paris in 1993 and "La soglia interna" at the Museo nazionale di Antropologia e Etnologia di Firenze in 1992/94, to name only a few.

Two more recent projects clearly indicate that the practice of placing a museum collection in the hands of an artist is becoming more and more common:

Hans Haacke undertook an extensive transformation of the Museum Boijmans Van Beuningen in Rotterdam. Opting for a serial, anti-hierarchical mode of presentation for the entire collection, he exhibited the works in the museum rooms, emphasizing several ideologically provocative encounters.

For its reopening in 1993, the MAK (Museum Angewandter Kunst) in Vienna invited several artists to stage presentations of selected objects from the collections, each in a separate room. This clearly contemporary approach to objects from the past led to Jenny Holzer's critical intervention in the hall of Empire and Biedermeier art. She had a kind of "memory, to speak about what was produced for whom and why" shown on a screen. Barbara Bloom built a central gangway with two large screens upon which she projected shadow images of chairs by Thonet and other chairs in the *art nouveau* style, which were exhibited on the other side of the screens.

Donald Judd reconstructed a white room for a decorative ensemble and baroque furniture. He then placed the room in another very large room as a white-walled box around which visitors could walk.

The historicist approach remains so predominant that one tends to forget that the past can only be seen in the light of the present. Any attempt, no matter how ambitious, to revive the past in some museums inevitably collides with the fact that the product of such efforts can only be perceived through the eyes and sensibilities of the present. Roland Barthes analyzed the meaning of myth in contemporary society, stating that it works only by reinterpreting the past as a function of the problems of the present. As André Malraux pointed out, our perception of the art of poetry does not proceed from Villon to Mallarmé but from Mallarmé to Villon, who was rediscovered thanks to this retrospective view of things. What could be better for museums often caught up in a rigidly past-oriented discourse and resistant to new impulses than to be revitalized by the confrontation of old works and contemporary art?

And this becomes all the more urgent in light of the fact that a capacity for aesthetic judgment can be developed only on the basis of comparison. It is much more stimulating to compare dissimilar, heterogeneous works than those which form a homogeneous whole. Such an opportunity has an invigorating effect upon the eye, which otherwise tends to tire in museums. Surely, the freshness of certain juxtapositions borders on impertinence; yet freshness is an element of creativity and youth. It pays tribute to the past, not in the form of conventional obsequiousness in the presence of past ancestors but by promoting the survival of a living tradition that is capable of self-renewal without bowing in humble imitation. The interest of the artists is focused as often on the ideas and the spirit transported by an object as on its external form. But old forms can be reused and recycled, particularly in a time when we seem doomed to suffocate under a flood of images. Today, more than ever before, the individual is subjected to a constant bombardment of visual images. We should not forget that a peasant under the *ancien régime* lived in a very limited iconographic world – a few paintings and portraits seen in churches, occasional stereotypically pious pictures distributed by door-to-door peddlers or illustrated stories with commentaries presented by traveling entertainers in the marketplace.

Today, pictures originate in advertising and the media as often as they do in art. In fact, we are witnesses to a reverse incorporation of art into media, whether by virtue of their essential forms or through the repeated use of the millions of images from the immense collection contained in our encyclopedia.

Like Warhol in his exhibition of museum warehouse inventory, we see the artists moving back and forth between individual objects and series. And this makes the confrontation between contemporary art and a museum of ethnology all the more interesting.

Aesthetics have proven extraordinarily flexible in recent years, making it possible to view many things from an aesthetic standpoint which would have been regarded only a short time ago as the exclusive domain of ethnology, anthropology or sociology. The number of anthropological studies on western art devoted to a better understanding of the creative process and its social function has grown, and it is only logical that they now turn their attention to contemporary art as well. The desire to derive meaning from a juxtaposition of objects at the expense of considerations of beauty presupposes an understanding of the symbolism and the meaning inherent in those objects. The surplus of images and objects is so great that it is easy to understand artists' resistance to creating even more of them and thus contributing to the further expansion of this immense body. When Tony Cragg arranges a number of extravagantly shaped, colored plastic liquid detergent bottles in a row, he is questioning the motivations that led to their production. What role does the designer's initiative play, and what part is attributable to market imperatives? What are the implications of the invasion of such containers into our environment? Claes Oldenburg, who transposed specific everyday objects into sublimated monumental forms, says that he must assume a "primitive" attitude in order to approach them from the necessary distance. The more he succeeds in abstracting them from their functional context, the better they are, he says. What remains is the question of how this affects our minds and emotions.

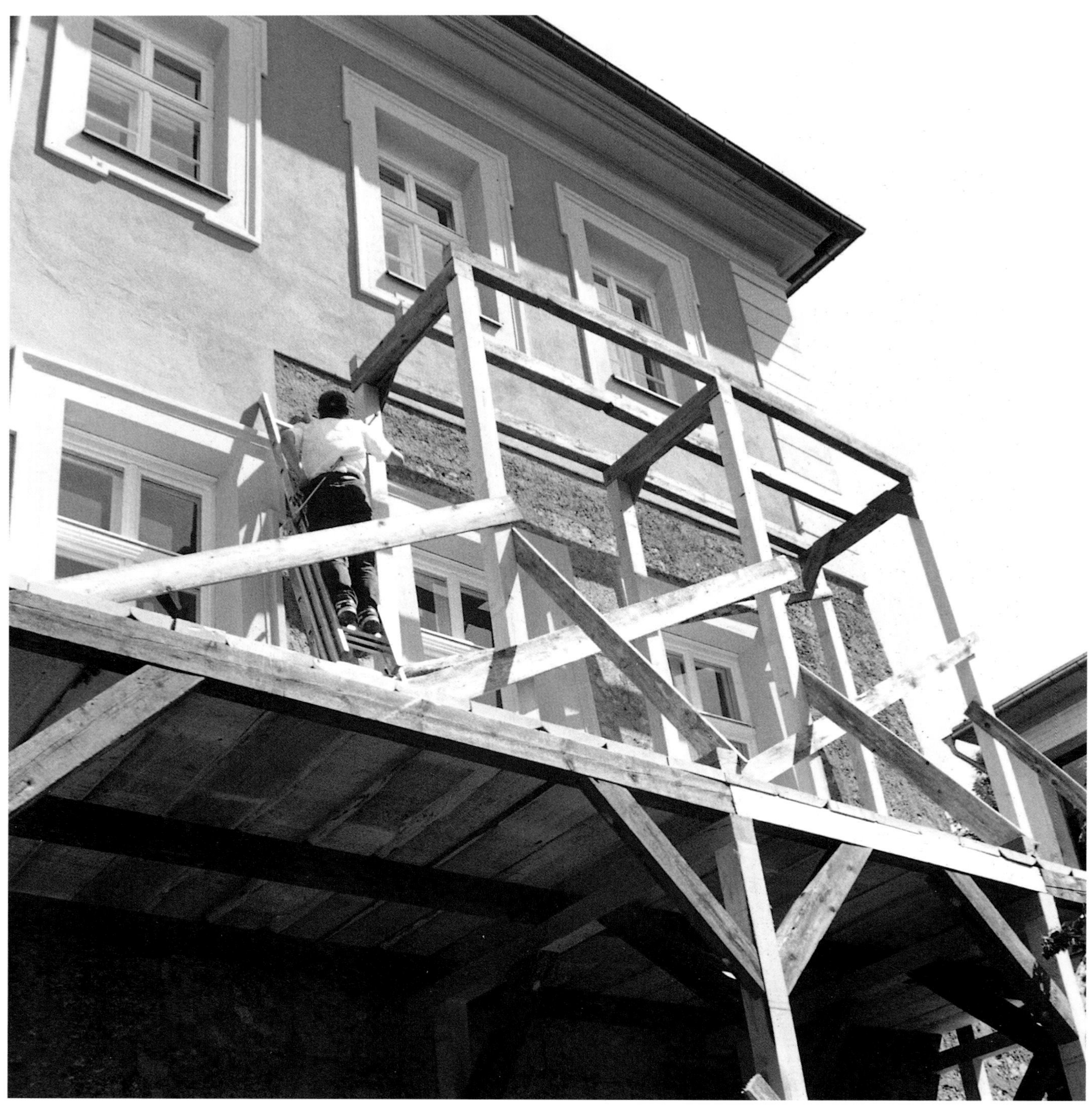

Installation in progress (Magdalena Jetelová's "Zwischenraum")

The Cultural Politics of Preservation

Saul Ostrow

A *parergon* is a framing device which at once encloses and enhances its object, much in the way museums do. Such constructs are attached to the things they house – surrounding and forming a context for them, without becoming an intrinsic aspect of their form. In the case of art it sets it aside, demarcating its interiority and exteriority. The problem which arises is that the frame which is meant to be subsidiary comes to communicate its contents to the outside world in such a way that it and the object it contains merge. Immanuel Kant uses the concept of the *parergon* in his *Critique of Judgement* to define what is proper to art and what is not. This concept is taken up by Jacques Derrida, who sets out to dismantle such differentiations that would separate an object from its context. It is the nature of the act of framing that I have used to open to interpretation the subject of this exhibition. I am interested in how this insertion of contemporary art within the cultural and institutional bounds of a museum that is specifically for folk arts and crafts affects our understanding of the parameters of each.[1]

Regardless of their stated purposes or objectives, *museums* are defined by practices which are themselves circumscribed by patterns of thought – world views – and ideologies which in turn inscribe themselves on their contents. The strategies and categories of accumulation and display employed both conceal and implement the reason and logic that organize the museum itself. As an institution it therefore exists in conflict both within itself and with what it houses. Dispassionately, as a matter of form, it appropriates material artifacts by mediating their potential meaning (being). The museum's unstated function is to delimit the contents of its holdings by deforming its subject in the very act of actualizing it. In this manner, the museum is to be thought of as a machine that produces subjects by reconsigning value.

The process of recontextualization supplies the material evidence used to validate the representative narratives of a given culture – be they of science, nature, history, art, etc. It is these narratives that both order and are ordered by the various networks and discourses which in turn come to constitute the museum's representation of its content. Of course this function is implicit, for most institutions are not in the business of undermining their authority – like magicians they only reveal how the trick is accomplished if it heightens the illusion. By holding in reserve a model of a culture, its peoples, practices and values, the museum is not only an institution of presentation and preservation, but also a political one – its representation displaces others. Technically the museum accordingly functions as a tool turning culture into a subject organized in accordance with its material remains. This economy of substitution and reification is neither benign nor non-intrusive, as it constitutes a clandestine participation in the discourses of power. The museum in this context makes history and culture supplement to lived experience, something informative and enriching rather than a component of lived experience.

In the case of a museum of folk art and crafts, we must assume that there is an intent to portray a way of life that is no longer accessible to us; but how is it that that life also comes to be idealized, its virtues and qualities made to appear closer to nature and therefore inherently good? The material displayed is meant to inform us of the aesthetic form that life took. Yet its residue is presented in such a manner that the communities from which it is derived appear to be built on a rational and familiar foundation. Of course these structures are not the product of their times, but of our own for, as with all acts of interpretation or translation, what is lost or made senseless must be reconstructed

[1] *The Parergon in the Truth in Painting*, University of Chicago Press, 1987.

to conform to its new situation. In such cases something else is inserted, be it an approximation or a fabrication so that an illusionary seamlessness of meaning is maintained. In the museum, as in the writing of history, this has a normative function giving it both control and authority over its subject by defining which aspects of its being are to be sustained and which are to be denigrated or ignored.

When dealing with historically closed periods, both beginning and end are known, everything seemingly is explicable and can be made clear. Correspondingly, what becomes excluded, marginalized or denigrated has been so, for the simple reason that it does not serve the chronological or comparative narratives that organize a museum's collection, be it of artifacts, fossils or art. Subsequently the simulacra produced by the museum's illusionary neutrality gain a semblance of authority and authenticity by which still other propositions or perspectives come to be grounded. This situation only reveals itself when those elements that have been absented seek their representation during periods of social and intellectual change within the restrictive cultural narratives.

Interestingly, the fact is that the Volkskunstmuseum was not a hindsight, but actually a forethought – an act of historization in which living traditions came to be preserved and then objectified. It should be apparent that no museum seeks to portray life as it is lived but only as it is imagined, that is at its best. Therefore this museum at its inception was an intervention, for it began to organize for future viewing not only the past but also its present (the late 19th century) just at the moment when it was becoming apparent that the existing craft and folk traditions could no longer resist the effects of modernity. Industrial society had totally encroached upon all aspects of daily life, not only changing material life by making available a glut of cheap mass-produced goods, but also by reordering social and economic relations.

Centralization and urbanization were on the rise, and the natural order of community, identity and the senses was being fragmented. All that seemed correct and natural was being challenged and rationalized in the name of progress. The museum's task was to preserve, promote and sustain the old traditions thus supplying a link to a way of life that could no longer sustain itself economically, but would continue to play a role in the construction of a cultural and regional identity. To this end it began to collect the material evidence necessary to sustain a false memory of a time when the sacred and the profane existed in harmony and as complementary components of a community that was bonded together as an organic whole. By means of preserving the signs of this unity, future generations would come to appreciate it. History, which all museums implement, after all is not only to be learned from, but also affects the discourses of subjecthood and power.

What romance such representations supply us with – here is evidence of a time before the orientation induced by the coming of the machine age. In room after room what we are presented with are things – we are made to look at them not as a reconstruction but as a construction of the quaintness of domestic life. Each object, garment, tool, room makes itself understood as a sign of simplicity, concern and common interests. Embodied in this is the logic which makes the pastoral life of the pre-industrial a tragic casualty of progress. Here are the possessions of its sweet victim, who only meant well and that industrialization had laid low. How simple and good things were when life was a cycle of work, family and religious ritual. What nice things they had, so fine that now only the rich can posses them. This is the idyll that the museum paints for us. It is through such acts of transformation that divergent elements from differing periods are generalized and actually formed into a subject capable of carrying this message. In turn, these same objects distract us so we will not realize that we are being misdirected, deprived of the means by which to judge, not the objects presented, but how we are made to understand them.

The fact that the circulation of desire and power that originally furnished the artifacts housed in this museum with meaning is not preserved indicates that they are removed not only by time but also by intent from the lived logic (consciousness) of those who made them. What is concealed by this absence is the world of rigid class distinctions, superstition, provincialism with its poverty, arbitrariness as well as a religious intolerance that threatened torment in the hereafter. This was the natural environment of what the museum has recontextualized as signs of wealth and sophistication. This is the reality that lurks behind the benign and picturesque cultural wealth represented by collections of carnival masks, traditional costumes and craft objects. It is this that makes it unimaginable that in their day, the passing of the regime associated with these objects would not have been met with a sense of relief and liberation rather than that of loss.

One wonders if – at the time of its founding in the late 19th century – this museum was not viewed as a reminder of how far things had progressed – a way to say, "just yesterday we lived in a world of the hand crafts and manual labor, today we have new customs, new wealth, a new world view – a new reality – a new sense of self." Remember, history is to be learned from, it is a record of the lessons we have learned in the past. Paradoxically, the newness of the Industrial Revolution puts in no appearance, here. It is under erasure, left outside at the front door, forgotten. The effect of this is that it relieves us of a burden to reflect on our own condition, allowing us instead to appreciate these old ways without being reminded that our own era is vulnerable to such change. However, it is this very message which in the last decade has come to concern Western culture and society – as we now prepare for the day when there will be a museum summing up our "Modern Era."

These reflections are provoked by the fact that Theodor Adorno optimistically viewed loss as a mechanism capable of inducing within us, individually as well as collectively, the ability to recognize and acknowledge, not only the role things play in constructing our sense of authenticity, but also their effect on the formation of the social, political and subjective technologies by which we put ourselves conceptually in the world. It is this possibility of loss becoming something unexpectedly "other," rather than being understood as merely a negation or inversion, that allows us to see beyond the perception of the standards and values that things provide us with. The museum therefore is a problematic institution for it records change yet stands in contradistinction to the project of endless revision, for it fixes things as standards of measure. For it to do its job it must remove things from the flux of time and change, hold them in reserve, and maintain the authority that they have been imbued with.

In our society, which is increasingly defined by the spectacle of simulated power and desire, the museum becomes another location that lends itself to the aestheticization of everyday life. Obviously, one of the consequences of this process is that the newly fashioned objects, values and conceptual models come to take on a familiarity which instantaneously historicizes them, promising that someday they will also have museum value. Such acts of aestheticization and historization of the everyday lend themselves to a sense of detachment and alienation which comes to be experienced as a loss of "self." Perhaps it is endemic to the ideal of preservation, for it seems to always engender a sense of loss that cancels out the aura of opportunity often associated with change.

None of what I have attributed to the institution of the museums is new. Both Clark Clifford[2] and Donald Preziosi[3] have written at some length as to how such institutions imbue their contents with aesthetic and historical meaning. I only reiterate these points concerning the nature of the museum in order to fully articulate not only the material, but the ideological environment into which these contemporary "artists" are introducing their work. While it is apparent from this that "The Bird of Self-Knowledge" exhibition intends to both intensify and disrupt the normalcy of the

[2] Clark Clifford, "Histories of the Tribal and the Modern," and "On Collecting Art and Culture," both published in *The Predicament of Culture, Twentieth Century Ethnography, Literature, and Art,* Harvard University Press, 1988.

[3] Donald Preziosi, "The Question of Art History," *Critical Inquiry*, #18 (Winter 1992), University of Chicago Press.

representation of both the museum and its contents, what may come as a surprise is the fact that the terms and conditions by which these artists ground their work will also be undermined.

The contemporary concepts that distinguish between "art," craft and other cultural products are the consequences of the separation and fragmentation of the sectarian world view of the 18th century. The regimes instituted by the Enlightenment sought to establish by reason and logic the essential nature of all things. In the case of art, which was constantly threatened with becoming merely an object of taste, this required that it seek its area of competence within the realm of aesthetics. So, rather than succumbing to the loss of community and values that beset folk culture and the craft tradition, art in the highly secularized world of the 19th century came to have the double burden of specifying itself and dispensing with its aura of worthlessness. These goals became the rationale for the *parergon of modern art* that theoretically encloses and fixes "art" in its place and has become an intrinsic aspect of art's practice.

The work of the artists represented in this exhibition, despite the differences of their age, nationality, approach and media, are the product of a practice that since the mid-19th century has defined itself by its willingness to surrender its craft in the pursuit of more firmly entrenching art in its area of competency. Behind a veneer of risk, bravado and nihilism, artists took it to be their task to avoid at all cost art's culpability while adapting to its rootless state. Through a process of trial and error, negation and absorption, art unfolded and unformed itself as well as its aspiration to be of more than metaphysical value or a sign of status. This was done first in the name of preserving art, then in defining itself, then in the name of its self-consciousness, and now in the name of understanding its power to reinvent itself.

Each sacrifice, trauma or gain was cause for scandal and celebration, for art was extending beyond its traditional material and aesthetic bounds. By this method art came to be more and more detached from lived life, though its means moved ever closer to it. The result has been an art defined by neither a criteria of skill or media, but instead by those discourses that it comes to significantly participate in or represent. It was found that for art to secure its identity it would have to serve philosophy. In this dynamic, contemporary art's practices respectively came to be circumscribed within a theoretical institution that delimits its contents and forms while deforming its subjects in the very act of actualizing them.

Perhaps the tension and debates that have evolved from art's role as social text and object of connoisseurship are a result of having outlived other traditions thought to be more essential and vital. As the inaccessible and accessible fetish of an institution both dedicated to the public good and to self interest, art's very existence denigrates and challenges what has come to be accepted, appreciated and oppressive. Like the survivors of the death camps who justify that they lived by incorporating into their narratives the lives and experiences of those who died so as to bear witness, art came to incorporate into its existence the displacement, fragmentation and indeterminacy that the standardized order of industrial society imposed upon all things.

Now, after 150 years, as the clock-work gears and pounding pistons of the machine age find themselves coming to an end in the hum, clicks and glow of the computer terminal, we may read art's presence in the context of a folk art and craft museum to be an announcement that its search for self has come to an end. This does not mean that art is being re-integrated into everyday life, for its practices continue to resist such reformation, though we now recognize that even the concept of self and autonomy are themselves determined and stated in terms defined by the intellectual, political and social life of Western society. This acknowledgment that art's frame cannot keep the outside world out is a result of the consciousness achieved in pursuit of its goal of detachment.

The interjection of contemporary art into the Volkskunstmuseum short-circuits the binary opposition of art and craft, museum and everyday life. Structurally defined as a set of frames within frames, "The Bird of Self-Knowledge" results in each element slipping from its frame, setting their contents into play, producing new situations, subjects and interpretations. In this context we are reminded of art's vulnerability and that of its function: as a form that gives objectification not only to the standards, values and criteria of society, but also its internal conflicts and changing modes of self-conception. This exhibition creates a netherworld in which our contemporary conception of art is destabilized. The intervention this exhibition constitutes within the presumed normalcy of the institutions of art, history and the museum does not remove the frame that defines each, but actually links them like Siamese twins. Each seemingly infringes on the other in ways in which various aspects that differentiate one from the next migrate, revealing unexpected relationships despite the uncertainty that the task of connecting them entails.

Each room, each object, each installation of this exhibition, offers multiple and often conflicting beginnings and ends. It is this philosophical and ideological opening – unraveling – that is consequential, for it makes explicit the indeterminacy of the status of each category as constituting nothing more than the relationships that exist between artifacts from the same culture. Through this convergence and the resulting inconsistency, the *parergons* that divide art from other aspects of material culture result in what Jacques Derrida refers to as an "undecidable" – an either/or that exists between either and or – and that liquidates the hierarchical distinctions posited in the differentiation of the categorical imperatives of each category, returning them to a general and undifferentiated state of cultural activity. The result is shared boundaries become internal edges, dividing each category, their unity and wholeness becoming unperceivable.

Culture in this state of self-knowledge seems destined to exist under the sign of the ambigram, an image that contains more than one possible reading – a woman before a mirror that can also be seen as a grinning skull. This sign allows the divergent and diverse elements of culture to exist in alternating states, rather as they had under the reign of the old modernism, both literally and metaphorically, exclusive of one another. This suspension of the institutional claims of differences confront us with two choices: either the propositions inherent in this exhibition concerning culture's self-knowledge are inane, just another example of cultural decay, necessitating that each practice, each subject, each category must return to its proper place, or they are proof that we must wrench ourselves out of a habitual way of looking at ourselves and our worlds. So here art again continues to go on by emphasizing its difference, its flexibility, its indifference, its rootlessness and its ability to adapt, but not be adapted.

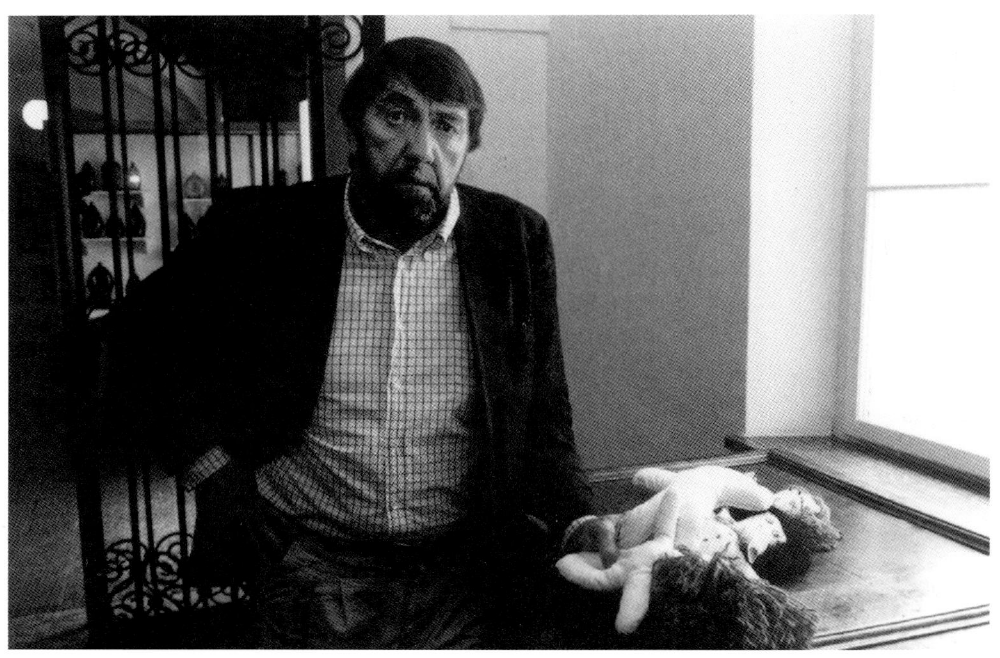

Anton Christian, author of the exhibition concept

Folk and Art = Folk Art? Remarks on the Fringe Areas

Marie-Louise von Plessen

What intertwining relationships of meaning will appear in the museum of the former Franciscan monastery when objects of everyday culture – items from the realms of domestic life and work gathered from the cycle of seasons in this alpine region – are altered through unheard-of media juxtapositions and unfamiliar material contexts? As mediatized ecclesiastical space, the monastery architecture of the Tiroler Volkskunstmuseum is already a "junction" between mission and the application of its own purpose. The interventions and interactions of visual artists are intended to estrange the material legacy of archaic Christian values and lifestyles, while making them accessible to the curiosity of contemporary viewers through the symbolic language of contemporary art. They expose the time that has elapsed between past origins and the present, time that imbues these objects with a presence which transcends their utility value, and they mark the boundary lines between the elements of "utility," "meaning" and "piety" in their use, approaching them from the viewpoints of sober work, utilitarian content and pious belief in the healing power of material things. Exposed to the disintegrating, liberating gaze of the artist, symbol becomes object, relic turns to material and ornament is transformed into element.

In their approach to the object-world of folk art, contemporary artists examine the relationship between "folk and art" in the secularized museum space with its sequential hierarchy of similarities: bedframe to box, plane to knife, mask to votive image. Unabashed by its stubborn autonomy, the artist dissolves, adds, outlines, illuminates, questions, changes, demystifies and penetrates the particularity of the object. If the attempt is successful, the transitory displacement of this culture of things will re-integrate itself into the presence of our sense perception and give new suspense to the imperfect equation of folk and art with its bland affinity to emotional kitsch and the cult of niches.

1. Utility

By 1888, the year in which the Tiroler Gewerbeverein resolved on the occasion of the 40th anniversary of the reign of Emperor Franz Joseph I to establish a museum of trades and handicrafts, manual trades and handicrafts had already given way for the most part to the machine in the alpine region. In order to maintain the old techniques for posterity, a collection of models was to be established for the purpose of ensuring the continued practice of traditional handicrafts and the preservation of related trades and customs. The "Museum für tirolische Volkskunst und Gewerbe" was opened in 1929. Objects, furniture, hand-crafted items made of glass, majolica, forged iron, wood and textiles outlasted their time as a collection of materials. Above and beyond their actual value as utilitarian objects, they are ordered and arranged as a meaningful legacy of everyday culture and religious belief of the past like fossils from layers of memory. In magnificent vividness, memory spaces and collection pieces bear witness, between worldly and heavenly realms, between sacrifice and redemption, regional and local worlds of belief, to the life and work of humans and animals in the "mountain country."

2. Meaning

When the orderly structure of objective hand-crafted art from the spheres of the secular and the sacred, preserved in alpine mid-winter and pre-Lenten customs into our time, is disrupted by the interventions of visual and conceptual artists, unusually intimate relationships of meaning emerge. The artist's intervention, regardless of the medium through which it is accomplished, reveals new complementary aspects of the object, which by virtue of this "visual interference" becomes recognizable in its traditional objective sense and in its meaning as an aesthetic, utilitarian or religious object as well. The artist generates emotional tension between the "waste product" cast off in the history of culture as a document of past symbols of meaning and its instrumental use, thus imbuing the decorative or utilitarian value of the old thing with new energy. The anonymous ethnographic artifact, its creator unknown, which was nevertheless preserved as a collection item out of respect for its intended purpose, encounters the individual skill of the artist. Selecting and acting subjectively, the artist intervenes in the scientific system of museum classification in open space, in the showcase or on the wall to expose new values and relationships of meaning in the system of material things.

3. Piety

With a new view of the old, the categorically subjective attitude of the artist, who disturbs the ethnographic and geographical order of the system of material things, helps us to discover buried, suppressed identities, longings, anxieties, desires, insights and curiosity about ruins, relics and remains. Thus, for example, Hermann Nitsch or Daniel Spoerri confront objects of everyday religious art and its rituals with highly personal fetishes and magical disenchantments in social spheres of violence and death that remain taboo even in our time. Interweavings of this kind expose the archaic nature of matter used in the ecclesiastical context as raw material for the projections of faith and devotion. The secular linking of artists' positions to the cultural legacy from the life of "the people" is not exaggerated in this way to the point of parody or grotesque distortion of the object of devotion – such an approach would be equivalent to theatrical dramatization – but instead for the purpose of making a visible and meaningful distinction between the union of "utility" – the utilitarian value of the object – and "piety," its character as a fetish and medium for belief, love, hope and eternal life. Yet the museum object thus cast in this new light is not assigned to the value system of the art world. The artist's intervention merely gives the artifact new life, while destabilizing the categories of traditional cultural value systems.

Bourgeois comfort releases handicrafts and the prayer chapel into the wake of insecurity about the cultural legacy, which has lost its vitality through integration into the museum setting. *The Bird of Self-Knowledge* grasps its olfactory organ, its nose, and recognizes the world of things as a subjective system of meaning in a continuous process of revolution in the relationship between science and the unknown.

On Self-Knowledge: Art as the Heiress of Alchemy

Beat Wyss

Cultural Work and Publicity

Never before has our world been so colorful, so full of music and so open to contact as it is today: music in the elevator, television in the railway station, online access in the supermarket. We live in such a highly entertaining generator of images and sounds that we would hardly notice at all if art were to disappear. The media projection machine has been expanding its reach for decades; it has become an even denser and more closely interwoven network, to the point that now – startled, as if the last windows offering a view to the pre-media landscape were closing – we begin to engage in nervous discussion. In panel discussions, talk shows and newspaper columns the question arises again and again: What becomes of art in the era of digital production? The prevailing tone is either euphoric or suggestive of capitulation, frequently a mixture of both – in the style of intellectual masochism that voluntarily retreats in the face of the overwhelming power of technology. The arguments offered by conservative cultural pessimists and futurist techno-enthusiasts are not so terribly far apart, and one often encounters people eagerly switching from one pole to the other. The notion of the "destruction of culture" is expressed on both sides – as a warning from the one, an appeal from the other. If we pause to look back to the early years of this century, we find similar responses in the attitudes of Oswald Spengler and Tommaso Marinetti, in their *pas de deux* of machine-age pathos and classicism. And thus, to the accompaniment of both jubilation and lamentation, we have been casting tradition onto the flames of the funeral pyre as both a dangerous and an endangered heritage for a full century.

Neither lamentation nor euphoria serves the needs of a re-evaluation of our relationship to our cultural heritage. Indeed, both attitudes are merely symptoms of that re-evaluation. What is needed in the current phase is sober analysis. Two values which have developed in the course of the modern era offer themselves for scrutiny: the concepts of work and publicity [i. e. the quality of being public, trans.]. Of course it would be presumptuous of me to attempt to describe the complex social, economic and technological interrelationships generated by the rationalizing impulse of new information technology. As an art historian I can address only the aesthetic aspects of this epoch-making upheaval; as a contemporary I can examine only its practical impact on our lives. Viewed from this limited vantage point, the re-evaluation of the concepts of publicity and work is distilled down into a phenomenon generally known today as "virtualization." Translated into terms applicable to everyday experience this means that actual personal presence is becoming increasingly superfluous. We are interconnected; as workers, as active and interactive individuals, we experience a process of estrangement in our relationship to the objects of our work, our actions and our interactions. Our theater of operations is the computer screen. The new communications technology enables us to impact upon the world without entering it. Work, action and interaction take place in the absence of the public. Information technology, in the words of Mitscherlich, favors work that leaves no traces.

What does this have to do with art? A great deal. For the development outlined above affects the substance of art, if we define art as a public activity and our efforts to deal with art as a way of learning to work with its material. In western culture before the media revolution, art was quite naturally a matter of public interest. In his aesthetics, Edmund Burke described the pursuit of beauty as a social act. Beauty promotes social interaction, for where else was it to be found in the 18th century, if not in churches, theaters and concert halls? One had to leave one's gloomy chambers, pass through the brownish-gray monotony of sandstone, mortar and feces in the narrow streets, and throw open a heavy portal, where it suddenly appeared: the shimmering glass window of the cathedral, with its precious array of colors that outshone even the brocade garments of the richest ladies in the city. Or one emerged from a coach on a rainy evening to find one's senses overwhelmed by the aspect of a festive hall, with the twinkling lights and scent of a thousand candles, while the raw acoustic ingredients produced by the instruments bubbled as the orchestra tuned in the orchestra pit, from which finally music would rise, like Creation from the womb of chaos.

Since the invention of radio and television, the beauty of art is available at the press of a button in the bedroom. The colorful, cacophonous generator that surrounds us on all sides may indeed satisfy our need for beautiful impressions immediately and perfectly. Yet there is one thing that, in contrast to art, it cannot do, and that is to bring us together in the pursuit and enjoyment of beauty. The electronic media privatize aesthetic experience by making themselves available to consumers in non-public context via cable and antenna. The pursuit of beauty is thus stripped of its social significance.

The sensual quality of art deserves particular emphasis in contrast to its media competition. The seemingly superficial context of gallery openings and concert intermissions can be perceived as the social foundation of aesthetic experience. The social interaction that takes place in and around the art scene should make us conscious of the fact that we have come together to enjoy and to judge art – despite the claims of purists, who treasure only the intellectual value of art. Art is a communion of the senses. It possesses, to cite Burke once again, a social character in its capacity to bring people together. In the pursuit and appreciation of art we preserve the idea of publicity. As a counterbalance to electronic media, art offers us the necessary deceleration of communication to the pace of the human being, whose needs and sensibilities remain stubbornly analog. As physical beings we cannot be digitized.

Aesthetic Knowledge and Technology

The above arguments are offered in opposition to the view held by media enthusiasts that art will simply be swallowed up by information technology. The unification of art, technology and science is one of the modern utopias whose realization would have fatal consequences. Admittedly, art was once the intuitive science of sense perception, a finely trained capacity paired with a command of the technical possibilities of its time. Leonardo gained his fame as a lutist, a poet and an engineer. The Neumanns, a family of architects, descended from a dynasty of wartime canon-makers and peacetime bell-makers. A 17th-century painter having his camera obscura built by a cabinet-maker could look over the craftsman's shoulder during the process and exercise an influence on the outcome; he would have had acquired his own experience with optical instruments. The spread of serially manufactured products soon left little room for the fulfillment of artists' special wishes, however. There is nothing left to modify in a camera bought in a photo shop.

"Autonomous" art is a reflexive response to industrial development. The artist remained a manual craftsman; his own discourse separated itself from the discourse of science and technology. With respect to the world of industry that supplied him with material for his art he could assume only an aesthetic point of view. Suspension bridges in the evening light, the atmosphere of a steam-filled railway station, the sounds of traffic and factory whistles provided art with new motifs. Just as art today can relate to modern science only through mimesis, it is itself a consumer of industrial processes. In most cases, technology has already achieved what artists can only dream of. Their enthusiasm for progress lags far behind the real achievements of progress. The artists of the avant-garde approached the problems of industrial culture from a much too artistic standpoint. As "artocrats," their intention was to reinvent the wheel – through art. The Russian Constructivists elevated Lenin's political formula – "Soviet plus electrification equals Communism" – to a program for textile design and coffee cups at the reformed schools of arts and crafts. Vladimir Tatlin went so far as to appropriate mankind's eternal dream in attempting to build a flying machine with which, according to the myth, the master Daedalus escaped in flight from the labyrinth of Knossos.

Modern technology and science, however, originate in the insight that nature is subject to laws that bear no similarity whatsoever to those that govern organic life. Development of the airplane did not become possible until the study of bird flight was abandoned and inventors turned their attention to the laws of aerodynamics. The first people to witness the liftoff of such machines were astonished at the sight of the rigid, bare skeleton made of iron, wood and canvas and the droning sound of its gasoline motor that had nothing at all in common with the warbling of swallows. Electricity was not harnessed for human use until after Galvani's concept of it as a manifestation of living energy was rejected.

As Foucault suggests, modern epistemology broke away from thinking in analogies. Yet analog thinking has been preserved in art. Modern science dissects nature, whereas art attempts to empathize with it, to put itself in nature's place. Art is concerned with analogies between natural laws and human proclivities, as Goethe describes in his *Selected Affinities.* Comparative perception rests upon the foundation of ancient natural philosophy and alchemy. From a scientific point of view, the work of Paracelsus may indeed by obsolete, yet his methodological approach to the world has retained its validity in the sphere of art. A central aspect of alchemy is the concept of imagination, which Paracelsus also called the "inner constellation." Like a magnet, the imagination pulls impressions of things as they are perceived into the mind of the scientist, whose experimental structures are distilled and clarified as ideas. The alchemist's experiment is a process of purification. The seven metals – lead, tin, iron, copper, mercury, silver and gold – correspond to the seven planetary spheres – Saturn, Jupiter, Mars, Venus, Mercury, sun and moon. These must be penetrated in order to elevate the mind to the highest level of knowledge.

Painters were in contact with chemists and aware of their speculations, for they, too, were concerned with procuring, compounding and separating matter in the production of paints. Musicians made use of descriptive geometry and mathematics, which were also applied in the science of astronomy. The laws of harmony were in tune with the wondrous beauty of the night sky. Music set the silent spheres of the heavens to resounding, and their proportions, in turn, corresponded to those of the human body. From these, architects took measurements in inches and feet and translated the relationships thus obtained into the "frozen harmonies" of architecture.

Art's insights into nature have remained pre-scientific. But does that necessarily make them wrong? This essay is meant as an appeal for acceptance of two mutually exclusive programs of thought for an interpretation of the world. Science behaves analytically; art behaves mimetically with respect to nature. The former paves the way for a technical approach to production, the latter for an imaginative one. Both processes are equally valid and should not be intermixed without careful consideration. There is no going back to a time in which art and technology shared the same knowledge, when artists were decorators of princely magnificence and technicians of war. Under the industrial conditions of the modern era the royal dream of a union of art and science threatens to culminate in totalitarian systems. A clear separation of powers between technical and imaginative production prevents the intermingling of euphoria and capitulation of which I spoke at the outset. The one approach points to technocracy, the other to the ecological niches of the esoteric. Recognition of the incompatibility of art and science must lead us to different insights and models for action.

Perhaps the maxim of a separation of powers between art and science finds support in the sober assessment of Hegel, who spoke of the inevitably anachronistic character of art. Its very significance lies in the fact that, viewed from the vantage point of science, it represents an "outdated" medium through which to view the world. Thus, for example, the flowering of emblematic painting went hand in hand with the decline of alchemy, as speculative naturalists and scientific laboratory chemists began to go their separate ways in the early 17th century. The spiritual tendency was represented by the "Brotherhood of the Cross of Roses," a group of Protestant theology students whose theories laid the foundation for a literary spiritualism that would later emerge in full bloom during the Romantic period.

As an anachronistic conceptual model, art develops powers of creative renewal as it rubs against the grain of technology. The reciprocal fertilization of imaginative and technical practice is revealed in the field of reproduction techniques. The many inventions in the field of information reproduction gave rise to questions very similar to the issues underlying the contemporary media debate. Does advancement in reproduction technology make art superfluous? The type of thinking exhibited by today's media technocrats is anticipated in the attitudes of frugal Calvinists of long ago. The possibility of disseminating the Gospel in large printings at low cost made visual art, as a medium for transmission of the word of God, a pure waste of money for the faithful. Everyone could now own a clear-text version of the Bible. In Zwingli's view, art was a "crutch for the ignorant." Yet the penny-pinching Reformers did not have it their way in the end. Books did not replace the visual image. On the contrary, as a means of transporting graphic prints, theoretical approaches to art and theories on art history, the printed text laid the groundwork for the visual art of the Renaissance.

Technical progress in reproduction has generated innovative approaches to traditional techniques employed in art. To name only a few modern examples: Photography influenced painting by stimulating the avant-garde to experiment with montage techniques and Cubism. Film exercised a similar influence upon the theater, which, inspired by the rhythms of the cinematographic image, liberated itself from the confining corset of the peep-show stage. Have people stopped going to concerts since the advent of recorded music? Reproduction technology has exercised a powerful influence in this area as well. The sound recording preserves the transitory musical event and makes historical interpretive analysis possible. It reaches new sectors of the public, promoting monopolies of taste and the cult of stardom on the one hand, but also providing – through subculture CD production, for example – a platform for young artists.

Through reproduction, art becomes recognizable as a medium in which technical and imaginative processes appear to interact. Thus media analysis has become an indispensable part of an artist's training. Insight into the media character of art is of interest not only for tactical reasons, but for creative ones as well, as it enables the artist to undermine the realm of technical production through creativity. Technical achievements are never intended to benefit art. The radio and the computer, indispensable tools for the production and dissemination of music, were developments of wartime research. In exploiting them for its own purposes, art engages in a counter-discourse with technology using the resources of technology. It estranges the instrumentality inherent in the material and thus underscores the necessity of relating to the world not only in practical but in aesthetic terms as well. Imaginative production disrupts technical production. It transforms the instrumental relationship based upon the exploitation of nature into a working relationship of mimesis. Although artists may benefit from the use of state-of-the-art digital equipment, their relationship to the means of production remains alchemistic, empathetic.

The cosmological model of Creation, the *megas anthropos* or great human, in whom we, as "small humans" are inscribed as like images with similar proportions, harmonies and elements, remains a valid aspect of artistic discourse. Art is one of the humanities, disciplines in which the world is viewed from the standpoint of mankind. A "humane" world is regarded as a good world. Belief in the possibility of influencing nature for the good, in the sense of "humanitarianism," is an aspect of art that cannot be explained scientifically. Technical production is concerned with the question "how" – *how* can something be produced faster or cheaper and made more useful? Progress in science derives from analytical skill in converting *why* questions into *how* questions. Art and the humanities, on the other hand, ask *why*, because it is part of their anachronistic nature to bring the issues of metaphysics into the scientifically demystified world.

Technically and practically speaking, artistic production establishes an alternative position in opposition to the world of science and industry. In both its methods and its theories, it perpetuates the heritage of alchemy in the shadow of and under conditions created by modern science. The artist is to industrial reality as the midwife is to the modern hospital. There is an anthropological constant in artistic processes – concern with an animistic, magical discourse on the basic questions of human existence: Where do we come from? Who are we? What are we to do? Where are we going? Science provides no answers to these questions. It can only solve problems, as its role in life is purely technical. Regardless of how completely it rules our lives in a practical sense, technical knowledge cannot satisfy our stubbornly surviving metaphysical need. Knowledge about art relates to life through the imagination. It involves a conception of the world based upon the macrocosmos-microcosmos model developed by natural philosophy. Thus it is no wonder that we find in every work of art, no matter how surprisingly novel it may be in expression and technique, questions of meaning that strike us as familiar and close to the heart.

These two programs of thought – scientific knowledge and aesthetic knowledge – require a cultural contract based upon the separation of powers. Presently, we note currents in science and technology exercising claims to possession of the sole key to the solution of the great questions of meaning – from genetic engineering to space travel. The monoculture of technical production exhibits a tendency to conceal industrial necessities and economic interests behind a veil of New-Age posturing. But metaphysics is the domain of art!

A Plea for the 21st Century: No Salvation, Please

At the threshold to the 21st century we must learn from the mistakes of the 20th. The modern era failed in its goal of reconciling art and technology. The catastrophes of our century have been the product of blind attempts to find a universal formula for all of the world's problems and to apply it in practice through totalitarian policies. The ideals of ethnic and national purity and the theory of party dictatorship left behind mountains of corpses. The instrument of these political *gesamtkunstwerke* was technology, tooled as an industrial machine to shape the working masses into marching production columns or columns marching into destruction. The futurist-poetic state was consumed in the flames of the wars of attrition and the waves of bombardments that inundated Europe. Modern art failed, to the extent it was involved as a prophet or an agent of the fantasies of omnipotence and final solution that have characterized the era.

It is to be hoped that the 21st century distinguishes itself from the 20th by refusing to strive for total works of art. Acceptance of the incompatibility of aesthetic and technical knowledge can serve as preventive medicine to protect against a recurrence of the errors of modernism. The danger of a repeat performance of the 20th century is real; signs of it are evident in the mixture, mentioned above, of unquestioning media euphoria and the detachment of cultural pessimism. And we have seen it all before. These are the two failures of modernism.

First, we recognize the growth of an enthusiasm for technology that has either learned nothing from the past or forgotten everything. Conceivably, the art of the future may be created not by artists but by genetic technicians, information scientists and engineers. Who knows? Perhaps our museums will soon begin exhibiting cloned animals, sensations that relegate the good old multiple and Mike Kelley's teddy bears to some dusty corner. Biologists will offer newly patented hybrid creatures or miniature versions of large mammals as artistic knickknacks. Next to these, the biomorphs of Surrealism will look like objects of children's handicrafts.

Since the beginning of the modern era art has undoubtedly regarded itself as the agent of nature in its striving to create beauty, which is present only in rudimentary form in Creation. Works of art are placed alongside those of imperfect nature as objects of ideal beauty. The artist who created an improved version of the world did so in the spirit of morality. The artist-technocrats of the future, however, will improve upon nature in the spirit of feasibility and utility. If this trend is sustained, we shall find ourselves subject to the compulsion of the modernist mentality to repeat the past. The difference would be that 21st-century fantasies of omnipotence would no longer be realized through politics, whose mechanics we presently observe, but through the utilitarian cynicism of the technocrats.

What I would now wish to avoid is a return to the second of the two failings of modernism – rightist cultural pessimism and leftist rejection of civilization. It should suffice to sketch the history of these attitudes in brief in order to facilitate recognition of what distinguishes them from separation of powers and the cultural contract between art and technology called for here. As already suggested, cultural pessimism and rejection of civilization accompanied the technical euphoria of the 1920s and 1930s like a shadow and became dominant after 1945, as intellectuals retreated into the corners untouched by progress to sulk. Heidegger and Adorno, the philosophical opponents of the era, were united in their condemnation of jazz and the cinema. The intellectual climate of the post-war period was characterized by rejection of the base "culture business." Art focused upon the "authentic," upon the bulky, cumbersome work that defied all attempts to instrumentalize it. A critical view of civilization prevailed among European artists; art underbid technology, now that the utopias of overbidding had perished in the flames of the real politics of industrially-induced destruction. Primitivism, already present in classical modernism, grew during the post-war period into anarchism. Artists read the epic of Gilgamesh and gazed in awe at the cave paintings of Altamira and Lascaux. Art followed a path that led from Picasso's African mask to the fat-and-felt corner of Joseph Beuys. What artists found interesting in industrial culture was its waste – its junk. Marcel Duchamp's *ready-made* experienced a revival in the Fluxus movement of the 1960s. Technology was ridiculed by art. Artists undermined utilitarian logic by returning to Shamanism. The "savage discourse" of Lévi-Strauss, the language of hand-crafted magic, found its ideological niche in the "white" room of the art gallery, where patrons and clients from the world of industry and commerce atoned for their utilitarian mentality through charitable demonstrations of appreciation for art.

Cultural pessimism and rejection of civilization are products of the disappointed hopes for salvation placed in technological progress. I fear that we shall be forced to repeat the history of technology as an intellectual history of catastrophe if we give in too quickly to media euphoria. One can easily imagine the disastrous consequences. Let us take a precautionary look back upon the great milestones of the technical revolution: Luther coupled the invention of printing with the liberation of the faithful from the spiritual oppression of the Church; Marx hoped that the socialized machine would free the working masses; the apostles of Bill Gates preach the doctrine of global brotherhood through media networking. Luther was followed by the Thirty Years' War, Marx by the devastating wars of our century. What will come after Bill Gates? The world has never become a better place because of technology. The paradises promised by the prophets and advocates of technological revolution have never been achieved in the course of real history.

I do not wish to be redeemed by the computer. The information society is not our salvation but simply a fact of life. Art and the humanities must participate in the discourse on technology. We can no longer wander off into the ecological niches of denial or content ourselves with Gnostic counterproposals as alternatives to the world as it is. We must take up information technology and make it intelligent in our own sense of the word, but we must at the same time expose its social and cultural limitations.

Ethics and Information

Human society needs the anachronism of art in order to survive, and this not only because it would otherwise lose sight of sense and meaning. Indeed, profit maximization and the acceleration of production per se do not create intellectual or spiritual quality of life. Loss of meaning would lead to the disintegration of society. The information society threatens to deteriorate into a system that excludes the public. Highly informed, chronically overworked minorities would be enthroned in glass office complexes looking down over a sea of urban misery. Data channels would reach those up above through detours around the collapsing city quarters and districts. As is already the case in Rio de Janeiro or Los Angeles today, the few who control the reins of the information society would return each evening to their fortress-style bungalow developments, their country clubs and Jacuzzis guarded by private militia. Their sons would study at Harvard, since state educational institutions would have become obsolete. The information society would pay no taxes, and so it could afford to pay for its social services on a private basis. Similar scenarios have already become reality in countries in what we generally refer to as the Third World. We are well on the way to conformity with this standard. The only question that remains is how long the information society will be able to survive in its insular existence once the network of social services has collapsed entirely. Revealing insights with implications for a possible future in Europe can be gained from news coverage of hunger revolts and gang wars in the bankrupt Tiger States of Southeast Asia. Information technology and know-how alone do not create a societal network. Being online is not the same as being involved. And what is more, most of the people in the world do not even have an electrical socket – the technical prerequisite for membership in the information society.

The information society is post-traditional. Its manifestations are the same all over the world: in Hong Kong, New Delhi or Houston, Texas. At best, regional culture and history are preserved for the benefit of tourists. Indeed, the crowning achievement of the globally networked information society is its success in severing the bonds of its own cultural origins.

The information society needs art, if at all, only as an object of investment in things used to decorate bank foyers. There is no public discourse. The media entertainment industry makes museums, theaters and opera houses, those outdated, expensive institutions of a middle-class public, superfluous. We are offered shrunken forms of public promotion of the arts: Pavarotti as Don Giovanni online from the Scala in Milan on a gigantic screen on the stage of an open theater – in Milwaukee, for example. Despite the lack of money to maintain its theater ensemble, there is still a clientele that occasionally enjoys showing up in evening clothes.

Art needs publicity – and not only in the form of an audience gathered to view it. Art needs publicity in the form of reviews, reports and debates. In the discourse on art, aesthetic experience is joined with issues of ethics. The old-fashioned phrase is "stumbling blocks in the path of unfettered progress." The term itself contains an element of an insistent reference to something "past." *Ethos* means custom, morals, folkways. Ethics is the study of standards of behavior that appear justified through age and tradition. *Ethos* is the traditional core of every culture, to the extent that we define culture as the totality of all manifestations with which a society governs the life interests of its subjects according to custom, morals and folkways.

The Tiroler Volkskunstmuseum in Innsbruck presents an exhibition of utilitarian objects which, when not in use, share similarities with objects of art. The older the tools, the less crass is the impression of separation between technology and art we gain from them. As an implement ages, that magical impulse that precedes the urge to achieve command of nature becomes visible. The exhibition entitled "The Bird of Self-Knowledge" is dedicated to this insight. The emblem selected, a hybrid creature comprising a stork and a human head, might well have escaped from the *Horapollon,* the ancient work on hieroglyphics that provided the foundation for the language of signs used in alchemy. Contemporary art engages here in a dialogue with utilitarian art and illuminates the inner quality they share: the legacy of imaginative knowledge. Technical knowledge will have to accept our asking how long it will be before the first computers appear as obsolete tools in museums of folk art. Technological forms developed for the solution of practical problems become outdated; in contrast, the questions confronted by art remain perpetually new, for they are always the same and always unanswerable.

Artists' Biographies

The artists' biographies have been kept brief by design. A bibliographical reference is cited for each artist, wherever possible. Only solo exhibitions since 1990 are listed; group exhibitions are not included.

Anton Christian

1940 Born in Innsbruck, Austria.
Lives and works in Natters/Innsbruck, Austria.

1942–50 Forced to resettle in the small village of Oberau, Austria during the war, shortly before his parents' home is bombarded.
1959–63 Studies at the Akademie der Bildenden Künste, Vienna, Austria
1964–66 Stay in Paris, France; intermittent studies at the Académie des Beaux-Arts
1969–71 Stay in London, United Kingdom
1980 Visiting artist at the University of Houston, Texas
1989–92 Studio in New York City

Selected Solo Exhibitions
1990 Tiroler Landesmuseum Ferdinandeum, Innsbruck, Austria (catalogue)
1991 Galerie Matthias und Mark Stähli, Oberdiessbach/Bern, Switzerland
University Museum, San Diego State University, San Diego, California (catalogue)
1992 University Museum, California State University Fullerton, Los Angeles, California (catalogue)
Stift Wilten, Innsbruck, Austria
Wiener Messepalast (Galerie Hilger), Vienna, Austria
1993 Südtiroler Kulturinstitut, Waltherhaus Bolzano, Italy (catalogue)
1994 Kunstverein-Kunsthaus Steyr, Austria (catalogue)
Haus Borchert, Bochum, Germany
1996 479 Gallery, New York City (catalogue)
Martin Rathburn Gallery, San Antonio, Texas
Galerie Schmid, Reith/Alpbach, Austria
1997 Galerie Esther Hufschmid/Jörg Stummer, Zurich, Switzerland
Galerie Sechzig, Feldkirch, Austria

Literature
Renetzeder, Evelin, *Anton Christian Das Malen – das Schreiben,* Innsbruck, 1996.

Heinz Cibulka

1943 Born in Vienna, Austria.
Lives and works in Ladendorf, Austria.

1957–61 Graphische Lehr-Versuchsanstalt, Vienna, Austria
since 1972 Photo series and pictorial poems, objects and object images; visual work, lyrical and conceptual texts and performances
1981 Awarded the Österreichischer Förderpreis für Photographie
1982 Co-founder of the Austrian Photo Archive
1985 DAAD grant, Berlin, Germany
1989 Co-founder of the FLUSS NÖ-Fotoinitiative
Awarded the Rupertinum Photopreis
1994 Awarded the Niederösterreichischer Landespreis
Several classes in photography at the Internationale Sommerakademie Salzburg, Austria and at the Weinviertler Fotowochen, Austria; workshops and lectures in Austria and abroad; organization of various events for the FLUSS-NÖ-Fotoinitiative.
1997–98 Visiting Professor for Art Photography at the Hochschule für Angewandte Kunst, Vienna, Austria

Selected Solo Exhibitions
1993 Museum for Photography, Antwerp, Belgium
Niederösterreichisches Landesmuseum, Vienna, Austria
Centre Nykyaika, Finland
1994 ULUV, Prague, Czech Republic
Angel Row Gallery, Nottingham, United Kingdom
Galerie J. et J. Donguy, Paris, France
1996 *Prospect 96,* Frankfurt am Main, Germany
Studio Morra, Naples, Italy
1997 Austrian Cultural Institute, London, United Kingdom
Centro del Imagen, Mexico City
Galerie Hummel, Vienna, Austria

Literature
Cibulka, Heinz, *Aus Nachbars Garten,* Vienna (Gumpoldskirchen), 1998.

Mario Cravo Neto

1947 Born in Salvador Bahia, Brazil.
Lives and works in Salvador Bahia, Brazil.

Selected Solo Exhibitions

1990 Galerie Springer, Berlin, Germany
Canon Image Center, Amsterdam, The Netherlands
1991 Galería del Teatro General San Martin, Buenos Aires, Argentina
Ada Galeria, Salvador Bahia, Brazil
1992 Houston FotoFest, Houston, Texas
Galeria Módulo, Lisbon, Portugal
Fahey/Klein Gallery, Los Angeles, California
Witkin Gallery, New York City
1993 Vision Gallery, San Francisco, California
Kathleen Ewing Gallery, Washington, D.C.
Fisher Gallery, Los Angeles, California
1994 Museum of Photographic Art, San Diego, California
Frankfurter Kunstverein, Frankfurt am Main, Germany
1997 Witkin Gallery, New York City

Literature

Weiermair, Peter (ed.), *Mario Cravo Neto,* Edition Stemmle, Kilchberg/Zurich, 1994.

Braco Dimitrijevic

1948 Born in Sarajevo, former Yugoslavia.
Lives and works in Paris, France and New York City.

1958 First solo exhibition at the age of 10
1968–71 Studies at the Academy of Arts, Zagreb, former Yugoslavia (MA)
1971–72 Grant from the British Council
1971–73 Postgraduate studies at St. Martin's School of Art, London, United Kingdom
1976–77 DAAD grant, Berlin, Germany

Selected Solo Exhibitions

1990 Pat Hearn Gallery, New York City
1990 Nicole Klagsburn Gallery, New York City
1994 Galerie de France, Paris, France
1994 Museum Moderner Kunst Stiftung Ludwig, Vienna, Austria
1994 The Israel Museum, Jerusalem, Israel
1995 Hessisches Landesmuseum, Darmstadt, Germany
1996 Moderna Galerija, Ljubljana, Slovenia
1996 Kunsthalle Düsseldorf, Germany
1997 Pièce Unique, Paris, France
1998 Musée National d'Histoire Naturelle – Jardin des Plantes, Paris, France

Literature

Harten, Jürgen, *Konstellationen,* Kunsthalle Düsseldorf, 1996.

Gloria Friedmann

1950 Born in Kronach, Germany.
Lives and works in Aignay-le-Duc and Paris, France.

Selected Solo Exhibitions

1992 Museum Moderner Kunst Stiftung Ludwig, Vienna, Austria
1993 Le Consortium, Dijon, France
1994 Villa Arson, Nice, France
Musée d'Art Moderne, Strasbourg, France
1995 *Pour qui, contre qui,* Museé National d'Art Moderne, Paris, France
1996 City Art Gallery, Wellington, New Zealand
1997 Städtische Sammlung, Augsburg, Germany
Annely Juda Fine Arts, London, United Kingdom
1998 Cent 8 Galerie, Paris, France
Galerie Academia, Salzburg, Austria

Literature

I.Q./E.Q., Annely Juda Fine Arts, London/Augsburg, 1997.

Statement

Craftsmen, makers of traditional garb, farmers, housebuilders are like me – converters of raw material – and thus they are my colleagues. I see the proximity of the symbol-bearing things exhibited here as a plus. The important thing is what is universally available to people. Alongside the utilitarian objects are the unequal partners bones and blood, the equation of man and animal, the human being's journey from here to the beyond. This "gene pool" I can understand; here we find alternatives to the anonymity of mass society.

Martin Gostner

1957 Born in Innsbruck, Austria.
Lives and works in Innsbruck, Austria.

Selected Solo Exhibitions

1987 Forum Kunst, Rottweil, Germany
1988 *Monza,* Amraserstraße 28, Innsbruck, Austria
1989 *Effi Briest,* project with Thomas Kling and Udo Kittelmann, Atelier P.B., Klapperhof, Cologne, Germany
1991 Galerie Christian Gögger, Munich, Germany
1992 Förderkoje Art Cologne, Cologne, Germany
1993 Studio Oggetto, Milan, Italy
1994 *Thesen der Gegenreformation,* Forum Stadtpark, Prague, Czech Republic
1995 *I.M. Zebra,* Galerie Sophia Ungers, Cologne, Germany
1996 *Stepping Into the Shit of History,* Galerie Giorgio Persano, Turin, Italy
1997 *Öde Galle,* Villa Merkel/Bahnwärterhaus, Esslingen, Germany
1998 Kölnischer Kunstverein, Cologne, Germany

Literature

Metzger, Rainer et al., *Martin Gostner,* Turin, 1998.

Quotation
When at last melancholy has no specific object
but spreads itself over the whole of life;
then it is a kind of introversion, a retreat,
a gradual disappearance of the will, whose visible manifestation,
the body,
it even undermines, quietly but deep within, whereby the human
being senses
a certain loosening of its bonds, a gentle intimation of the death that
dissolves both the body and the will;
which is why this grief is accompanied by a secret pleasure that is,
as I believe,
what the most melancholy of all peoples has called the joy of grief.

Arthur Schopenhauer, *The World as Will and Idea*

Rolf Iseli

1934 Born in Bern, Switzerland.
Lives and works in Bern, Switzerland, St. Romain, France and Jávea, Spain.

1950–54 Apprenticeship as a photographer and photolithographer

Selected Solo Exhibitions
1990 Musée Cantonal des Beaux-Arts, Lausanne, Switzerland
1992 Centre Culturel Suisse, Paris, France
Galerie Philip, Paris, France
1993 Galerie Jan Krugier, Geneva, Switzerland
Casa Rusca, Locarno, Switzerland
1996 Galerie Larry Rubin, Zurich, Switzerland
Galerie Ditesheim, Neuchâtel, Switzerland
Kunsthalle Burgdorf, Switzerland
1998 Galerie Krugier-Ditesheim, Geneva, Switzerland

Literature
Holz, Hans Heinz, *Rolf Iseli: Woher – wo – wohin,* Kunsthalle Burgdorf, 1996.

Magdalena Jetelová

1946 Born in Semily, former Czechoslovakia.
Lives and works in Düsseldorf and Bergheim, Germany.

1965–67 Studies at the Academy of Arts, Prague, Czech Republic
1967–68 Studies at the Accademia di Brera, Milan, Italy
1968–71 Continuation of studies at the Academy of Arts, Prague, Czech Republic
1985 Emigration to the German Federal Republic.
Grant awarded by the city of Munich, Germany
1986 Awarded prize at the competition Dimension V of the Philip Morris GmbH, Germany
1987 Grant awarded by the Institut für Auslandsbeziehungen, Stuttgart, Germany
1988 Awarded the Glockengasse 4711 prize, Cologne, Germany
Visiting professor at the Akademie der Bildenden Künste, Munich, Germany
Awarded the Overbeck-Preis für Bildende Kunst, Lübeck, Germany
1989 Professor at the Sommerakademie, Salzburg, Austria
Art award from the city of Darmstadt, Germany
since 1990 Professor at the Staatliche Kunstakademie, Düsseldorf, Germany
1991 Awarded the Max-Lütze-Preis, Stuttgart, Germany
since 1992 Honorary member of the Academy of Arts, Berlin, Germany
1993 Consultant to the Prague Castle Council
1997 Awarded the Robert-Jacobson-Preis, Stiftung/Museum Würth, Germany

Selected Solo Exhibitions
1990 John Weber Gallery, New York City
Städtische Galerie, Göppingen, Germany
Hällisch-Fränkisches Museum, Schwäbisch Hall, Germany
Galerie Jule Kewenig, Frechen, Germany
1991 Cornerhouse, Manchester, United Kingdom
The Henry Moore Sculpture Trust Studio, Halifax, United Kingdom
Mellon Gallery, Pittsburgh, Pennsylvania
Mala Galerija, Moderna Galerija, Ljubljana, Slovenia
1992 *Domestizierung einer Pyramide,* Museum für Angewandte Kunst, Vienna, Austria
Zwei Räume, Galerie Christine König, Vienna, Austria
1993 *Iceland Project,* Belveder, Prague, Czech Republic
1994 Kaiser's Pfalz, Paderborn, Germany
1995 Galerie Harthan, Stuttgart, Germany
Galerie Lüpke, Frankfurt am Main, Germany
Bunkerprojekt, Museum Lemvig, Germany
1996 *Translocation II,* Institut Mathildenhöhe, Darmstadt, Germany
Dislocations, Museu d'Art Modern, Barcelona, Spain; Kings Cross, London, United Kingdom

Literature
Wolbert, Klaus (ed.), *Orte und Räume – Locations and Spaces,* Institut Mathildenhöhe, Darmstadt, 1996.

Kazuo Katase

1947 Born in Shizuoka, Japan.
Lives and works in Kassel, Germany.

Selected Solo Exhibitions
1991 *Eclipse of the Earth,* The New Museum of Contemporary Art, New York City
1993 *Rainhouse,* The Douglas Hyde Gallery, Dublin, Ireland
Geworfene Schatten, The Shoto Museum of Art, Tokyo, Japan
Downtown Train, Tramway, Glasgow, Scotland
1994 *Schlafende Sterne,* Westfälischer Kunstverein, Münster, Germany
1995 "Behind the Light," *Japan today,* Louisiana Museum of Modern Art, Humblebaek, Denmark (traveling exhibition)
1996 *Das Blaue Haus (Die gefangene Zeit),* Museum Wiesbaden, Germany
1997 *Götternacht,* Kasseler Kunstverein, Alte Brüderkirche, Kassel, Germany
1997 *Regenstein,* St. Nicolai, Alfeld, Germany
1998 *Winterreise,* Oberbeck-Gesellschaft, Lübeck, Germany
Geistes Gegenwart: "Nachtasyl," Diözesanmuseum, Freising, Germany

Literature
Räume der Gegenwart, Cantz, Stuttgart, 1997.

Quotation
Stavrogin: "... in *Revelation,* the angel announces that there should be time no longer."
Kirillov: "I know. That is what it says – emphatically, in unmistakable clarity. When everyone has achieved happiness there will be no time, because it will no longer be needed. A very true thought."
Stavrogin: "But where will it be hidden, then?"
Kirillov: "It won't be hidden anywhere. Time isn't a thing, you know, but an idea. It will be extinguished in the mind."

F. M. Dostoyevski, *The Possessed*

Michael Kienzer

1962 Born in Steyr, Austria.
Lives and works in Vienna and Graz, Austria.

1977–79 Studies in sculpture at the Kunstgewerbeschule, Graz, Austria under Professor Josef Pillhofer
1979–82 Stay in Berlin, Germany, collaboration at the Kunst- and Kulturzentrum Kreuzberg
1985 Grant from the state of Steiermark, Austria for contemporary art
1989 Grant from the state of Upper Austria for visual arts
Grant from the city of Graz, Austria for art
1990 Grant from the state of Steiermark, Austria for visual arts (3rd place)
1993 Awarded first prize at the Graphikwettbewerb Innsbruck, Austria
Awarded to visual arts from the Diocese of Graz-Seckau, Austria
1987–89 Stage designs for the Westfälisches Landestheater Castrop, Germany: *Die schmutzigen Hände,* Jean Paul Sartre; *Kabale und Liebe,* Friedrich Schiller; *Transit,* Anna Seghers; *Der Reigen,* Arthur Schnitzler; *Don Juan oder die Liebe zur Geometrie,* Max Frisch

Selected Exhibitions and Projects
1998 Galleria Stefania Miscetti, Rome, Italy (with E. Erjautz)
Galerie Eugen Lendl, Graz, Austria
Kunstraum Mezzanin, Vienna, Austria (with E. Erjautz)
Phänomen des Flüchtigen, kultur.raum.spitalskirche, Lienz, Austria; ArtForum Galerie, Merano, Italy
Skulpturen, Galerie Elisabeth und Klaus Thoman, Innsbruck, Austria
Die Normalen, Österreichisches Kulturinstitut, London, United Kingdom

Literature
Niegelhell, Franz et al., *Zwischendurch,* Triton Verlag, Lübeck, 1995.

Nikolaus Lang

1941 Born in Oberammergau, Germany.
Lives and works in Bayersoien, Germany.

1958–60 Carving school, Oberammergau, Germany
1960–66 Studies at the Akademie der Bildenden Künste, Munich, Germany
1966–67 DAAD grant, Camberwell School of Art and Crafts, London, United Kingdom
1967–69 Teacher at the Camberwell School of Art and Crafts, London, United Kingdom (sculpture)
1971 *Short Walk,* Wimbledon Common, London, United Kingdom
1971–72 DAAD grant for a stay in Tokyo, Japan
1975 Awarded the Staatlicher Bayerischer Förderungspreis, Germany
1976 Awarded the Villa Romana prize, Florence, Italy
Spaziergang durch einen Steinbruch bei Palagio, Palagio, Italy
1979 Stay in South Australia
1980 Grant from Glockengasse 4711, Cologne, Germany
1981 Stay in Malmö, Sweden
1983–84 Stay in Berlin, Germany
1986 Awarded the Defet Kunstpreis
1986–89 Stay in South Australia
1987 Working grant, awarded by the South Australian College of Art, Adelaide, Australia

1989 Full member at the Bayerische Akademie der Schönen Künste, Munich, Germany
1993 Stay in South Australia
Commission for the Design Center, Linz, Austria
1995 Stay in South Australia
Commission for ASER, Adelaide, Australia
1996 Two stays in northwest Australia
1997 Honorary award from the Friedrich-Baur-Stiftung, Bayerische Akademie der Schönen Künste, Munich, Germany

Selected Exhibitions
1991 *Nunga und Goonya,* Kunstraum München e.V., Munich, Germany; Städtische Galerie im Lenbachhaus, Munich, Germany; Kunsthalle Bremen, Germany; Stadtgalerie, Saarbrücken, Germany
1992 *Nunga und Goonya,* daedalus, Vienna, Austria; Institut für Auslandsbeziehungen, Stuttgart, Germany
Terra Nullius, Kunstverein Ruhr, Essen, Germany; Kunstraum Wuppertal, Germany
1993 *Nunga und Goonya,* The Douglas Hyde Gallery, Dublin, Ireland
1995 *Druckstock 1, 1980,* Sprengel Museum, Hanover, Germany
1998 *Points of view,* Neuer Berliner Kunstverein, Berlin, Germany

Literature
Lang, Nikolaus et al., *Nunga und Goonya,* Kunstraum München and Städtische Galerie im Lenbachhaus, Munich, 1991.

Pieter Laurens Mol

1946 Born in Breda, The Netherlands.
Lives and works in Breukelen and Amsterdam, The Netherlands.

1959–63 Apprenticeship as a carpenter
1963–65 Studies at the St. Joost Art Academy, Breda, The Netherlands

Selected Solo Exhibitions
1990 Galleria Mikkola & Rislakki, Helsinki, Finland
Louver Gallery, New York City
1991 Galleria Sperone, Rome, Italy
1992 *Once I Existed,* Galerie Franck & Schulte, Berlin, Germany
Once I Existed, Louver Gallery, New York City
1993 Stedelijk Van Abbemuseum, Eindhoven, The Netherlands
Ferro Fever, Institute of Contemporary Art, Amsterdam, The Netherlands
La Charge Utile, Centre d'Art Contemporain, Geneva, Switzerland
IVAM, Centro del Carme, Valencia, Spain
Zeichnungen, Galerie Franck & Schulte, Berlin, Germany
1994 MIT List Visual Arts Center, Boston, Massachusetts
Centre Saidye Bronfman, Montreal, Québec
Contemporary Arts Museum, Houston, Texas
Galerie Paul Andriesse, Amsterdam, The Netherlands
Contemporary Arts Center, Cincinnati, Ohio
1995 Galerie Paul Andriesse, Amsterdam, The Netherlands
1996 *Lure of Thumb,* Galerie Paul Andriesse, Amsterdam, The Netherlands
Sean Kelly, New York City
The Museum of Modern Art, New York City

Literature
Schwarz, Gary et al., *Grand Promptness* (monograph on the artist's work), Artimo Foundation, Breda, 1996.

Hermann Nitsch

1938 Born in Vienna, Austria.
Lives and works in Prinzendorf, Austria.

1957 Idea for the "Orgien Mysterien Theater," a six-day theater pagent that occupies him constantly from this time forward and on which all of his efforts and hopes are focused. The "Theater" is a new form of *gesamtkunstwerk,* in which real events are staged. Spectators are encouraged to engage all five senses.
1960–66 Action and exhibition activities in Vienna, Austria, triggering several trials and three periods of imprisonment.
1966 *Destruction in Art,* symposium, London, United Kingdom, performance of the 20th action
1968 Cinematheque, New York City, performance of the 25th and 26th actions
1971 Acquires Prinzendorf castle
1974 Performance of the 24-hour 50th action (first day and night of the six-day pagent) in Prinzendorf, Austria
1984 Performance of the 72-hour 80th action (three days and three nights of the six-day pagent) in Prinzendorf, Austria
1987 20th painting action at the Wiener Secession, Vienna, Austria
since 1989 Professor at the Hochschule für bildende Kunst, Städelschule, Frankfurt am Main, Germany
1995 Involved in design and direction of the opera *Hériodiade* by Jules Massenet at the Wiener Staatsoper, Vienna, Austria
since 1966 Actions, exhibitions, lectures and concerts in various cities in Europe, the US and Australia
1996 Perforamnce of the 96th action (12 hours) in San Martino, Naples, Italy
38th painting action, Schömerhaus, Klosterneuburg, Austria
1997 40th painting action, Museum des 20. Jahrhunderts, Vienna, Austria
1998 Six-day theater pagent, Prinzendorf, Austria

Continued work on projects for the "Orgien Mysterien Theater;" expansion of the painting and theater concept to include architectural and musical aspects.

Literature
Weiermair, Peter (ed.), *Die Sammlung Morra,* Kunstraum Innsbruck, 1997.

Luigi Ontani

1943 Born in Montovolo di Grizzana/Bologna, Italy.
Lives and works in Rome, Italy.

Selected Solo Exhibitions
1990 Galleria Massimo Minini, Brescia, Italy
1992 Studio d'Arte Bernabò, Venice, Italy
1993 Galleria Gian Enzo Sperone, Rome, Italy
Castello Di Volpaia, Radda (Chianti), Italy
1994 Studio d'Arte Raffaelli, Trento, Italy
Sperone Westwater Gallery, New York City
1995 Galleria Scudo, Verona, Italy
1996 Frankfurter Kunstverein, Frankfurt am Main, Germany
Galleria d'Arte Moderna, Trento, Italy
1997/98 *Versus 2000,* Museion Bozen, Bolzano, Italy

Literature
Weiermair, Peter (ed.), *Retrospektiv,* Frankfurter Kunstverein, Frankfurt am Main, 1997.

Claudio Parmiggiani

1943 1943 Born in Luzzara, Italy.
Lives and works in Bologna and Torrechiara, Italy.

Literature
Claudio Parmiggiani, Mathildenhöhe, Darmstadt; Galerie Hlavniko Mesta, Prague, 1992.

Pedro Proença

1962 Born in Lubango, Angola.
Lives and works in Lisbon, Portugal.

1986 Diploma at Escola de Belas Artes Lisboa (ESBAL), Lisbon, Portugal
Author of essays, poems and articles.

Selected Solo Exhibitions
1990 Galería Miguel Marcos, Madrid, Spain
Galería Rita García, Valencia, Spain
Galeria Graca Fonseca, Lisbon, Portugal
1992 Galeria Pedro Oliveira, Porto, Portugal
1993 Scuderie dell Palazzo Ruspoli, Rome, Italy
Galeria Pedro Oliveira, Porto, Portugal
1994 Fundacão Calouste Gulbenkian, Lisbon, Portugal
Galería Rita García, Valencia, Spain
1995 *Uma Salada Alegórica,* Gilde, Guimarães, Portugal
1996 *Big girls don't cry.* Galeria Pedro Oliveira, Porto, Portugal
Da Interpretacão, Galeria Ad Hoc, Vigo, Portugal
Galería Xavier Fiol, Palma de Mallorca, Spain
1997 *Antiphonte & Ophélia,* Casa Fernando Pessoa, Lisbon, Portugal
1998 *Anacorese Galante,* Galeria Pedro Oliveira, Porto, Portugal

Literature
Weiermair, Peter (ed.), *Pedro Proença, Eccentric Drawing,* Frankfurter Kunstverein, Frankfurt am Main, 1998.

Néstor Quiñones

1967 Born in Mexico City.
Lives and works in Mexico City.

Self-taught artist

Selected Solo Exhibitions
1990 *Madora,* Galería OMR, Mexico City
1992 *Principio interior,* Galería OMR, Mexico City
1993 *Aquietamiento,* Museo de Arte Carrillo Gil, Mexico City
1996 *Paso de conocimiento,* Drexel Galería, Monterray, N.L., Mexico
1997 *Tambor,* Galería OMR, Mexico City

Literature
Néstor Quiñones, Museo de Arte Carrillo Gil, Mexico City, 1993.

Statement
The *Towel-Holder* perfectly symbolizes the intent behind this installation. It mirrors the natural essence of mankind, and at the same time I recognize in it the duality upon which culture is based: the challenge posed to all humans to sharpen their perceptions while raising their ethical standards and intensifying their sensibilities in the face of imponderable mysteries such as the transformation of matter and the natural evolution of all things. We are the products of culture, whether we are conscious of the fact or not. Only the moment counts in the no-man's land between present and future. It is this moment I wish to make palpable in my work.

Arnulf Rainer

1929 Born in Baden/Vienna, Austria.
Lives and works in Vienna, Upper Austria, Bavaria, Germany and Tenerife (Canary Islands), Spain.

Self-taught artist

since 1954 Overpainting
1978 Awarded the Großer Österreichischer Staatspreis, Austria
1981 Awarded the Max-Beckmann-Preis der Stadt Frankfurt am Main, Germany
1981–95 Teaches a master's class in painting at the Akademie der bildenden Künste, Berlin, Germany
Member of the Österreichischer Kunstsenat, Austria

Selected Solo Exhibitions
1990 Castello di Rivoli, Turin, Italy
Gemeentemuseum, The Hague, The Netherlands
Saarland Museum, Saarbrücken, Germany
1991 Malmö Kunsthall, Malmö, Sweden
1992 De Menil Collection, Houston, Texas
Stedeljik Museum, Amsterdam, The Netherlands
1994 Museum Moderner Kunst, Stiftung Wörlen, Passau, Germany
1996 Centro Galego de Arte Contemporáneo, Santiago de Compostela, Spain
1997 Kunstmuseum Bonn, Germany
1998 Nationalgalerie Prague, Czech Republic

Literature
Catoir, Barbara, *Übermalte Bücher,* Prestel Verlag, Munich, 1989.

Pavel Schmidt

1956 Born in Bratislava, former Czechoslovakia.
Lives and works in Munich, Germany and Solothurn, Switzerland.

1966–68 Stay in Mexico
1977 Diploma from the Deutsches Gymnasium, Biel, Switzerland
Studies in Chemistry at the University in Bern, Switzerland
1982 Master student under Prof. Hans Baschang; Diploma, First State Examination at the Akademie der Bildenden Künste, Munich, Germany
1983–89 Academic assistant at the Akademie der Bildenden Künste, Munich, Germany, under Professors Rudolf Seitz and Daniel Spoerri
1989–91 Temporary professorship
1992 Collaboration on Daniel Spoerri's project "eaten by" for the Swiss Pavilion at the World Exposition in Seville, Spain

Selected Solo Exhibitions
1992 *W(h)ale,* Städtische Galerie Bremen, Germany
Partnerschaften, Suermondt-Ludwig-Museum, Aachen, Germany
1993 Galerie Sabine Wachters, Brussels, Belgium
1994 Galerie Medici, Solothurn, Switzerland
Ohne Titel oder Gold log, Centre Pasquart, Biel, Switzerland; Städtische Galerie Regensburg, Germany
Pied à Terre, Centre Culturel Suisse, Paris, France
1995 Musée du Ranquet, Clermont-Ferrand, France
Galerie Rigassi, Bern, Switzerland
1996 *Entgleitungen und Heilungen,* Schloß Karlsruhe, Galerie Alfred Knecht, Karlsruhe, Germany
Altes Kurmittelhaus, Merano, Italy
Die fünfte Himmelsrichtung, Singen, Germany
Cerveira Biennial, Portugal
1997 Galerie Sabine Wachters, Brussels, Belgium
1997 *Mitnichten und Schlechthin,* DG, Munich, Germany
1998 *Davide saluta la Venere,* Villa Romana, Florence, Italy

Statement
Where this-and-that shakes hands with whatever
A few quick and non-profound thoughts on the above-mentioned works group in the Tiroler Volkskunstmuseum.

This group of works is the outcome of an attempt to establish links between the objects in the existing museum collection and selected aspects of the artist's intervention. The things in the museum have been stripped of their functionality and their ritual utilitarian character. Exhibited on walls or in showcases, they appear estranged from their original context and at the same time closer in some way to the more or less or totally uninitiated viewer and museum visitor.

What has been left to these items is their unique, finite form, which may well testify to their specific symbolic content, on the one hand, and their fascinating aura within the context of cult activity, on the other. We know and sense intuitively that both are deeply rooted in religious belief, which is itself tightly interwoven with local popular beliefs and superstitions. That this has been preserved along with folk art – in spite of the unabating influence from the outside and the endless flow of through-bound traffic, in spite of changing political conditions and national affiliations – is an astounding, stimulating and laudable state of affairs.

Tyrol, with its Brenner Pass, one of the oldest and most important north-to-south passages in the Alps, is one of those very special regions (like those of the Splügen, Gotthard, Simplon, Great St. Bernhard and other passes), where cultures have traditionally met and, to a certain extent, intermingled. Mediterranean culture meets alpine culture and the cultural regions north of the Alps – each with its own respective mythologies. Venus encounters the decorative garden dwarf, so to speak (to mention only one of the conceivable confrontations of mythologies).

Expressed in even more simple terms, it is the region where the wine culture collides and co-exists with the beer culture – or the wine-myth topos with the beer-myth topos. …

The product of the artist's intervention, consisting of four object-figures, seeks in the encounter to expand upon the real thing (as it exists in the museum). This expansion is meant to attain a level at which both the autonomy and the existence of the two (the museum piece and the work of art) are maintained but where a "temporary marriage" may be celebrated as well.

And thus the Saltner (vinyard watchman) gains a lady companion after all his years as a museum exhibit. …

And the beautifully carved and painted beds will be brought to life by a couple, for a while. …

The singular hand-made tools, once fashioned in an attitude of respect for the handcrafting trades that is particularly striking to us today, receive as guests their envious descendants from European building supply stores.

Pablo Siebel

1954 Born in Santiago de Chile.
Lives and works in Madrid, Spain.

Selected Solo Exhibitions

1992 La Galería, Santiago de Chile
1994 Museo de Salamanca, Salamanca, Spain
1995 Galerie Arte Giani, Frankfurt am Main, Germany
Sala de exposiciones de la Biblioteca de Castilla y León, Valladolid, Spain
Galería Coscoja, Segovia, Spain
1996 Galería Montalbán, Madrid, Spain
Casa de Cultura de El Espartal, Madrid, Spain
1997 Galerie Arte Giani, Frankfurt am Main, Germany
Centro Cultural Las Dehesillas, Leganés, Madrid, Spain

Statement

In the beginning was the cradle. As a native of Chile, I must wrestle with the problem of reconciling my European roots with Latin American mysticism. My Innsbruck installation is a fleeting image of this tension. Rising from the seven Tyrolean cradles are the wooden steles that mirror my perception of the world.

Al Souza

1944 Born in Plymouth, Massachusetts.
Lives and works in Roswell, New Mexico.

Selected Solo Exhibitions

1990 Moody Gallery, Houston, Texas
1991 Quint Contemporary Art, La Jolla, California
1992 Moody Gallery, Houston, Texas
Gallery Paule Anglim, San Francisco, California
1994 Condeso/Lawler Gallery, New York City
Moody Gallery, Houston, Texas
1996 Moody Gallery, Houston, Texas
1997 Moody Gallery, Houston, Texas
1997 Quint Contemporary Art, La Jolla, California
1998 Moody Gallery, Houston, Texas

Literature

Littlejohns, Joanna, *Al Souza,* Guernsey College, Guernsey, 1996.

Daniel Spoerri

1930 Born as Daniel Isaac Feinstein in Galati, Romania.
Lives and works in Seggiano, Switzerland.

1950–54 Studies in classical ballet in Zurich, Switzerland and Paris, France
1950 Co-founder of the "Nouveau Réalisme"
1968 Establishes the Spoerri Restaurant
Appointment to the Akademie der Bildenden Künste in Munich, Germany
1993 Awarded the Grand Prix National de la Sculpture

Selected Solo Exhibitions
1990 *Palettes d'artistes,* Galerie Beaubourg, Paris, France
Faux puces, Galerie Beaubourg, Paris, France
Rezeptmappen, Goethe Institut/Galerie Conde, Paris, France
1991 *Salute. Daniel Spoerri,* Künstlerwerkstatt Lothringerstraße, Munich, Germany
Corps en morceaux, Galerie Raab, Berlin, Germany
1992 *Seville series "eaten by…,"* Expo 1992, Swiss Pavilion, Seville, Spain
1994 *Cabinet Anatomique,* Centre d'Art, Montbéliard, France
1995 *Le Cabinet Anatomique,* Galerie Yvon Lambert, Paris, France
1996 *Carnaval des Animaux,* Galerie Yvon Lambert, Paris, France
1997 Perrigeux (Dordogne), France
1998 *Vendredi treize,* Centre Culturel Suisse, Paris, France

Literature
Violand-Hoby, Heidi (ed.), *Daniel Spoerri,* Munich, 1998.

Antoni Tàpies

1923 Born in Barcelona, Spain.
Lives and works in Barcelona, Spain.

1944 Studies in law in Barcelona, Spain (breaks off studies shortly before completion)
Studies in drawing for two months at the Academia Valls, Barcelona, Spain.
1945 Devotes more and more time to painting. First experiments with dense materials
1948 Growing interest in Surrealism, psychoanalysis and modern sciences

Selected Solo Exhibitions
1991 Royal Garden of the Castle, Micovna Pavilion, Prague, Czech Republic
1992 *Tàpies und die Bücher,* Schirn Kunsthalle Frankfurt, Frankfurt am Main, Germany
Millares, Saura, Tàpies, Museu Sztuki, Lodz, Poland
1993 Valenicano de Arte Moderno, Valencia, Spain; Serpentine Gallery, London, United Kingdom
Retrospective of the graphic work, Museum of Modern Art, New York City
1994 Pace Gallery, New York City
Rinzen, Spanish Pavilion, XLV Venice Biennial, Venice, Italy (awarded the Golden Lion)
Retrospective, Schirn Kunsthalle Frankfurt, Frankfurt am Main, Germany
Tàpies. Celebració de la mel, Fundació Antoni Tàpies, Barcelona, Spain
1995 Retrospective, Prins Eugens Waldemarsudde, Stockholm, Sweden
Waddington Galleries, London, United Kingdom
Antoni Tàpies. Obra grafica 1947–1990, Palacio de Sástago, Zaragoza, Spain
Galerie Nationale du Jeu de Paume, Paris, France
Picasso – Miró – Tàpies. Keramische Werke, Hetgens Museum, Düsseldorf, Germany
1996 Retrospective, Solomon R. Guggenheim Museum, New York City
Recent Work, PaceWildenstein Gallery, New York City
Graphic work, Museo de la casa de la Moneda, Madrid, Spain
1997 Retrospective, Marugame Genichiro Inokuma, Kagawa, Japan; Niigata City Art Museum, Japan
Retrospective, Auditorio de Galicia, Santiago de Compostela, Spain; Centro Cultural de Belém, Lisbon, Portugal
Waddington Galleries, London, United Kingdom
Edicions T Galeria d'Art, Barcelona, Spain
Face à l'Histoire. L'artiste moderne devant l'événement historique, Centre Georges Pompidou, Paris, France
Retrospective, Centro per l'Arte Contemporanea Luigi Pecci, Prato, Italy
Galleria Christian Stein, Milan, Italy

Elmar Trenkwalder

1959 Born in Weißenbach am Lech, Austria.
Lives and works in Innsbruck, Austria.

1978–82 Studies at the Akademie der Bildenden Künste, Vienna, Austria, under Professors Max Weiler and Arnulf Rainer
1986 Invitation to the Ateliers Internationaux à Fontevraud, F.R.A.C. Pays de la Loire, France
1993 Awarded the Anton-Faistauer-Preis for painting by the state of Salzburg, Austria

Selected Solo Exhibitions
1991 Galerie Jean-François Dumont, Bordeaux, France
Galerie 60, Feldkirch, Austria
1992 Galerie Altnöder, Salzburg, Austria
1994 Galerie im Traklhaus, Salzburg, Austria
Exhibition at the Salon des Bundesrates, House of Parliament, Vienna, Austria
1995 Galerie im Taxispalais, Innsbruck, Austria
La Chaufferie, Ecole des Arts Décoratifs de Strasbourg, France
Hipp-Halle, Gmunden, Austria
1996 Galerie 60, Feldkirch, Austria
Galerie Maniero, Rome, Italy
Galerie Krinzinger, Vienna, Austria
1997 Galerie Jean-François Dumont, Bordeaux, France
Ursula Blickle Stiftung, Kraichtal, Germany
1998 Galerie du Collège Marcel Duchamp, Châteauroux, France
La Box, Ecole Nationale des Beaux-Arts, Bourges, France
F.R.A.C. Limousin, Limoges, France

Henk Visch

1950 Born in Eindhoven, The Netherlands.
Lives and works in Eindhoven, The Netherlands, and Stuttgart, Germany.

1968–72 Studies at the Royal Academy for Art and Design, The Hague, The Netherlands
1984–87 Professor at the Rijksakademie voor beeldende Kunsten, Amsterdam, The Netherlands
since 1995 Professor at the Staatliche Akademie der Bildenden Künste, Stuttgart, Germany

Selected Solo Exhibitions
1990 *Henk Visch,* Kunstverein Hanover, Germany
Op een tafel in Maastricht (with John Körmeling), Jan van Eyck Academy, Maastricht, The Netherlands
1992 *I see, I understand, I know, I remember, I do,* P. S. I., New York City
Her brother his husband, Spalova Galerie, Prague, Czech Republic
1993 *Henk Visch Sculpture 1989–1992,* Domaine de Kerguehennec, Centre d'Art, Locmine, France
1994 Produzenten Galerie, Hamburg, Germany
There is always another way of doing things, Wako Works of Art, Tokyo, Japan
1995 *Juan Muñoz und Henk Visch,* Kunstverein Hamburg, Hamburg, Germany
1996 *In het park,* Openlucht Museum voor Beeldhouwkunst, Middelheim, Antwerp, Belgium
Rauch im Himmel, Galerie Patricia Schwarz, Stuttgart, Germany
1997 Wako Works of Art, Tokyo, Japan
Arte del '900, Palazzo Grassi, Venice, Italy
1998 Muka International Youth Prints, Auckland, New Zealand
Zeichnungen, Sprengel Museum, Hanover, Germany
Zeeziek, Galerie Ferdinand van Dieten, Amsterdam, The Netherlands

Literature
In het park, Openlucht Museum voor Beeldhouwkunst, Middelheim, Antwerp, 1996.

Authors' Biographies

Wolfgang Brückner

Professor Dr. Wolfgang Brückner, born in 1930; Ph. D. 1956; professor 1964; professor and Director of the Institut für Volkskunde at the University of Frankfurt am Main, Germany in 1969; since 1973 professor of German Philology and Folklore at the University of Würzburg, Germany; corresponding member of the Academy of Sciences and the Royal Gustav Adolf Academy in Uppsala, Sweden. Co-editor of numerous scientific journals and manuals. Major fields of research: "culture" and "folk" as theoretical constructs; the relationship of word and image in law, religion and art; phenomena of the popularization of art; people, trends and fashions; forms of religious cultural moulding; the problematics of history and histories; the world of real things in the realm of ideas.

Jean-Hubert Martin

1944 Born in Strasbourg, France.

1971–82 Curator, Musée National d'Art Moderne, Paris, France
1982–85 Director, Kunsthalle, Bern, Switzerland
1987–90 Director, Musée National d'Art Moderne, Paris, France
1989 "Magiciens de la terre"
1991–95 Conservateur Général du Patrimoine, Art Director, Château d'Oiron, France
1993 Commissioner for the French participation at the Sydney Biennial, Austrialia
since 1994 Director, Musée National des Arts d'Afrique et d'Océanie, Paris, France
1995 Commissioner for the French participation at "Africus," Biennial in Johannesburg, South Africa
1996 Commissioner for the São Paulo Biennial, Brazil

Saul Ostrow

Lives and works in New York City.

1972 Master of Fine Arts, University of Massachusetts

Saul Ostrow is an artist, critic, an organizer of exhibitions, the Art Editor for *Bomb Magazine* (a quarterly magazine of art, literature, theater and film), Co-Editor of *Lusitania Books* (publishing anthologies focusing on cultural issues) and the General Editor of the book series *Critical Voices in Art, Theory and Culture,* published by Gordon and Breach Arts international. His own writings have appeared in *Flash Art International, Art Press* (France), *Neue Bildende Kunst* (Germany), *The International Review of Art* (Columbia, SA1.) *Arts Magazine, World Art* and *The New Art Examiner* (USA) as well as numerous journals and exhibition catalogues. Since 1997 Saul Ostrow has curated over 40 exhibitions in the US and Europe. He teaches a seminar in Critical Theory and Art History at School of Visual Arts, Parsons School of Design, as well as at New York University, where he is also acting co-ordinator for the Master of Fine Arts studio program. In 1994 Saul Ostrow took a sabbatical from his role as artist – and if time permits will return to his studio before the year 2000.

Countess Marie-Louise Plessen

1950 Born in Neustadt (Holstein), Germany.
Lives and works in Berlin, Germany and in the Loire valley, France.

Studies in History, Philosophy and Sociology in Munich, Germany

1974 Awarded Ph. D.
Historian, author, curator and director of international exhibitions of art and cultural history.

1977 *Le musée sentimental,* Centre Georges Pompidou, Paris, France
1979 *Le musée sentimental de Cologne,* Kölnischer Kunstverein, Cologne, Germany
1981 *Le musée sentimental de Prusse,* Berlin Museum, Berlin, Germany
1987 *Berlin-Berlin – die Ausstellung zur 750 Jahrfeier,* Martin Gropius Bau, Berlin, Germany
1990 *Bismarck – Preußen, Deutschland und Europa,* Martin Gropius Bau, Berlin, Germany
1991 *Mozart – Zauberflöte,* Künstlerhaus Wien, Vienna, Austria
1992 *Die Elbe – ein Lebenslauf,* Deichtorhallen, Hamburg, Germany; Hygiene-Museum, Dresden, Germany; National Museum, Prague, Czech Republic
1993 *Sehsucht – das Panorama als Massenmedium des 19. Jahrhunderts,* Kunst- und Ausstellungshalle Bonn, Germany
1995 *Das Russische Museum St. Petersburg in Bonn (Große Sammlungen III),* Kunst- und Ausstellungshalle Bonn, Germany
1996/98 *Marianne und Germania 1789–1889. Deutschland und Frankreich: Zwei Welten – eine Revue,* Berliner Festwochen, Berlin, Germany; Musée du Petit Palais, Paris, France
1999 *Zeitreise Weimar Kulturstadt Europa.* Concept and direction of an interactive cultural-historical tour as a constructed complex consisting of 25 stations. Weimar in history and memory.

Peter Weiermair

1944 Born in Steinhöring, Germany.
Lives in Salzburg, Austria.

Studies in German, Philosophy and Art History at the Universities of Innsbruck and Vienna, Austria.

since 1966 Editor (Allerheiligenpresse)
1968 Founder of the "forum für aktuelle kunst," Innsbruck, Austria, which he directed until 1979
1968–79 Curator, Tiroler Landesgalerie, Galerie im Taxispalais, Innsbruck, Austria
1979–80 Teacher at the Akademie der Bildenden Künste, Vienna, Austria
1980–98 Director, Frankfurter Kunstverein, Frankfurt am Main, Germany
since 1986 Curator, *Prospect* triennial, Frankfurt am Main, Germany
since 1990 Professor, Hochschule für Gestaltung, Offenbach, Germany
since 1990 President, IACCA (International Association of Curators of Contemporary Art)
since 1998 Director, Salzburg Museum of Modern and Contemporary Art, Rupertinum (Salzburger Landessammlungen für moderne und zeitgenössische Kunst Rupertinum), Austria

Beat Wyss

1947 Born in Basel, Switzerland.

Studies in Art History, Philosophy and German Literature in Zurich, Switzerland; Berlin, Germany and Rome, Italy.
Visiting Scholar at the Getty Center, Santa Monica, California

since 1990 Professor, Art History, Ruhr-Universität Bochum, Germany
1996 Visiting Professor, Cornell University, New York City
since 1997 Director, Kunsthistorisches Institut, Universität Stuttgart, Germany

Author of: *Trauer der Vollendung, Zur Geburt der Kulturkritik* (1985), 2nd printing, Cologne, 1997; *Peter Bruegels Landschaft mit Ikarussturz, Humanistischer Pessimismus,* Frankfurt am Main, 1990; *Ein Druckfehler,* Cologne, 1993; *Der Wille zur Kunst, Zur ästhetischen Mentalität der Moderne,* Cologne, 1996; *Die Welt als T-Shirt, Zu Ästhetik und Geschichte der Medien,* Cologne, 1997.

Works provided on loan by

Staatliche Museen zu Berlin
Nationalgalerie
Eigentum des Vereins der Freunde der Nationalgalerie

Frankfurter Kunstverein
Frankfurt am Main

Tiroler Landesmuseum Ferdinandeum
Naturkundliche Sammlung
Innsbruck

Galerie
Franck & Schulte
Berlin

Galerie Lelong
Zurich

Studio Raffaelli
Trento

Jost Thoma Collection
Zurich

Franziska Baer Collection

and lenders who wish to remain anonymous

This book is published in conjunction with the exhibition entitled "The Bird of Self-Knowledge – Folk Art and Current Artists' Positions," presented at the Tiroler Volkskunstmuseum Innsbruck from June 27th to October 26th, 1998, and the symposium "Schnittpunkte zeitgenössischer Kunst – Volkskunst" at the ORF Landesstudio Tirol, October 9th and 10th, 1998.

Exhibition concept: Anton Christian
Exhibition curator and catalogue editor: Peter Weiermair, on behalf of the Freundeskreis des Tiroler Volkskunstmuseums
Realization and installation: Klaus Thoman, Stefan Bidner
Organization and marketing: Helene Forcher, Angelika Kaufmann

Editing: Esther Oehrli, Hubert Bächler
Translations from the German: John S. Southard
Art direction: renntypo, visuelle kommunikation, Teufen, Switzerland
Lithography: von Känel Co. AG, Zurich, Switzerland
Printing: Kündig Druck AG, Baar, Switzerland
Binding: Buchbinderei Burkhardt AG, Mönchaltorf, Switzerland

ISBN 3-908161-64-9 English book edition
ISBN 3-908161-63-0 German book edition

Front cover illustration:
Der Vogel Selbsterkenntnis, Tiroler Volkskunstmuseum Innsbruck
Back cover illustration:
Pedro Proença, The Sense of Imperfection, 1998